Nonverbal Learning Disabilities at School

Companion volume

Nonverbal Learning Disabilities at Home
A Parent's Guide
Pamela B. Tanguay
Foreword by Byron P. Rourke, FRSC
ISBN 1 85302 940 8

of related interest

Asperger's Syndrome
A Guide for Parents and Professionals
Tony Attwood
ISBN 1 85302 577 1

Non-Verbal Learning Disabilities
Characteristics, Diagnosis and Treatment within
an Educational Setting
Marieke Molenaar-Klumper
ISBN 1 84310 066 5

**Relationship Development Intervention
with Young Children**
Social and Emotional Development Activities
for Asperger Syndrome, Autism, PDD and NLD
Steven E. Gutstein and Rachelle K. Sheely
ISBN 1 84310 714 7

**Relationship Development Intervention
with Children, Adolescents and Adults**
Social and Emotional Development Activities
for Asperger Syndrome, Autism, PDD and NLD
Steven E. Gutstein and Rachelle K. Sheely
ISBN 1 84310 717 1

**Addressing the Challenging Behavior of Children with
High-Functioning Autism Asperger Syndrome in the Classroom**
A Guide for Teachers and Parents
Rebecca A. Moyes
ISBN 1 84310 719 8

Nonverbal Learning Disabilities at School

Educating Students with NLD, Asperger Syndrome, and Related Conditions

Pamela B. Tanguay

Foreword by Sue Thompson, MA, CET

Jessica Kingsley Publishers
London and Philadelphia

First published in the United Kingdom in 2002 by
Jessica Kingsley Publishers Ltd,
116 Pentonville Road, London
N1 9JB, England
and
325 Chestnut Street,
Philadelphia, PA 19106, USA.

www.jkp.com

© Copyright 2002 Pamela B. Tanguay
© Foreword copyright 2002 Sue Thompson

Second impression 2003

Library of Congress Cataloging in Publication Data
A CIP catalog record for this book is available from the Library of Congress

British Library Cataloguing in Publication Data
A CIP catalogue record for this book is available from the British Library

ISBN 1 85302 941 6

Printed and Bound in Great Britain by
Athenaeum Press, Gateshead, Tyne and Wear

Contents

To my daughter Stef,
whose tenacity and strength
inspire me

To my husband Ray,
who made this work
possible

I love you both
Always

Acknowledgements

As with all children, when it comes to educators, our daughter has been exposed to the good, the bad, and the ugly. Fortunately, there have been more good teachers than bad, and a few who were truly extraordinary. Without the help and support of each of you at critical periods in Stef's education, I truly don't know what we would have done, or what might have become of our wonderful little girl. I would like to take this opportunity to thank the following individuals for caring:

> *Gail Ladney, who swept Stef under her mother hen's wing, nurturing and protecting her, and creating a safe haven during the early grammar school years.*

> *Marylyn Darling, a wonderful teacher, who skillfully and lovingly instilled confidence in our daughter so that her talents could begin to unfold.*

> *Linda Childress, a brilliant and creative teacher who was always there for Stef, as both teacher and mentor, but also as a loving lioness protecting our cub. Not only did you teach our daughter to write, and write well, but more importantly, you taught her to believe in herself.*

> *The entire King's School staff, and Kathy Peck in particular, who "got it" right from the beginning. It has been a joy to watch our daughter blossom under your collective care.*

Stef will soon be graduating from high school, and moving on to college and adulthood. Her ability to do so, and to realize her wonderful potential, has been because of what each of you contributed, in your own unique way, to Stef's formal and informal education. Thank you all from the bottom of my heart.

I'd also like to thank a few special friends who helped me, so that I could help my daughter:

> *Joan Scott for sharing the highs and lows, and being more of a sister than merely a friend.*

> *Sue Thompson for being my mentor as I learned how to become a facilitator and teacher.*

> *Liane Holliday Willey for being a dear friend, and helping me more fully understand the world she shares with my daughter.*

You have each made a huge difference in my life. Your encouragement and support has helped me to maintain my strength and perspective. To each of you, my fond and heartfelt thanks.

Foreword

Parenting a child with NLD (Nonverbal Learning Disorders) can be an awesome challenge. It often entails learning about hitherto unfamiliar disciplines, such as educational modes and methods, so that you can be prepared to make informed decisions about your child's education. This is exactly what Pamela Tanguay has done. A devoted parent and long-time advocate for her child, what began for her as a recounting of her own daughter's school experiences in elementary and middle school, has evolved into an expanded treatise of universal relevance. *Nonverbal Learning Disabilities at School* will serve as an easy-to-read guide, offering suggestions for getting and staying on top of your child's educational program. This book contains practical advice on a number of the issues a student with NLD is likely to encounter at school, as well as providing an extensive listing of resources for further research.

When you are the parent of a child with NLD, you often have few or limited opportunities to "swap recipes" with other parents who share similar circumstances. Pamela Tanguay is a parent who is not only willing to share her wealth of experience and exhaustive research with you, but has painstakingly compiled her findings in an easily assimilated format that can help provide perspective, as well as information and guidance. It is important for parents to learn as much as possible about the nature of a child's learning disorder. Reading *Nonverbal Learning Disabilities at School* is a good place to start. This book will probably reinforce some of the "gut" feelings you've always had about your child's difficulties at school. By first educating yourself, you will be in a much stronger position to make informed decisions regarding your child's educational pursuits.

As well as being a parent, you need to begin thinking of yourself as a manager whose job it is to coordinate and oversee your child's educational journey. Remember, it is the right and responsibility of all parents to be actively involved whenever decisions about your child's education are being determined. You should endeavor to educate yourself by attending conferences, reading available literature on NLD, and networking with other parents who have "been there." Pamela Tanguay has done all of the above. She has been networking with other parents for nearly a decade, culminating in the formation of a website which she co-administers. As the parent of a child with NLD, you need to learn as much as possible about NLD, so that you can become an effective advocate on behalf of your child while he or she is attending school. However, in this day and age, merely understanding your child's NLD will not usually prove to be enough. You, the parent, will also find it useful to become aware of some of the modifications to their child's educational program which will be necessary in order to ensure his or her success at school. This book is chock-full of examples of appropriate modifications for the student with NLD.

Most educators undergo years of formal academic and empirical preparation before entering their own classrooms. In educational psychology courses, future teachers are exposed to the major theories of how children typically develop and learn. Educators with additional special education background have more in-depth, specialized training in exceptional development. Unfortunately, though, the majority of teacher training programs today (in both regular and special education) offer little, if any, training in the area of interventions for the student with NLD. When a teacher is lacking in information about NLD, and is also unfamiliar with your own child's unique profile, this teacher may impose the same expectations on your child that he or she has established for all students. The results, in this event, can be disastrous for all involved.

As the parent of a child with NLD you should, therefore, be prepared to communicate information about your child's educational needs, as well as his or her neurological condition, to the school-based teams who are involved in planning your child's individual education program and arranging for his or her educational placement. Once specific accommodations appropriate for your child's particular pattern of assets and deficits are determined, they can be easily implemented by his or her teacher, and, in this way, both the child and the teacher can achieve their respective goals, without unnecessary turmoil. By first educating yourself, and then letting the professionals who teach your child know what works best for his or her specific circumstances, you will greatly increase the likelihood that your child will respond more readily to the demands of school and, hence, be able to learn more effectively.

Parents are a child's first and best advocates when it comes to education. You need to be actively involved with your child's schoolwork and homework. Go over every assignment your child brings home from school – all those crinkled dittos, red-penciled tests, and dog-eared workbook pages at the bottom of the backpack. Save representative samples to bring with you to meetings at school, as written documentation of your child's progress (or lack thereof) throughout the school year. Also, use these work samples to do your own error analysis. For example, you may discover that your child's failing grade on an exam is not reflective of his or her misunderstanding of the concept, but rather the result of confusion caused by the visual presentation of the material. Pamela Tanguay gives several examples of the right and wrong ways to present material to students with NLD. When you recognize that the format (and not the material) is causing your child's difficulties, it is time to request a meeting with your child's teachers.

Many parents find that their efforts to crusade for a more appropriate learning situation for their child are frustrated by teachers and school staff who are unfamiliar with the educational implications of NLD. Friction often arises between educators and parents because both parties lack sufficient information about how the student with NLD learns best. The child is caught in the middle and suffers immeasurably. Knowing in your heart that your child's needs are not being met in his or her current educational placement is not enough. You must be well versed in the most appropriate educational interventions for your child, in order to be able to evaluate the recommendations made by teachers, principals, and other staff members at his or her school. If you are to successfully advocate for your child with NLD, you need to make sure you are familiar enough with your child's abilities, strengths, and weaknesses, as well as physical, emotional, and social development, that you can understand and, when necessary, counter, any statements made by educational professionals that you know to be untrue or unacceptable. Your best defense is always knowledge.

In my many years as an educational therapist, I have found that the parents who have the most success working with schools have done their homework before approaching their child's teachers. In addition to learning about NLD and familiarizing yourself with the current body of research (readily available at the websites listed in Tanguay's References and nicely summarized in her Introduction), above all, it is important that you know your own unique child. Take time to observe your child in the classroom, in the community, and at home. Not everything in *Nonverbal Learning Disabilities at School* will apply to every child with NLD. However, many of the suggestions in this book will surely ring true for your child. Focus on the areas where he or she is presently having the most difficulty. Your child may not be experiencing any noticeable social problems, but may have untold difficulty getting around at school and transitioning between classes. In this case, focus on the suggestions for visual-"spatial"-organizational intervention. On the other hand, your child may be compensating very well for his or her visual-"spatial"-organizational deficits, but be experiencing a great deal of difficulty with social interactions. In this case, social skills training should be at the top of your priorities. If need be, seek the support of outside evaluations and opinions from qualified professionals such as child psychologists, educational therapists, occupational therapists, developmental pediatricians, and others who are trained in both the areas of child development and NLD.

When you, as parents, are informed about NLD and how it impacts your child, you will not be derailed by misguided or misinformed allegations made by your child's school staff. You will not allow your child to be labeled as "uncooperative," or "lazy," or "a behavior problem," or "emotionally disturbed." You can point to authoritative information contained within the current body of literature to support the neurological incompetencies your child is experiencing which are still often misunderstood by educators. But first, you must educate yourself, so you can be armed with accurate information. Successful parents (such as Pam Tanguay) don't take a submissive approach. They work assertively to educate the school staff regarding the needs of their child.

Attending school can be a frightening and sometimes outright painful experience for the child with NLD. It doesn't need to be. The student with NLD requires an educational environment that will nurture his or her gifts, serve his or her needs, and provide the emotional support needed to deal with his or her inconsistent behavioral tendencies. Minimizing the amount of stress this student encounters while at school should be a top priority for everyone involved with his or her education. Pamela Tanguay has compiled many ideas and suggestions which will ease the trauma this child can experience at school when no one understands his or her needs. After reading Nonverbal Learning Disabilities At School, you will certainly be empowered to better manage your child's education.

Sue Thompson, M.A., C.E.T.
January 31, 2002

Introduction

Nonverbal Learning Disabilities (NLD), also known as Nonverbal Learning Disorder, is not what we commonly think of as a learning disability. NLD is a neurological condition that is considered to be a developmental disability. It is far more pervasive than learning problems typically seen in the classroom, affecting virtually every aspect of the individual's life. Although this syndrome was initially identified almost forty years ago, it has been slow to receive recognition due to its low incidence among the student population. Like other developmental disabilities such as autism, it is on the rise.

A child may have NLD alone, or in combination with another condition. Dr. Byron P. Rourke of the University of Windsor and Yale University, who is the world's leading researcher in the field of NLD, has identified a cluster of conditions that share the NLD neuropsychological profile.[1] In his 1995 publication, *Syndrome of Nonverbal Learning Disabilities: Neurodevelopmental Manifestations,* he and his associates identify the following as having virtually all of the assets and deficits of NLD:

° Asperger Syndrome

° Callosal Agenesis (uncomplicated)

° Velocardiofacial Syndrome

---

1   Please read the *Syndrome of Nonverbal Learning Disabilities: Neurodevelopmental Manifestations,* edited by Byron P. Rourke, for a full explanation of the disorders, diseases and dysfunctions that result in NLD. Additional information on this book can be found in the Annotated Bibliography (Appendix II) at the back of this book.

- ° Williams Syndrome

- ° de Lange Syndrome

- ° Hydrocephalus (early; shunted)

- ° Turner Syndrome (45, X)

- ° significant damage or dysfunction of the right cerebral hemisphere

Although each of these conditions, including NLD, would individually be considered a low-incidence disability, when grouped together under the NLD umbrella, clearly the numbers are greater, and growing. The material contained within this book applies to the unique educational needs of a child with any of these neurological conditions.

NLD is by definition a syndrome, consisting of a cluster of assets and deficits. Although the neuropsychological pattern is present in each person, the mix of strengths and weaknesses comes together somewhat uniquely in each child. Some children may be more physically awkward, while others may have more social deficits, and still others may have significant impairment in all deficit areas of the syndrome. Another variable is the age of the NLD child. A youngster in first grade may appear more capable than when she reaches adolescence. And finally, a child with an exceptionally high I.Q. may be able to compensate somewhat better than a child of average intelligence.

The purpose for publishing this book is to provide teachers and parents with information specific to the education of the NLD child. The primary areas of deficit with these youngsters are in the nonverbal domains, thus the name. There is also another group of children who, although they do not have the NLD syndrome, do have learning disabilities in one or more nonverbal domains. Students with dyscalculia (math disability) fall into this group. Teachers should consider NLD educational strategies, where they apply, for this second group of students.

Historically, teachers have had very little training specific to learning disabilities in the nonverbal domains. Therefore, it is often difficult to know which teaching strategies would be effective for NLD students. Most teachers will be familiar with many of the techniques that are presented in this book, and may consider quite a few to simply be good teaching practices. However, these good teaching practices are critical to the success of the NLD student. This book is not intended to teach teachers how to teach, but rather to identify the teaching strategies in their repertoire that are particularly effective for NLD students. Also included are some techniques designed specifically for this student population, which teachers may also find useful for other youngsters.

Clearly no one book can address all of the educational issues of any student. The material presented within this book focuses on the unique educational issues of the child with NLD from kindergarten through middle school. However, many of the strategies which are covered will continue to apply throughout the student's high school years.

As with my first book, I have taken editorial license in two areas. The first is gender reference. Today, the politically correct way to address gender is to alternate between the use of male and female. However, since this work is dedicated to my daughter, I chose to use the female gender throughout the book. The second issue also relates to political correctness. You will note that I use the phrase 'NLD child or children.' Some people prefer the phrase 'child with NLD' because they believe that it is more appropriate to put the child before the disability, rather than characterize the child by their disability. I think that this is a fair point. However, the use of 'NLD child' seems less stilted and more personal than 'child with NLD.' I hope that I do not offend anyone by my choices.

– Pamela B. Tanguay

Chapter 1

NLD – What Is It?

Educators are often misled by the term Nonverbal Learning Disabilities (NLD), sometimes assuming that these children are nonverbal, which is incorrect. In children with Nonverbal Learning Disabilities, the primary areas of deficit are in the *nonverbal* domains. These children's strengths lie predominantly in the verbal domains. NLD is considered a syndrome, meaning that the disability is comprised of a cluster of skill deficits. These deficits impact virtually every aspect of the individual's life. As a result of the pervasive implications of NLD, it is a serious, and sometimes profound disability.

NLD is not a learning disability in the traditional sense, but rather a life learning disability. It is far more appropriate to consider NLD in terms of a pervasive developmental disability, rather than a learning disability. The definition of a pervasive developmental disability is quite global in nature. It assumes a severe, chronic disability that is present before the individual reaches the age of twenty-one. It further assumes substantial functional limitation in areas such as self-care, receptive and expressive language, learning, self-direction, and mobility, as well as the capacity for independent living and economic self-sufficiency. This definition is certainly a closer description of the implications of NLD than what we generally understand a learning disability to be.

Our traditional understanding of a learning disability is much narrower in scope (e.g. dyslexia), and is considered to affect primarily academic learning. NLD, on the other hand, affects the individual's ability to learn academic *and* life skills. Children with more traditional learning disabilities do not face the social and athletic difficulties of NLD youngsters. Most youngsters with a learning disability are able to enjoy social and athletic pursuits as part of their educational experience. NLD children have challenges with academic, motoric, social, emotional, and self-help skills. There is little in the school environment that these children readily grasp, except those activities that are purely verbally-based.

When first hearing the term Nonverbal Learning Disabilities, many parents and teachers may believe that the problem should properly be addressed exclusively in the classroom. Although NLD is called a learning disability, it is a pervasive and potentially debilitating disorder. In order to provide appropriate intervention for the NLD child, it is important to understand the global nature of the disorder. Although there *are* many academic issues, there are also many other functional limitations which must be addressed if the child is to succeed. The NLD child will likely need support from a multi-disciplinary team, and her needs will change across developmental cycles.

Much of the available literature describing NLD is technical in nature, and difficult for parents and teachers to understand. You will read about social-emotional and adaptational deficits, tactile difficulties, psychomotor coordination problems, and so on. Although these are some of the inherent deficits of the disability, throughout this book we will attempt to use more "user-friendly" terminology.

STRENGTHS AND WEAKNESSES

The primary strengths of NLD children are auditory and verbal. Most will develop a sophisticated vocabulary before they enter school, often well beyond their peers. Generally they have excellent attention and memory for what they *hear*, unless the material is complex. These strengths may not be as noticeable in the younger NLD child, but will become more obvious as she matures. By the time that NLD children reach the upper elementary and middle school grades, it should be apparent that they are auditory learners.

Although each child is unique, students with NLD will have varying degrees of difficulty in the following areas:

Tactile (touch) and Visual Attention and Perception

She may be unable to correctly process what she touches or sees, with poor attention for both. (Example: The child may be unable to identify something familiar by touching or holding it, or recognize her classroom by appearance alone.)

Psychomotor Coordination (physical awkwardness)

The child may have difficulty getting her body to do *what* she wants it to, *when* she wants it to, and *how* she wants it to. (Example: Hopping, skipping, jumping, catching and throwing a ball, riding a bicycle, and handwriting are all psychomotor coordination activities which will likely be a challenge.)

Adaptability

She will almost certainly have considerable difficulty adapting to changes in her established routine. The child does *not* have the ability to "wing it." (Example: If there is a substitute teacher, a change in the daily schedule, or a fire drill, the student may have significant difficulty coping with the situation. She finds comfort and security in routine, and changes will likely be anxiety-provoking.)

Spatial Orientation

She will likely have significant difficulty knowing where she is, or other objects are, in space. (Example: She may appear clumsy, and finding her way around the school will almost certainly be problematic.)

Mental Flexibility

This child learns and thinks very concretely, and processes information in a black-and-white manner, not understanding shades of gray. She thinks in logical terms, and abstract concepts will be difficult or beyond her ability. In all likelihood, she will do poorly with open-ended questions. (Example: If asked, "how was your vacation?" she may not have a response. There are too many variables in the question of "how," and since she can't figure out what you mean, she won't answer. However, if asked a concrete question such as "did you bring your library book to school?" she can respond, because she has a clear understanding of what is being asked.)

Executive Function and Organization

She will have difficulty prioritizing and organizing both her thoughts and her work. (Example: If called on in class, she may know the answer, but be unable to quickly pull her thoughts together to provide a response. If the child is given a large assignment in school, she will not be able to break it down into its component parts, or determine the sequence of tasks, i.e. which task must be completed before another can be accomplished.)

Pragmatic Language

Pragmatic language is defined as the functional use of language. These children cannot "read between the lines" or interpret other nonverbal communication. Although she may have a well developed vocabulary, there will probably be significant communication difficulties because her expressive and receptive language is based on words alone. (Example: If you say "I have to run down to the office," the neurologically typical (NT) child will know that "run" is a figure of speech. The NLD child might say "but we aren't allowed to run in school.")

Generalizing Information

The NLD child is unable to apply prior learned knowledge to a new but similar topic or situation. (Example: This child generally learns to spell quite well. However, this skill may be slow to generalize to other academic areas. A word correctly spelled during a spelling class, may then be spelled incorrectly when written during a social studies test.) (Example: If you teach the child what information should be written at the top of her social studies paper, such as name, subject area, and so forth, you will have to explain it again when you give her a math assignment. She will not automatically assume that you want all papers done consistently, unless you directly tell her to do so, and are specific as to what information belongs at the top of each paper.)

Social Skills

Difficulties with pragmatics, inference and generalization result in pronounced social problems. The child does not understand our culture, or the social rules governing appropriate behavior. (Example: At recess, or during unstructured activity, the NLD child may *seem* uncooperative, and act in a very immature way. She may have difficulty with turn-taking, because she doesn't understand the concept, not because she is willful by nature. If you ask her if she is ready to join the group, she might innocently say no, because she *isn't* ready. She does not understand that you weren't really asking, but rather telling her what you wanted her to do.)

Emotional Stability

Due to the child's inability to order her world, adapt to new situations, and comprehend nonverbal messages such as voice inflection, body language, etc., she may be riddled with anxiety, which will likely increase with age as her environment becomes more complex. (Example: The young NLD child may often cry when at school, or seem confused much of the time, because she is! The adolescent may become quite withdrawn and depressed as academic and social demands increase.)

Although this child is likely highly verbal, her overall communication skills are actually quite deficient. Research indicates that less than 35% of all human communication is conveyed verbally, with the remaining 65% or more being transmitted nonverbally. In order to fully understand what someone is telling us, we must listen to the words, *and* interpret facial expressions, body language, tone of voice, context, process inconsistencies, and determine what the individual *meant* to communicate. The NLD child will only process the words. For instance, if you say "Nice job!," you are probably pleased, have a lilt to your voice, and a smile on your face. The child interprets that she did well. If a peer says "Nice job!," is frowning, using a sarcastic tone of voice, and attempting to convey displeasure, it is likely that the NLD child will misperceive the message. She will hear the words, but miss the voice inflection, facial expression and intent. Unfortunately, she will decipher the message as having done well.

WHAT CAUSES NLD?

Dr. Byron P. Rourke of the University of Windsor in Canada, and Yale University in Connecticut, is the preeminent researcher in the field of Nonverbal Learning Disabilities. After decades of research, Dr. Rourke and his associates have determined that the disorder is caused by damage to white matter in the brain (Rourke 1989, 1995).

A very simplistic definition of white matter is that it is brain tissue made up of nerve cells that connect various parts of the brain to each other. It is called white matter because the nerve fibers are coated with myelin, which is a light-colored fatty substance that acts as insulation. In essence, white matter is the brain's wiring system. The myelin sheath (the fatty substance) can be compared to the plastic coating we find on electrical wires, and allows for rapid and accurate transmission of information within the brain. If the myelin sheath is damaged (as Dr. Rourke indicates is likely the case with NLD), the child's processing speed is reduced, and the signal may not be sent accurately, or arrive at the proper destination. Therefore, although the information centers within the brain may be intact, the transmission of signals is not working properly. In other words, there is a "short circuit" somewhere in the child's brain. Information about the brain tells us that there is a disproportionate amount of white matter in the right hemisphere of the brain versus the left. Therefore, the disability is sometimes referred to as Right Hemisphere Syndrome, meaning that the right hemisphere is dysfunctional.

In contrast, it appears that function in the left hemisphere remains relatively intact. Therefore, language, step-by-step reasoning, and other like skills that are processed by the left hemisphere are more preserved. The right hemisphere, dealing with spatial, abstract, intuitive, and other "nonverbal" aspects, is impaired. Also, since higher-order thinking skills require the use of both hemispheres to integrate complex information, these skills are also impaired because one of the hemispheres isn't working properly.

For a more thorough understanding of Dr. Rourke's research into white matter dysfunction and Nonverbal Learning Disabilities, there are two books in particular that you will find helpful: *Nonverbal Learning Disabilities: The Syndrome and the Model,* and *Syndrome of Nonverbal Learning Disabilities: Neurodevelopmental Manifestations.* Information on both of these books is included in the Annotated Bibliography (Appendix II) at the end of this book.

NLD IS OFTEN MISDIAGNOSED

Unfortunately, due to limited awareness of NLD, many children, especially when they are young, are commonly misdiagnosed. Because of their poor planning and organizational skills, their apparent problems with impulse control, and their inability to attend to tactile and visual information, educators and other professionals often misdiagnose NLD children as having ADD/ADHD. Tactile and visual modalities are probably the most commonly used educational strategies in the first few years of school. These are areas of deficit for NLD children who would naturally appear to be unable to "attend" to tactile and/or visual material, resulting in the erroneous assumption that the child has ADD or ADHD.

Another common misdiagnosis within the NLD population is anxiety or panic disorder. It is true that many of these children have very high levels of anxiety, however their anxiety is the result of their disability (NLD).

BRIGHT AND LEARNING DISABLED

If the child is young, say five to eight years old, it may be difficult to comprehend the magnitude of this disability, and how significantly it will affect her in just a few short years. Although you will see problems in the young child that are disturbing – her inability to put on her jacket or sweater, stay within the lines on her papers, use a pencil or a pair of scissors – you also see that she is bright, articulate, and engaging, particularly when she is interacting with adults. Since she is so bright, articulate and engaging, how can there be a problem? Parents and teachers see an inquisitive child, with an excellent vocabulary, who reads well (although some NLD children have early reading difficulties), spells well, and learns basic math facts. Although the child's handwriting may be poor, that is not unusual for students in their early school years. Her social skills appear immature, but that is also not unusual for this age group. Clearly, because of her obvious verbal strengths, it is difficult to grasp how significant the disability is while she is young.

To make matters worse, the verbal strengths of the child, coupled with the *appearance* of academic competence, may present a false illusion of giftedness. At this stage, it may be particularly difficult for school personnel to appreciate that NLD is a debilitating disorder, whose full impact may not be realized until she is 9, 10, or

11 years old. It has been said that this is a disability that a child "grows into," which makes a certain amount of sense. The skill deficits of these individuals are not seriously challenged until the upper elementary grades, when teaching begins to move away from the child's areas of strength, i.e. simple rote memory, vocabulary, spelling, and single-word decoding skills. As academic challenges increase, and the child can no longer depend on her compensatory skills, difficulties in school become apparent. As is often the case with children that have learning difficulties, the first sign may be the child's anger and frustration. It will take a skilled clinician to properly evaluate and diagnose NLD.

INTERVENTION IS CRITICAL

Understanding NLD, and its implications, is the key to appropriate intervention. It is a *very* serious disability, but there are excellent prospects for the child if it is identified early and appropriate interventions are provided. These children can be taught just about anything. However, the operative word here is "taught." Children with NLD will not learn through observation, assimilating information along the way. They must be taught everything explicitly, in a verbal, scripted, step-by-step manner.

Example

The NLD child might not know how to do simple, everyday tasks. We don't generally have to consciously teach children how to do simple things such as turn on a faucet, flush a toilet, or close a door. Neurologically typical children seem to intuitively grasp these common everyday tasks. However, for NLD children, these tasks are not so common or "simple." Even if the child has been taught to turn on a faucet at home, it may work differently at school; flushing the toilet in the school restroom will surely be different than what they have been taught at home; they have not been faced with closing a bathroom stall door. Remember, this youngster doesn't generalize information, and her nonverbal problem-solving skills are deficient. As in all things, she must be specifically taught a task by verbally scripting each step in the order that it is to be done.

NLD children are generally bright kids, and some are very bright. They have a different learning style, and need to be taught in a verbally scripted manner. When taught to her learning style, the child may grasp some things quite quickly, often only needing to hear new material explained once. At other times, she may need repetition. With neurologically typical children, we aren't consciously aware of how often they watch us perform a task before they learn how to do it. At some point, we just realize that they have figured it out on their own. It probably didn't take any specific instruction, but with the NLD child it will. She will not learn through observation, and will need very specific information when she is given instruction. If she asks for clarification, it is because she truly did not understand what you said to her. Be patient, and explain again what you are trying to say, using simple, straightforward language.

SUMMARY

NLD is a pervasive, neurological disability which is caused by damage to the brain's circuitry, resulting in significant deficits which are remediated, in a step-by-step manner, through the child's auditory and verbal strengths.

This child responds well to a relatively small, quiet, well-organized environment, with a teacher who is articulate, even-tempered, and enthusiastic. Neuropsychological deficits include the following:

Tactile and Visual

○ Tactile perception and attention – she does not have the ability to identify something by touch alone or "attend" to teaching strategies which require touch.

○ Visual perception and attention – she does not have the ability to accurately scan the visual field or environment and process what is seen or "attend" to teaching strategies that use the visual modality.

Psychomotor and Spatial

○ Psychomotor coordination – her ability to have her body do what she wants it to, when she wants it to, and how she wants it to is impaired.

○ Spatial orientation – she is unaware of where she is in space and her physical proximity to other objects.

Social and Emotional

- ° Pragmatics – her functional and practical use of language is impaired.

- ° Social skills – her ability to interact appropriately, based on established social norms, is deficient.

- ° Adaptability – she is seriously limited in her ability to adjust to a new situation or change in circumstances.

- ° Emotional stability – because of her significant deficits, her emotional well-being is inconsistent.

Cognitive

- ° Generalizing information – she is unable to apply prior learned knowledge to a similar situation.

- ° Mental flexibility – her ability to assimilate and process new information or ideas that may influence the way that a person thinks about a topic or situation is impaired.

- ° Executive function and organization – she does not have the innate ability to organize, prioritize, and plan either her thoughts or her work.

Chapter 2

NLD Student Profile

This chapter covers the NLD profile of three developmental age groups of students: preschool and the early elementary grades, the mid to late elementary grades, and middle school. If a particular child has not yet been diagnosed, this profile may aid educators in identifying children who should be evaluated for NLD. In the case of a child who has been diagnosed with NLD, the profile should help parents and educators understand how the child is affected in a formal educational setting at each developmental level.

It would be ideal for NLD youngsters to be recognized when they are still toddlers. However, it is more likely that they will be identified later, after they have begun school. Although most NLD children are not diagnosed until age eight or older, there are warning indicators that may lead to an earlier diagnosis. The child's difficulties may be noted by her teachers and other school personnel, but assumed to be problems that she will outgrow. It is critical that educators be aware of the NLD student profile, so that the child can be identified for evaluation. Intervention significantly increases the likelihood of a successful long-term prognosis for NLD children. The earlier the child is identified, the earlier an intervention program is implemented, the better her long-term prognosis.

PRESCHOOL AND EARLY ELEMENTARY

Educators have seen these children for many years, but may not have understood what the symptoms represented. The following are characteristics which are commonly present in NLD children between the ages of five and eight.

Need for Structure/Predictability/Guidance

These children are very rule-driven, and may be preoccupied with what the rules are, continually asking for clarification, or saying that they don't understand the rules.

They are often easily confused, appearing to require additional guidance as to what they are expected to do. They may look to see what other students are doing, or look at the papers of the students sitting next to them in order to determine how to proceed. The NLD child might ask another child what she is supposed to do, rather than asking the teacher for clarification. If she does not receive the required clarification, she will likely become anxious.

NLD children do quite poorly in unstructured situations. They are unable to figure out what they should do, and generally react poorly to their uncertainty. They may respond to a situation by becoming anxious, or acting in a socially immature and/or inappropriate manner.

The lunchroom may overwhelm this child. She will likely need assistance in getting beverages and/or food in the cafeteria, especially if she has to handle money, if there are several selections, or if she has to stand in more than one line. If she brings her lunch from home, she might need assistance in taking her food out of the lunchbox or bag, in unwrapping the food, and putting a straw in her drink. You may also notice that she always has the exact same lunch throughout the school year, since she thrives on sameness. The social interactions at the lunch table will be difficult for her, as are all socially demanding situations.

NLD children seem to have immature self-help skills which, in fact, they do. Compared to her peer group, the NLD child will require more assistance in putting on her jacket or sweater, in zipping or buttoning it, and in tying her shoelaces, and will require help for a longer period of time than her age mates. She may not be able to tie her shoes until she is in fourth or fifth grade.

Motor Skills

The child will almost certainly have some level of difficulty with art projects. Staying within the boundaries of a picture when painting or coloring will be challenging, and handling paint brushes may be awkward. If the activity is finger-painting, due to sensory issues, she may resist the activity. She will likely have extreme difficulty using scissors, and will require assistance with cutting. Needle and thread activities, or stringing beads, may be beyond her ability. When completed, her arts and crafts efforts may look quite immature.

Holding a pencil correctly, and forming letters and numbers, may be arduous. Staying on and between the lines on the paper may be impossible. She may press very hard when writing, tearing the paper, or erase with too much force, again tearing the paper. Her penmanship attempts will appear immature. As she struggles with pen and paper tasks, she may begin to resist these activities.

The NLD child will almost always appear physically awkward, which will be apparent in her physical education class. She may have an unusual gait, which will affect her ability to run gracefully. There will likely be difficulties with hopping, skipping, and jumping, as well as climbing. The child may be totally confused when participating in a team sport, unable to follow the rules of the game.

Communication and Social Skills

The verbal skills of the NLD child are immediately apparent to adults. Her vocabulary is likely quite developed, and she may talk like a little adult. These skills may actually put off other children, and the NLD child may prefer to talk with her teachers rather than interact with her peer group. Often she will be more comfortable with adults than with children her own age. This is likely because adults are more predictable than children.

The NLD child consistently misinterprets what is said to her. She may misunderstand the teacher's instructions, or what another child says to her. She may tell her parent that the teacher or another child was mean to her, when there was no evidence that anyone was unkind. These misunderstandings will be an ongoing problem.

This child is socially awkward, and may or may not attempt to interact with other children. While other children are entering the classroom in the morning, chatting with each other as they put away their things, the NLD child may seem oblivious to the other children. She will likely come into the classroom, put her things away, go to her desk, and quietly await the start of the day. If she chooses to interact with one or more of the other students, her approach may be inappropriate, immature, or untimely.

Recess is likely to be particularly difficult for this child. The social demands may overwhelm her. Her weakness in social reciprocity will likely be most apparent on the playground. She may not relinquish a swing when her "turn" is over, or return a stray ball that another group of children are playing with. Over time, her peers may begin to reject her, so that she becomes isolated and on the periphery, and may begin to resist recess entirely.

Behavior

The NLD child generally has a thirst to learn that stands out from the other students, taking her school work very seriously, and may actually be a perfectionist. She may prefer to spend all of her time in the classroom, rather than participating in social activities such as recess, which she finds too challenging.

When the NLD child becomes anxious, it may be difficult to reassure and calm her. She may have to be removed from the classroom, or whatever activity she is involved in, so that she can pull herself together in a quiet location with a supportive adult.

These children do best in structured settings, such as their primary classroom, than in less structured environments, as might be found with art or physical education. If the child has different teachers for specials (art, library, physical education), her primary teacher may receive comments from other teachers regarding her behavior. This may seem out of character, especially if the child generally behaves better than her classmates when in her primary classroom. It is also likely that the primary teacher has intuitively developed a method of working with the child that the other teachers do not use.

Visual/Spatial/Organizational Skills

The NLD child may have significant difficulty copying from the board or from a book. She may make what appear to be careless mistakes, which are in fact due to her visual processing deficits.

Most NLD children have significant spatial difficulties and get lost very easily. They will have difficulty navigating the school, remembering their way to and from their classroom, how to get to the bathroom, and should never be assigned the responsibility of line-leader. On field trips, unless an adult keeps an eye on the NLD child at all times, she may become separated from the group.

The child will likely have problems understanding concepts of time, including telling time, as well as days of the week, number of days in a month, months in a year, number of days in a year, and so on.

This child's organizational skills are likely very poor, and her desk may be the messiest in the classroom. She may forget to turn in her completed assignments, and lose everything that isn't attached to her.

Other

Although the NLD child may be bright, she may be slow to complete her work, or unable to finish an assignment or test within a given period of time.

Deficits in visual and tactile areas may lead to the erroneous conclusion that the child has ADD or ADHD. The reason for this assumption is often because much of early education is dependent on the visual and tactile modalities, and she is unable to attend to either because of her inability, or limited ability, to process information presented in either of these modalities.

Although the NLD child is often a precocious reader, this is not universal. Some NLD youngsters may have delayed decoding skills even though their vocabulary is well developed.

MID TO LATE ELEMENTARY

Many of the problems that NLD children have in preschool and early elementary grades are common to other students, and often accommodated by educators who are accustomed to working with young, less able or mature children. However, NLD students do not "outgrow" their difficulties as their peer group does, and by the middle elementary grades, appear far less able than their age mates. At this point, the teacher may feel it would be helpful to demand more of the student, so that she can become more independent. This is the worst thing to do to this child, who continues to need a high level of support due to her neurological problems. The following describes how this child will likely present in the middle to upper elementary grades.

Need for Structure/Predictability/Guidance

She will continue to be very rule-driven, and will likely resist any change to her schedule. She will respond poorly to substitute teachers, assemblies that create a change in her daily schedule, field trips, or anything that disrupts her routine.

The NLD child continues to do quite poorly in unstructured situations. In addition to her uncertainty, she may become embarrassed because she is now old enough to be aware that other children don't have the same difficulty in these circumstances that she does.

Lunch in the cafeteria may be the most difficult time of the day. The chaos of the environment, social demands, and expectations of independence combine to be exceptionally challenging for the NLD student. The assistance provided to many, if not all, children in the early elementary grades is no longer provided to this age group. However, the NLD child continues to need assistance in getting beverages and/or food in the cafeteria, especially if she has to handle money, if there are several selections, or if she has to stand in more than one line.

The NLD child's self-help skills may continue to be deficient. She may still require assistance with certain tasks, especially with tying her shoelaces. She will likely appear far less independent than her age mates.

Motor Skills

The child will almost certainly have some level of difficulty with finger dexterity. Art projects, especially those which require cutting will be challenging, as will other activities requiring precision. Penmanship exercises may be very frustrating, and the switch from printing to cursive may either be very difficult, or much easier than printing. However, she may continue with too much pencil or eraser pressure, resulting in messy or torn papers. If she finds pencil and paper tasks too arduous, she may object when assigned these activities.

The NLD child continues to appear physically awkward, which will be apparent in her physical education class. She may have an unusual gait, which will affect her ability to run gracefully. There will likely be difficulties with hopping, skipping, and jumping, as well as climbing. The child may be totally confused when participating in team sports, unable to follow the rules of the game.

Communication and Social Skills

Her vocabulary likely continues to be quite developed. Her verbal skills may actually put off other children, and the NLD child may prefer to talk with her teachers rather than interact with her peer group. Often she will be more comfortable with adults than with children her own age. This is likely because adults are more predictable than children.

Misinterpretations continue, and probably increase. Teacher communication is less concrete than with younger students, so there are more opportunities for the NLD child to misunderstand both classroom instruction and directions.

As less direct instruction is provided, the NLD student will be confused and frustrated. Casually moving from one academic subject to another will cause tremendous anxiety for this child. She continues to need verbal cues...

> "Okay students, we are finished with our spelling, so you can put your spelling book in your desk...take your arithmetic book out, and turn to page 25, and we are going to start at the top of the page, problem #1."

As in the earlier grades, if she does not receive the required clarification, she will likely become anxious, and/or ask another student for guidance.

This child is socially awkward, and may or may not attempt to interact with other children. While other children begin their day by chatting with each other as they put away their things, the NLD child may seem oblivious to the other students. As in earlier grades, she will likely enter the classroom, put her things away, go to her desk, and quietly await the start of the class. If she chooses to interact with one or more of the other students, her approach may be inappropriate, immature, or untimely.

Recess continues to be particularly difficulty for this child. The social demands become more complex, and her social awkwardness is likely apparent to her peer group. Her inability to comfortably join a group, or perform the physical games that are being played, may continue to isolate her. Other children may zero-in on her vulnerability, and begin to tease or bully her.

Behavior

The NLD child generally continues to display a thirst to learn that stands out from her peers, taking her school work very seriously, and may be a perfectionist. She may prefer to spend all of her time in the classroom, rather than participating in social activities such as recess, which she finds too challenging.

The NLD child continues to have problems with anxiety. She will be embarrassed by crying, and will want to remove herself from the classroom if she is overwhelmed. However, she continues to need a quiet place where she can pull herself together, and a supportive adult to assist her.

The child's need for structure likely increases, preferring her primary classroom to less structured environments, as might be found with art or physical education. If the student has different teachers for specials (art, library, physical education), her primary teacher may receive comments from other teachers regarding the NLD child's behavior. This may seem out of character, especially if the child generally behaves better than her classmates when in her primary classroom. It is also likely that the primary teacher has intuitively developed a method of working with the child that the other teachers do not use.

Visual/Spatial/Organizational Skills

As the demands for copying from the board or from a book increase, the NLD child's difficulty with these tasks becomes more pronounced. She may make what appear to be careless mistakes, which are in fact due to her visual processing deficits.

This child's organizational skills likely continue to be very poor, and her desk may be the messiest in the classroom. She may forget to take home what is required in order to complete homework assignments and forget to turn in her completed assignments.

The child may still struggle with concepts of time, including telling time, as well as the days of the week, number of days in a month, months in a year, number of days in a year, and so on, although there is some improvement over the early elementary grades.

The spatial challenges of NLD children likely become more pronounced. They will have difficulty navigating the school, remembering their way to and from their classroom, how to get to the bathroom, the gym, etc. As more independence is allowed in moving unaccompanied around the building, the NLD child's spatial deficits are quite apparent. On field trips, unless an adult keeps an eye on her at all times, she may become separated from the group.

Other

Although the NLD child may be bright, she may be slow to complete her work, or unable to finish an assignment or test within a given period of time. This problem may become more pronounced each year.

Deficits in visual and tactile areas may continue to lead to the erroneous conclusion that the child has ADD or ADHD. The reason for this assumption is often because much of early education is dependent on the visual and tactile modalities, and she is unable to attend to either because of her inability, or reduced ability, to process information presented in either of these modalities. However, as teaching becomes more verbal, the student's visual and tactile attentional deficits are less pronounced.

For those NLD youngsters who had early decoding difficulty, reading skills begin to improve. However, comprehension for nonfiction material is impaired.

MIDDLE SCHOOL AND BEYOND

The move from a supportive grammar school environment, to the demands of middle school, is a challenging transition for youngsters. However, for the NLD child, this move, if not handled with significant foresight and planning, is often disastrous. Even the exceptionally bright NLD student, who was able to develop compensatory strategies in grammar school, finds herself ill-equipped to handle middle school. She continues to need a very limited number of teachers, direct instruction, and significant support. However, the typical expectation of middle school students is that they are more independently able, and require less direct instruction than they did during grammar school. A further complication is that the educational principle of middle school and beyond is curriculum-driven, meaning that each subject is taught by a different teacher. The significant change in environment and student expectation overwhelms the NLD student, resulting in notably increased levels of anxiety and somatic complaints.

Need for Structure/Predictability/Guidance

The student with NLD continues to need structure and predictability, will be confused by the more complex schedule of middle school, and will likely resist any change to her established daily routine. She will respond poorly to multiple teachers, substitute teachers, field trips, or assemblies that create a change in her schedule.

The NLD child continues to do quite poorly in unstructured situations. In addition to her uncertainty, she will almost certainly be embarrassed by her limitations and acutely aware that other children don't have the same difficulty in these circumstances that she does.

Rather than cry, as was likely just a short time ago, she may act out or appear to shut down.

Lunch in the cafeteria will surely be very difficult for the NLD student. The increased chaos of the environment, increased social demands, and expectations of independence combine to be exceptionally challenging for this student. She continues to need assistance in getting beverages and/or food in the cafeteria, especially if she has to handle money, if there are several selections, or if she has to stand in more than one line. However, the assistance provided to elementary school children is not generally provided to this age group of children.

The NLD child's self-help skills may continue to be challenging. Although there has been progress in developing these skills, she is not likely to be adept, and will generally require additional time to perform tasks such as tying her shoelaces, and the requirement of a complete change of clothes for her physical education class is unrealistic. She clearly appears far less independent than her age mates.

Motor Skills

Fine motor skills have likely shown some improvement. However, the act of writing may still be difficult, her penmanship poor, and problems with writing fatigue are common. If she finds pen/pencil and paper tasks too arduous, she may object when assigned these activities. Or, she may produce very limited output.

The NLD child's physical awkwardness likely continues to be apparent in her physical education class. Dribbling a basketball, hitting a baseball, or activities which require more precise foot work are probably quite difficult. The child may be totally confused when participating in a team sport, unable to follow the rules of the game.

Communication and Social Skills

The NLD student's verbal skills lead adults to believe that she is far more able than she is. Misinterpretations continue, and probably increase. Teacher communication is less concrete than with younger students, so there are more opportunities for the NLD child to misunderstand both classroom instruction and directions.

As less direct instruction is provided, the NLD student will be confused and frustrated. However, the benefit to moving from class to class for each subject allows her to switch mental set between each, something that was difficult for her when she had the majority of her subjects in one classroom. However, she continues to need significant verbal cues. If she does not receive the required clarification, she will likely become anxious, and/or ask another student for guidance.

The social awkwardness of this student becomes more pronounced. Between classes, while other students are whooping it up in the hallways, the NLD student is focused on finding her way to her next classroom. She will likely come into the classroom, go to her desk, and quietly await the start of the class. If she chooses to interact with one or more of the other students, her approach may be inappropriate, immature, or untimely.

Hallways become the social nether land for middle school students. The chaos of switching classes, the resulting chatter and teasing, are generally beyond the social ability of the NLD student. As a result, other students often zero-in on this weakness of the NLD child. NLD youngsters are often a primary "target" of the class bully, and require the protection of adults.

Recess continues to be particularly difficult for this child. The social demands continue to increase in complexity, and her social awkwardness is likely apparent to her peer group. Her inability to comfortably join a group, or perform the physical games that are being played, may continue to isolate her. She is likely to be the perfect target for manipulative adolescents, who know exactly how to embarrass her. Fortunately for the NLD student, most schools eliminate recess at some point during middle school.

Behavior

The NLD child sees school as a place where she goes to learn, taking her school work very seriously, and may actually be a perfectionist. However, her work product may not reflect the considerable amount of time that she invests. Due to her slow pace, and the demands that she places on herself, her level of frustration may continue to increase, especially if her grades do not reflect her hard work.

The NLD child's difficulty with anxiety persists. When she is overwhelmed, she will prefer to remove herself from the classroom, rather than be embarrassed by crying. At some point, and in certain situations, her anxiety may present in the form of silliness rather than tears. She continues to need a quiet place where she can pull herself together, and may still require the assistance of a supportive adult.

Because there is no longer a primary classroom teacher who can develop a rapport with the child, and understand her needs and motivations, the NLD student's behavior, in whatever form it takes, is often misunderstood. It is common for the NLD adolescent to "shut down" during the middle school years, not participating in class. The child may adopt a "mask" in order to cope with her inability to perform, which, unfortunately, may be misinterpreted as a lack of motivation.

Visual/Spatial/Organizational Skills

The NLD student's significant difficulty copying from the board or from a book continues. She may make what appear to be careless mistakes, which are in fact due to her visual processing deficits.

This child's organizational skills are likely very poor, and her book locker may be a total mess, making it almost impossible for her to find what she needs. She may forget to write down her homework assignments, take home what is required in order to complete the assignments, and forget to turn in her completed work.

Long-term assignments will be extremely challenging, and the student will not demonstrate the requisite planning skills, or understand the necessary order of tasks, in order to complete the assignment. Projects which are completed will not reflect the amount of work which was invested, will likely have gaps, and lack flow.

Time concepts improve, but likely lag behind the expected level. Elapsed time, or the time necessary to complete a task, will continue to be a significant problem.

In middle and high school, the NLD student's spatial challenges cause her significant difficulty in navigating the environment. She will have trouble remembering her way to and from her classrooms, how to get to the bathroom, the gym, etc., especially when her point of reference changes. As more independence is allowed in moving unaccompanied around the building, this adolescent's spatial deficits are quite apparent. Field trips may pose a greater risk than in earlier grades because adults do not supervise this age group as closely as they do younger children, increasing the likelihood that the NLD student may become separated from her group.

Other

Although the NLD child may be bright, she may be slow to complete her work, or unable to finish an assignment or test within a given period of time.

As teaching focuses less on visual and tactile strategies, and more on lecture, the previous ADD or ADHD characteristics seem to disappear. However, even though this student is an auditory learner, she struggles with complex material no matter the domain – visual, tactile, and auditory.

Decoding, spelling, and vocabulary skills are strong. However, reading comprehension, especially in the subject areas of social studies/history and science, is deficient. Answers to essay questions are quite difficult, and expressive and other writing activities do not reflect the child's intelligence. Study skills are weak, and test results may not demonstrate the student's knowledge in a particular subject.

SUMMARY

This is an apparently bright child, with very strong verbal skills, who often misunderstands what is said to her. She has poor organizational and abstract skills, weak self-help skills, is socially inept, and demonstrates immature or inappropriate social interactions with her classmates.

The NLD child is a polite, rule-driven, and serious student, who has difficulty with change, is often confused, easily overwhelmed, frequently tired, and may have somatic complaints such as a headache or upset stomach. She is physically awkward, bumps into things, and gets lost easily.

Although she develops strong decoding skills, her reading comprehension is compromised by an inability to identify, and differentiate between, relevant versus irrelevant facts, and/or infer information that is not specifically stated. This student has excellent rote memory skills, especially for things that she hears.

Math facts may come easily, although calculations and operations may present a significant challenge. Penmanship and other fine motor tasks are impaired, but may improve with time and practice.

For those unfamiliar with NLD, the young child might appear to meet the criteria for Attention Deficit/Hyperactivity Disorder (AD/HD), however the two disorders are quite different. The physically awkward, anxious NLD child who has difficulty managing change is quite different from the physically adept, social AD/HD child who thrives on novelty.

Chapter 3

School Environment and Placement

The success or failure of most NLD children is based on the environment in which they are required to function. As a result of their unique problems, it is very difficult for these children to understand the requirements of a particular situation, as well as how to adapt to it. Parents generally respond instinctively to the eccentricities of their children, without giving it much conscious thought. Therefore, the parents of an NLD child have likely adapted the home environment to suit the unique needs of their child.

Once she begins school, the child's life becomes far more challenging. She no longer understands what is expected of her, and almost always has tremendous difficulty adapting to the new environment. Also, coping in multiple settings is quite difficult for this child. In addition to managing her home environment, she may also be required to spend a portion of her day in a before- and/or after-school daycare situation. The more settings that the NLD child is forced to cope with, the less able she will be to manage any of them well. Although it may not be possible, the ideal situation for this child is to have only two settings to cope with – home and school. If before- and/or after-school care is necessary, it would be best to have someone care for her in her own home.

Providing the right environment at home, and insisting on an equally appropriate one at school, will likely win the parent of an NLD child the irritating title of "overprotective." The fact is that you must be very protective of this child, and for quite some time. It is important for parents to "hang tough" when school officials tell them that their child is too dependent on them. The child's parents are her anchor, and she needs to know that someone will "protect" her when the need arises.

This chapter will address the environmental issues at school that need to be considered in order for the NLD child to function effectively, as well as the appropriate educational placement for her. Environmental issues cover things such as the physical layout of the classroom and school, the cafeteria, lights and sounds, crowds, routines and schedules, etc. Placement relates to which educational option you decide is most suitable for your NLD child. There are basically three placement options to choose from. The first is the public school system. This may be either a program for learning disabled youngsters, or a regular education program. The second option is a private school, whether it is one that is specifically geared to learning disabled children, or has primarily a regular education program. The third option is homeschooling, where the parent is both teacher and program coordinator, and has the freedom to create an environment specifically designed for his or her child.

The needs of these youngsters change over time. Actually, let me correct that. The NLD child's needs remain constant, but the demands of a typical school change over time. In a traditional program, student support is withdrawn at the same time that demands increase and the child's environment becomes more complex. What we normally see in schools is that, for the early years, there is a considerable amount of concrete direction, the children are with one teacher for the majority of their school day, do everything together, and are always accompanied by an adult. As children get older, directions become less concrete, students are with multiple teachers during their school day, schedules become more complex, and children are expected to be more independent in the learning process. As support is being withdrawn, and demands increase, the NLD child will be unable to adapt. She is unable to respond to the demands of a traditional educational environment after the early elementary years. Usually the warning signs of her inability to adapt are fairly apparent by third or fourth grade, and generally quite pronounced when she is required to make the transition to middle school, which unfortunately often coincides with adolescence. It is absolutely critical to accommodate this student's needs in order for her to develop both scholastically and emotionally.

ENVIRONMENT

The unique needs of this child may not be readily apparent in the younger years, but that doesn't mean that they aren't real. Although she may look like a typical five- or six-year-old, she is not at the development level of her age mates. It is important to understand the disorder and its implications in order to provide the appropriate environment for her. Don't be fooled by this child's well-developed vocabulary, or even apparent giftedness. As a society, we often equate intelligence with language skills. Because of her early strength in this area, the NLD child may appear to be far more able than she actually is. Remember, she is using her strength (verbal skills) to compensate for her deficits in other areas. Her developmental disability is a major impediment to her learning and must be accommodated in order to meet her particular needs. The following are recommendations appropriate for this child's school environment.

Educational Setting

The NLD youngster requires a tremendous amount of consistency. She needs a highly structured day, which is very predictable. During the early years, the maximum class size should be between six and eight children, with fewer children being the ideal. There should be both a teacher and an aid, so that one of them is always available to assist the NLD child when she is struggling.

It is very difficult for the NLD student when her primary teacher is replaced by a substitute teacher. She does not understand the expectations or teaching style of the substitute teacher, and generally, the substitute teacher does not understand the needs of the NLD student. To address this situation, there should be one individual identified as a consistent substitute teacher for the class. The primary teacher should educate the identified substitute teacher at the beginning of the school year about the particular needs of the NLD student. Providing this continuity will alleviate the undue stress placed on the NLD student by having to cope with a change in circumstances.

As the child progresses through her elementary years, her need for a relatively small class size continues, as does the need for a classroom aid to be available to assist her as the need arises. Unfortunately, this option may not be available. The appropriate placement for the NLD child may be a regular education class. If so, it is likely that there will be between 22 and 25 students in the class. However, it is important to understand that every step that is taken away from what this child needs – in this case, a small number of students – compromises her ability to succeed. If she is required to participate in a regular education classroom of 22 to 25 students, it is *imperative* that an aid be in the classroom at all times, with specific responsibility to assist the NLD child. The aid must be qualified to teach, since the NLD youngster will often need individual instruction in a particular assignment.

When the child reaches middle school, which is generally in sixth or seventh grade, the traditional educational environment becomes totally overwhelming for an NLD student. It is absolutely imperative that this student continue to have the same type of consistent, predictable, highly supportive environment that was required for her elementary education. Many school systems are able to meet the needs of a one-teacher class, with a limited number of students, and an aid during the elementary school years. However, most are not equipped to readily provide this environment for middle school and beyond. If the school does in fact provide small-class instruction, the classes are generally designed for either behaviorally challenged students, or for those who are academically below grade level. Neither of these situations is appropriate for the NLD student. She should not be placed in a class with such students in order to meet the requirement of a small class. Either placement would seriously undermine her education.

Classroom Setting

In the early elementary years, activities are often conducted with the children seated on the floor in a circle, which is sometimes referred to as "circle time." Since this is not an effective teaching environment for the NLD child, she will benefit from direct guidance from an adult. During "circle time," she should be seated directly next to the teacher or aid.

Most classrooms for young children are highly decorated, providing significant visual stimulation. For the NLD student, these decorations are serious barriers to learning. What most youngsters find appealing – pictures on the walls, items suspended from the ceiling, bulletin boards with work samples scattered about – the NLD child finds distracting and frustrating. The most effective way to deal with this situation is to seat the NLD child in the front row of the class, keeping the front wall clear of distracting material. The blackboard should be kept clean of any extraneous writing or other material, only having information that is directly relevant to the lesson that is being taught.

The classroom should be arranged so that all of the children sit at desks that face forward, rather than being grouped in pods. It is important to remember that the NLD student is an auditory learner, whose related issues must be accommodated. A seating of front and center is best, with quiet students seated on both sides and behind her. The NLD child must always be seated facing the teacher, and not be distracted by the children around her. Desks should not touch each other, as she may feel crowded – her personal space invaded. Since this child is an auditory learner, her hearing is likely to be acute so that normal classroom noises are amplified and far more distracting. Therefore, she should not be seated next to a fidgety child who is constantly shifting around in his or her chair, so that the chair/desk makes scraping sounds on the floor. Nor should she be seated near a student who continuously taps a pencil, or makes other distracting noises that will interfere with her ability to concentrate on what the teacher is saying.

The classroom setting that is required during the early elementary years remains necessary for the NLD student through middle school and beyond. The classroom should be arranged with all desks facing forward, and not touching. The child should continue to be seated front and center, with quiet students around her. Visual distractions should be confined to the side and rear walls, leaving the front wall uncluttered, and the blackboard free of everything except the material related specifically to the class instruction.

Other Considerations

Due to the NLD child's social and communication impairment, she should not be left unsupervised during unstructured time. Whether she is at recess, in the corridors before and after school, or eating in the cafeteria, an aid should be assigned to observe her. If she is having difficulty with social interactions, or with independent skills such as getting hot lunch or milk, the aid should step in and assist her. NLD students are most vulnerable while in unstructured settings, and will need assistance for quite some time. Initially, the aid should be more involved with helping the child, and as she becomes somewhat more independent, the aid can "shadow" her, only stepping in when it is clear that the situation warrants it. Remember that NLD children are targets for unkind youngsters and bullies and should be protected from harmful situations.

If the child is required to be transported to and from school on a bus, arrangements should be made for pick-up in front of her home. Due to her spatial and social difficulties, this should be an accommodation that is fairly easy to secure. A parent or other adult should observe the child while she waits for her bus, to insure that she is not teased or bullied by other youngsters. The NLD child should have an assigned seat on the bus, next to a kind child, and close to the bus driver. The driver should be aware of the child's disability and prevent any taunting or teasing of the child while on the bus. An adult should be available to meet the bus, again with drop-off in front of the child's home, or wherever she is cared for after school. If the child finds the bus ride stressful, she might enjoy listening to a music audiotape or CD during the trip, allowing her to relax and block out extraneous distractions.

"Specials," such as library, art, gym, and so forth, are generally less structured than other classes. Often, even in the earliest school years, children have these subject areas in a specialized location, rather than in their classroom. It is doubtful that teachers who only see the NLD child a few times a week, and possibly for only a few months during the school year, will understand her needs. Combined with the fact that these classes tend to be less structured than those in the student's primary classroom, the NLD child is left in a vulnerable position. An aid should be assigned to attend these classes along with the NLD youngster in order to insure that her needs are met, and provide assistance where appropriate.

To repeat…every step that is taken *away* from what the NLD child needs compromises her ability to succeed. *If the child displays unacceptable behavior, whether she is acting out or seems overly sensitive, the problem is almost certainly with the environment, and not with the child! Always look at the appropriateness of the demands and expectations being placed on her before assuming that there is a behavior problem. Determine what is causing the behavior, and then correct it. The behavioral problem will almost certainly disappear once the environmental problem is corrected.*

PLACEMENT

The ultimate decision-makers in the educational placement of the NLD child are always the parents. The parents know best what type of environment is most suitable for their child and compatible with the family's personal goals, such as educational philosophy, standards, values, or possibly religious principles. There are three available options for educating a child – public school, private school, or homeschool. If you select a public or private school, it is imperative that the teachers and other school staff members are supportive, flexible, and appreciate the pervasive nature of NLD. If they are new to the condition, they should be receptive to learning about it. The educational choice should be based on parental preferences, and not as a result of the public school system's failure to meet the special needs of the child. The following provides additional information on the three available educational placement options, and the implications for the NLD child.

Public School

It is the right of every school-aged child to receive a free, appropriate public education, which means that the student's education will be provided at the taxpayer's expense. Generally, this right is fulfilled through the public school system. The most common educational programs provided through the public school system are regular education and special education. Regular education is provided to those children who are not considered to need "special" assistance, and special education is provided for students who have been identified as needing "special" assistance as a result of a qualified disability, which significantly affects their ability to learn. Although we generally think of special education in relation to learning disabilities and academics, it also encompasses other disabilities, such as vision and hearing impairments, physically challenged youngsters, and serious health problems. It is important to understand that special education is a *process, not a place*.

For the young NLD child, a regular education program offered by the town's public school system may effectively meet her needs. Some youngsters will need additional support services such as special education and/or related services. School districts manage their special education programs in various ways. Some schools have self-contained classrooms for their special education students. Others have full inclusion programs, where special education students and regular education students are taught in the same classroom by two teachers – one being a regular education teacher and the other a special educator. Still other programs have resource rooms, where students spend the majority of their day in their regular classroom, and go to the resource room for special education or assistance in specific areas, such as reading, math, etc.

Services administered by the school's speech and language specialist may be indicated in order to develop the NLD child's communication skills (particularly pragmatics). Also, the services of an occupational therapist may be warranted in order to assist the child with her fine-motor difficulties and self-help skills. Although each child must qualify for these and other services, they are free within the U.S. public school system, and if provided, will be incorporated into the child's school schedule.

Many public schools have the ability to appropriately support the NLD child during the elementary school years, where a high level of structure and direction are the norm. However, most school districts, if not all, have far more difficulty meeting the needs of this student in middle school and beyond. The curriculum-driven approach in middle and high school, where there is a separate teacher for each subject, is contra-indicated for the NLD student, who does best with a single teacher. The typical environment of 1000 or more students, class and teacher changes for each period, complex schedules which often change from day to day, and the expectation of independent learning, are all inappropriate for the NLD student.

In order for the public school system to effectively accommodate an NLD student in middle and high school, they need to be creative. However, the constraints of their typical educational environment makes creativity difficult. The advent of charter and magnet schools may be one answer. Charter schools receive public funding, but are run separately from the traditional public school. They are managed by groups such as teachers, parents, or foundations, are free of many district regulations, and are often tailored to community needs. Magnet schools also receive public funding, and were originally designed to attract students from elsewhere within a school district. These schools generally place special emphasis either on overall academic achievement or within a particular area such as science, the arts, or technology. Charter and magnet schools are typically much smaller than regular public schools, and as a result of their smaller size, are able to be more flexible and creative than a traditional public school setting. If there are charter and/or magnet schools within the district, this may be a consideration for the NLD student. These public educational placement options should be considered when determining the most appropriate environment for the child, particularly in middle and high school.

Private School

Private schools are divided primarily into two classifications – independent schools and parochial schools (those with a religious affiliation). Within these two categories are both regular and special education schools. There are residential schools, day schools, and a combination of residential and day schools. Private schools are supported through student tuition, which varies tremendously from school to school. The choices can be overwhelming, making it difficult to select the appropriate placement for the NLD child.

As parents consider various schools, they need to keep the needs of the child in mind. Some schools are quite impressive, and we can forget what our original criteria was. The best placement for the NLD child may not be the most impressive school. In fact, many of the impressive private schools are too socially demanding for NLD youngsters. The ideal placement for this child has the following:

- A creative, flexible staff who is knowledgeable about NLD, or clearly excited about the prospect of becoming knowledgeable.

- A physical layout that is easy for the child to navigate within – straight corridors, well-marked doors, etc.

- A very small total student population, with 50 or fewer being ideal, but no more than 200.

- Very small class size, with 6 to 8 students and a classroom aid for the younger child, and 10 to 12 students and a classroom aid for the older student.

- Student continuity – students stay together from one year to the next, so that the NLD child can develop an understanding of the group dynamic, and form meaningful relationships.

- Teacher continuity – the student has the same teacher(s) for multiple years, and there are a limited number of teachers working with the NLD youngster.

- A school philosophy of teamwork, and a policy of zero tolerance for bullying.

Remember that although this is considered to be the ideal placement, each step taken *away* from the ideal will significantly compromise the education of the NLD student. Remain open-minded and flexible in looking at various placement options. You might unwittingly pass on a school that would have been an ideal situation for your child. For instance, you may determine that a special education school is the appropriate placement for your child. However, the school under consideration may be geared to more left-hemisphere learning disabilities such as dyslexia, have a large student population, and assign multiple teachers to your child. You may have rejected a small Christian school because your family isn't terribly religious, and they don't have a special education program. However, it may have a very small school population of fewer than 50 students, a caring and supportive staff with a philosophy to recognize and support the uniqueness of each child, a zero-tolerance policy on bullying, and require uniforms (enabling your child to fit in by looking like all of the other students)…a little gem of a school that could have easily been overlooked. It is important to consider all possible educational placements, because it is unlikely that you will find a perfect situation. First identify the most critical components, and then locate a school that most closely fulfills the criteria.

Generally, it is best to do the initial school research without directly involving the NLD child. She may become overly anxious about the prospect of change. On the other hand, if she is in a situation that is causing her extreme distress, it may be reassuring for her to know that there are alternatives to her current placement. Some private schools will accept a mid-year transfer, but most prefer, or require, that a student transfer at the start of a new school year. When considering a school, it is very important to have an on-site interview with the Director, a tour of the facility, and observe classes while they are in session. Above all else, trust your instincts!

Once the school search has been narrowed down to one or two potential placements, it is time for the NLD child to visit. No amount of research can replace the student's impression of the proposed environment. Only she can truly determine whether or not she will be comfortable there. The most important criteria for her will be whether or not she feels accepted and safe.

Homeschool

Homeschooling is an educational option which is exploding across the United States, and gaining in popularity around the world. Many parents who elect to homeschool their children do so for reasons other than a developmental or learning disability. However, it is often a viable option for NLD youngsters, and should not be discarded lightly as a temporary solution while a long-term program is being developed, or used in conjunction with a traditional educational program, or for an extended period of time.

Homeschooling is legal throughout the United States. Laws and regulations vary by state, and interpretations of the laws vary between school districts. The State Department of Education can provide information on state laws and local regulations. Some homeschool families prefer the convenience and security of having a prepackaged curriculum, while others choose to make their own decisions about what is important to learn and what materials they will use. Many colleges, universities and vocational institutes across the nation are accepting homeschooled students, and more will follow as the homeschool population continues to grow.

In most situations, the parent(s) of an NLD child will be faced with consideration of alternative education options at some point during their child's school years. For many, this happens at the point of middle school, when the demands of a traditional school overwhelm the NLD adolescent. The important parental consideration is to remain open to all available options if their child's educational environment can't be sufficiently modified to meet her unique needs.

Parents are justifiably concerned with how they might handle the challenge of homeschooling their child. There is quite a lot of available support if homeschooling appears to be the most appropriate educational alternative for the NLD child. Please refer to the appendices at the back of this book, and the website NLD on the Web! at http://www.nldontheweb.org, for homeschooling resources.

SUMMARY

Once the NLD child reaches school age, her world becomes incredibly difficult to manage. It is absolutely critical to accommodate this student's needs in order for her to develop both scholastically and emotionally.

Coping in multiple settings is quite difficult for this child. The more settings that she is forced to cope with, the less able she will be to manage any of them well.

The child uses her strengths, verbal skills and rote memory, to compensate for her many weaknesses. Her well developed vocabulary may present the erroneous illusion that she is far more capable than she actually is.

The components of a successful environment/ placement for NLD students, regardless of age, include:

○ Nurturing environment for the little ones, weaning to supportive, rather than independent, for the older students.

○ Small building, student population and class size.

○ Teacher and classroom paraprofessional/aid.

○ Limited number of teachers and class changes.

○ Continuity of teachers and students.

○ High level of structure, predictability, and routine.

○ Caring staff, accepting students, and zero tolerance for bullying.

○ Reduced visual and auditory distractions.

○ Supervision and assistance for social and spatial challenges.

There are various educational options to consider, from the public school system, including charter and magnet schools, to private schools, both independent and parochial, and finally, there is homeschooling. Although traditional public schools may be able to appropriately support the NLD child in the early to middle elementary grades, they are less able to do so in middle and high school.

Chapter 4

Teaching Strategies

Anyone who has worked closely with an NLD child has noted that she is often confused, overwhelmed, and anxious. This student has tremendous difficulty understanding the world around her, and although very eager to meet the expectations of others, she has significant difficulty understanding what those expectations are and/or how to meet them. The NLD student is often a perfectionist, which is likely due to the fact that she doesn't understand shades of gray. Where some youngsters will do as little as possible to get by, this child gives 100% effort to each and every assignment. Considering how difficult school is for this child, it is heartbreaking to see her struggle in so many ways, continue to work so hard, and not reach her potential. She deserves to be taught in a way that enables her to learn, demonstrate her strengths, and succeed.

There are several chapters within this book that are dedicated to specific aspects of the NLD student's needs. However, this chapter will deal with those across-the-board teaching strategies that apply to the student in all situations.

LEARNING STYLE

The NLD student is unusually concrete and literal, and needs very specific direction in order to function appropriately within an educational setting. The likelihood of this student's success is dependent upon the quality of information and direction that she receives from her teachers. When working with the NLD youngster, the on-going theme should be "say what you mean, and mean what you say." Rubrics and models are particularly helpful in demonstrating for this student what the performance expectation is.

Rubrics

A rubric is a scoring tool that lists the criteria for a particular piece of work…in other words, what counts. Rubrics are very effective for the NLD student, should be introduced early, and used consistently throughout her education. A rubric for an essay might indicate that the student's work will be judged on purpose, organization, details, voice, and mechanics. A rubric should also describe, usually based on a point scale, the levels of quality for each of the criteria. For example, the mechanics criteria might define the lowest level of performance as having grammar and punctuation errors and many misspellings, and the highest level of performance as having consistently accurate grammar, including how to use commas, semicolons, periods, and correct spelling. Rubrics take the mystery out of what the teacher's expectations are, which is why they are incredibly beneficial to the NLD student, who needs very specific guidance.

Models

A model is simply an example of the completed product for an assignment. Models are effective for demonstrating to students what a final report, essay, or research project might look like. It is helpful to provide several graded models per assignment so that the NLD student clearly understands the difference between poor, acceptable, and excellent work. Models are most effective for this student when used in conjunction with rubrics. Continuing with the rubric example above, students should be provided with models of an essay assignment showing varying degrees of quality. The class should receive instruction in how each essay is, or should be, rated according to the rubric. Models provide the NLD student with a concrete example of what she is working toward.

Avoid Competing Distractions

The NLD student should be seated close to the teacher, with as few distractions as possible. She should be surrounded by quiet children, and the front of the classroom should be free of extraneous decorations. These seating considerations apply to the child at all ages, from the early elementary grades through high school.

For the young child, much of the class instruction may be visual and tactile, areas of deficit for this child. Also, due to normal distractions within the classroom, it is difficult for her to remain focused on the teacher. The use of an FM receiver, also called an FM trainer, is sometimes very effective for the youngest NLD student. An FM system is a listening system designed to overcome the negative effects of distance between teacher and student and of competing noise. It has two parts, a receiver worn by the child, and a microphone/transmitter worn by the teacher. The microphone transmits the teacher's speech over FM radio waves to the student's receiver. The child wears headphones or an earbud. This system was originally designed for use by hearing-impaired students. However, it is now used for additional purposes, such as for children with central auditory processing disorders and learning disabilities. The use of an FM receiver enables the teacher to provide specific additional instruction to the NLD student, ask if the child needs additional help, and so forth. It is one way for a teacher to provide direct, one-on-one instruction to an NLD child within a regular education classroom, even if she is on the other side of the room. There is a similar system now in use for the older student, which serves the exact same purpose as the original FM system – to provide direct, one-on-one communication from teacher to student from across the classroom. The teacher's system is quite similar to the one used for the younger child, consisting of a microphone/transmitter. However, the receiver consists of a small speaker, about the size of a can of soda, which sits on the student's desk. Consideration of an FM system should be coordinated and supervised by the school district's hearing specialist.

Unimodal Instruction

The NLD student is typically a unimodal learner, unable to process information from more than one modality at a time. Neurologically typical students benefit from multi-modal teaching, such as simultaneous verbal instruction and demonstration. When this method is adopted with the NLD student, it is quite possible that she will be unable to process *either* the verbal *or* visual instruction. This may be especially true with the young child. It would be far more effective to verbally and explicitly explain the concept to be taught first, and *then* demonstrate it. It is important to remember that visual and tactile strategies are generally not effective with this student, so it is important to increase the amount of verbal instruction.

Although this student may often appear confused, she may also present as day-dreaming or inattentive. It is more likely that the perceived day-dreaming or inattention reflects this child's compensatory strategy to avoid eye contact when she is concentrating. This occurs most often at the middle and high school level where the student has determined that she is unable to look and listen simultaneously. Therefore, she will look out the window, or down at her desk so that she is better able to concentrate and process what the teacher is saying.

Unfortunately for the teacher, this student may not provide the typical cues of educational engagement, such as intently watching the teacher, smiling when eye contact is made, or other nonverbal communication such as nodding when she either understands or agrees with what is being said. However, her absence of facial affect does not mean that she is not learning. Although the child's tendency to avoid looking at the teacher, and provide little nonverbal feedback that she is attending, may be frustrating, it is the result of her disability. Rather than attempting to change these neurological traits, the teacher should use alternate means of determining whether or not the student is attending and learning. A simple touch on the arm while walking past her desk will assure the teacher that this student is focused on the instruction.

This student does not want to draw attention to herself, and often has difficulty organizing her thoughts, so that she may avoid traditional methods of self-advocacy, such as raising her hand. It would be helpful to develop some form of signal for the student to use when she does not understand, or needs additional help. A simple agreed-upon signal that the student may use to attract the teacher's attention can work very effectively.

Avoid anything that competes with the student's ability to listen to classroom instruction. She should *never* be required to write, or do any other activity, while the teacher is speaking. Notetaking should be avoided wherever possible. The student should be provided with notes *before* the beginning of an instructional segment. This will allow her to follow along, and highlight or note what the teacher indicates is very important material, without compromising her need to listen in order to learn. The exception to this practice may be for a high school student who has received specific instruction in how to take notes, *and clearly demonstrates the ability to do so without compromising her learning through listening.*

Parroting vs. Learning

The NLD student has strong rote memory skills, especially for material that is presented verbally. As a result, she tends to memorize information rather readily, and may appear to understand far more than she actually does, particularly when dealing with facts. In other words, she is parroting rather than learning. This is often reflected by excellent grades on her in-class papers and homework assignments, but failing grades on quizzes and tests. What is probably happening is that she is relying on her memory skills, but when the material is presented in a different format, or requires an understanding of the material, she is unable to perform. Strong rote memory skills are a strength in certain aspects of education, such as basic math facts, spelling and the rules of grammar. However, the NLD student tends to over-rely on her rote memory, so that she is unable to apply what she has apparently learned, but does not comprehend. To avoid simple parroting, continually check for understanding.

The following sections on frontloading and cooperative learning cover educational techniques that are excellent teaching strategies for the NLD student. Using these strategies will significantly increase this student's ability to understand material that is being taught, rather than her tendency to rely solely on her rote memory skills.

FRONTLOADING

The NLD student always needs to know the rules and expectations of her environment – both academic and personal. When a teacher begins a lesson by telling the students what they'll be expected to learn that day, "When you leave class today, I expect you to be able to identify an adjective and be able to use one to expand a sentence…", it provides focus – good for everyone, but absolutely essential for the NLD student.

Students with NLD are contextual learners. Frontloading an assignment is critical for this student, because it allows her to see the lesson in as much context as possible. As an educational specialist once said, "provide her with the closet so that she knows where to put the hangers." Frontloading begins by examining what the class already knows about the subject matter or theme that is being covered. A flip chart is helpful for jotting down "what we already know," and works much better than a blackboard, not just for the NLD student, but for the entire class because you can elicit a lot of information, flip back and forth between pages, and refer to them at a later time. The next step in frontloading is expanding the students' knowledge by providing related background information. Sometimes, this includes vocabulary; other times it includes references to works of art.

Example

Let us suppose, for instance, that I want to teach Longfellow's Paul Revere's Ride. Frontloading would include a determination of what the class already knows about the Patriot and Loyalist positions. Background building might include a discussion of Patriot's Day in Boston, a movie about the Battle of Lexington and Concord, a discussion about figurative language, and a look at a map of Boston to locate the Old North Church, the Charlestown Shore, and the Charles River. All of this activity may seem like a lot of time invested to make a poem understandable. However, these prereading activities increase the NLD student's (and all students') comprehension of the text, and is clearly time well spent.

Without the use of frontloading teaching strategies that provide contextual information, the NLD student will likely be unable to learn more than discreet facts. Left to her own devices, she will memorize pieces of information in isolation. She needs to be taught how to make connections…how facts, events, and information relate to one another.

COOPERATIVE LEARNING

Cooperative learning is a teaching strategy where small groups of students work together on an assignment in order to maximize their own and each other's learning. There are three basic classifications of cooperative learning:

1.   Base groups, which are established as long-term cooperative learning groups. The principal purpose for these groups is to provide support and encouragement for each member so that each gets the help that he/she needs in order to be successful in a course.

2. Informal cooperative learning groups are created for a specific purpose and last from a few minutes to one class period.

3. Formal cooperative learning groups are generally the most structured, and last from one class period to several weeks. The goal of these groups is for students to work collaboratively to achieve shared learning goals, and ensure that each member successfully completes the assigned learning task. Any assignment may be adapted for a formal cooperative learning group and can be implemented in any subject area.

Although an informal or base learning group would not be effective for an NLD student, a formal cooperative learning group can be particularly beneficial for NLD students whose strength is in the verbal/auditory modality. Let's look at what this particular teaching strategy looks like, and why it can be so effective for the NLD child.

The teacher first instructs the students in the dynamics of cooperative learning. He/she explains that the objective is for the team to complete an assignment, and that each student will be graded for their individual accomplishments *and* for the final team results. The teacher provides the students with the expectations for group learning, and provides a timeline for the students to follow. He/she clearly identifies what the assignment is, and how the students are to approach it from a team perspective. The entire team is held responsible for ensuring that all members participate throughout the activity. Individual roles are established for use within each group. For instance, each team might require a spokesperson, someone to take notes, someone to develop any visual material, a coordinator for research activities, and so on. Most importantly, the students receive instruction on how to provide constructive feedback to their team members. All of these requirements should be prepared by the teacher *in writing*, and provided to the students before starting their assignment.

The class is then divided up into small groups, with individual team members selected by the teacher, and particular care given to the members identified for the NLD student's team. The classroom is arranged to facilitate group interaction. Written expectations and team rules are provided to each team. The teacher continually monitors student interaction within the groups, and provides assistance and clarification as needed. The teacher provides on-going feedback to each team on their use of group skills and facilitates problem-solving when necessary.

The formal cooperative learning group, when properly structured and implemented, is ideal for the NLD student, *especially* when introduced at a young age. Why? Let's consider the following academic characteristics of NLD youngsters:

- They have impaired social skills.

- They are often isolated from their peers.

- They learn best when they are fully engaged.

- Although auditory learners, lecture classes which require notetaking create a hardship for them.

- They have very uneven skill sets.

- They have difficulty distinguishing between relevant and irrelevant information.

- Their reading comprehension is impaired.

- They are strong verbal learners.

- They have weak organizational skills.

Now let's consider how a formal cooperative learning model can be highly beneficial to the NLD student. First, the social "rules" have been established by the teacher, and the team is responsible for ensuring that each member actively participates. Therefore, if the NLD student is reticent, she will be drawn out by her peers, rather than being allowed to passively observe the interaction of other members. Since the teacher selects the members of each team, care can be taken to ensure that members are tolerant and supportive of the NLD youngster. The assignment has been clearly structured by the teacher, thereby mitigating the organizational difficulties of the NLD student, and further clarification may be provided by other team members. The NLD student is not solely responsible for a large assignment, but rather for a single task, where her strengths may be utilized. Any reading assignment required as part of the activity is discussed within the group. This enables the NLD student to gain an understanding of the material that she would likely not grasp on her own.

Not only do cooperative learning exercises aid in the NLD student's academic learning process, but they also foster social skills, provide an opportunity for her to display her strengths, thereby improving self-esteem, and with a little luck, provide a means for her to make friends.

To further enhance the cooperative learning experience for the NLD student, the following are additional recommended considerations:

° Teams should be identified at the beginning of the school year, with specific care taken to ensure that the NLD student is placed with a supportive group of peers. The teams should continue throughout the course of the school year so that the NLD youngster can form relationships within the group, and be more likely to take risks within the team.

° Once the NLD student becomes comfortable working within her team, the identified roles should be rotated so that the student is exposed to tasks that she would not normally feel comfortable performing. The support of fellow team members is crucial in this process.

° The team's feedback process is a critical component of the cooperative learning experience. Handled poorly, it is destructive for all students, but potentially devastating to the NLD student. In addition to very clear parameters established by the teacher (what is and is not allowed while providing feedback between students), evaluation forms should be developed by the teacher which reinforce an acceptable process. For each assignment, all team members would evaluate their own contribution, as well as the team's combined performance. In addition, each member of the team would be responsible for providing feedback to his/her team mates. Feedback would require several positive statements, and only one constructive recommendation for improvement (with zero tolerance for destructive statements). The teacher would also complete evaluation forms measuring the effectiveness of the team as a unit, and for each member's contribution.

A formal cooperative learning approach can be adapted and introduced as early as preschool. In order for the NLD student to benefit from this teaching strategy, it should be implemented no later than the upper elementary grades. It is important to recognize that no matter how beneficial a concept might be, success depends upon well executed implementation. For the typical student, a poorly implemented teaching strategy is merely ineffective. However, a poorly implemented cooperative learning environment would have disastrous results for the NLD student. The teacher must be well versed in all of the elements necessary to implement this learning strategy, as well as how it may benefit, or harm, the NLD student.

VISUAL PROCESSING

The NLD student has visual processing, tracking (moving the eye along a straight line), and planing (integrating information from the vertical and horizontal plane) deficits. She should not be required to copy material from either the board or a book, since she will almost certainly make mistakes during the transposition process, and will be unable to accurately complete the assignment. Instead, she should be provided with the material that has already been copied for her.

The amount of information on a page should be reduced for this student. She will become overwhelmed with too much (and too crowded) visual material, and be unable to isolate the specific details of the problem that she is required to answer. It may also be beneficial to block out everything on the page except the problem that she is working on, to aid her ability to visually focus on the pertinent data.

The use of flip charts and overheads are effective teaching aids for this student. Not only is the contrast easier for her to process than chalk on a blackboard, but the switch from one chart or overhead to another provides her with the cue to switch mental set from one topic or issue to another. Flip charts and overheads are especially effective for the middle- and high-school NLD student who has difficulty understanding what is important when she is taking notes. The student should be instructed that what is on the flip chart or overhead is important, and she should be provided sufficient time to copy the material when the teacher is not doing actual teaching. This assumes, of course, that the NLD student's handwriting has improved to the point that it is functional. If not, the teacher should provide the student with a paper copy of the overheads or information presented on the flip charts.

GRAPHIC ORGANIZERS

Graphic organizers are an excellent way to present information so that this student can both process and remember it. Although the visual modality is not this student's preferred learning style, simple icon representations are excellent memory enhancers for her.

Example

An effective way to help the NLD student remember the math concept "order of operations" is to provide her with an index card with the operational symbols presented in the order in which the problem should be performed. These index cards should be developed for every math concept that is taught. The student should be permitted to use her index cards when performing math problems.

Example

When students are introduced to essay questions, the NLD student should be allowed to provide her answer in graphic organizer format, rather than in prose. If a question asks what happened before and after a particular event, she should be taught to make a "T" chart – 'Before' would be the heading on one side of the chart, and 'After' would be the heading on the other side, with a vertical line drawn between the two. She would then list the events that belong in either column.

The use of graphic organizers are an effective strategy to "level the playing field" for this child so that she is able to demonstrate her level of knowledge or skill.

The teaching strategies that are covered in this chapter are effective not only for the NLD student, but for all students. Time and time again, teachers who have adapted their classroom instruction to use these strategies for NLD students have found that all of their students benefit significantly. They learn more, are better able to apply what they have learned and to work as a team.

SUMMARY

The NLD student is very concrete and literal, and has tremendous difficulty understanding the world around her. Although very eager to meet the expectations of others, she has significant difficulty understanding what those expectations are and/or how to meet them, and needs very specific direction in order to function appropriately within an educational setting. Rubrics and models are particularly helpful in demonstrating for this student what the performance expectation is.

The NLD student should be seated close to the teacher, with as few distractions as possible. Consider the use of an FM system that allows one-on-one communication from teacher to student. There are separate models for younger and older children.

The NLD student is typically a unimodal learner, unable to process information from more than one modality at a time. Visual and tactile teaching strategies are generally not effective for this student, so it is important to increase the amount of verbal instruction. Avoid anything that competes with the student's ability to listen to classroom instruction.

It is likely that what is perceived as daydreaming or inattention reflects this child's compensatory strategy to avoid eye contact when she is concentrating. A simple touch on the arm while walking past her desk will assure the teacher that this student is focused on the instruction.

The NLD student has strong rote memory skills, especially for material that is presented verbally. However, the NLD student tends to over-rely on her rote memory, so that she is unable to apply what she has apparently learned but does not comprehend.

Frontloading is a critical teaching strategy, because it allows the NLD student to see the lesson in as much context as possible. Without the use of frontloading teaching strategies that provide contextual information, the NLD student will likely be unable to learn more than discrete facts. She needs to be taught how to make connections... how facts, events, and information relate to one another.

Cooperative learning is an incredibly effective teaching strategy for NLD students. Small groups of students work together on an assignment in order to maximize their own and each other's learning. If implemented properly, a cooperative learning environment can be particularly beneficial for NLD students whose strength is in the verbal/auditory modality, and learn best through discussion.

Visual processing, tracking, and planing problems can be minimized by eliminating the task of copying material from either the board or a book. The use of flip charts and overheads are effective teaching aids for this student. The contrast is easier to process than chalk on a blackboard, and the switch from one chart or overhead to another provides the cue to switch mental set from one topic or issue to another. Flip charts and overheads are especially effective for determining the relevant parts of a lesson.

Although the visual modality is not this student's preferred learning style, simple icon representations are excellent memory enhancers. Graphic organizers are an efficient way to present information so that this student can both process and remember it, and demonstrate what she has learned.

Chapter 5

Social and Emotional Functioning

The child with NLD will generally be the cooperative student who is polite and anxious to please, most notably with adults. In fact, this may be the first thing that you notice about her. Socially, she may often be on the fringes, looking on, rather than participating in activities. You may quickly sense that the child is developmentally younger than her peer group. The reality is that this youngster needs a tremendous amount of structure in her interaction with others, whether it is a conversation with her teacher or at play with other children. What presents as politeness is, in actuality, a need to understand and follow the rules that govern her social environment. Even though she may possess strong verbal skills, the young child may be unable to initiate a conversation or interaction of any kind. The older student may attempt to initiate a conversation or peer interaction, but be inept or inappropriate in doing so. The NLD child often suffers from anxiety, which at times appears to be the primary difficulty. However, it is the underlying problems with communication and social deficits, coupled with other learning issues, that creates this student's anxiety.

This chapter will cover the topics of communication and social skills, along with suggested intervention strategies for both, as well as how best to manage this student's anxiety.

COMMUNICATION SKILLS

The NLD child will likely have expressive language skills which appear to be well beyond her peer group. The advanced vocabulary of this youngster, as compared to her age mates, will continue to be notable throughout her grammar-school years, and likely into the higher grades. In fact, the NLD child's vocabulary may be so well developed that her peer group is "put off" by the child's language, because of their inability to understand, or their lack of interest in, what she is saying.

A sophisticated vocabulary is one of the hallmarks of NLD, and as a result, adults often assume that the child is gifted. What is not so obvious is that this particular child is dependent almost exclusively on language, so that her vocabulary is disproportionately developed. This child does not learn from environmental clues, by watching other children or adults, or even from experimentation – she tends to use words and labels for everything. Since she relies so heavily on words, it is natural that her vocabulary and language skills would develop more rapidly than other children of the same age.

Nonverbal Communication

Vocabulary and language alone do not automatically result in effective communication skills. The fact is that 35% or less of all communication is verbal, with the remaining 65% or more being comprised of nonverbal communication. It is in the area of nonverbal communication that the NLD child struggles. Nonverbal communication includes things such as gaze, facial expression, body language, and tone of voice. Even in young children, nonverbal communication plays a major role. Young babies respond to their mother's smile and tone of voice, and toddlers will point to what they want, or take someone by the hand in order to show them something. NLD children do not have the advantage of these nonverbal communication skills.

Most of us are unaware of how much we rely on nonverbal communication. The following are examples of what this child faces daily, and is unable to process.

Example no. 1

The students are in class, but no teacher is present. They take advantage of the lack of supervision and begin to socialize, toss things around the room, and generally act like kids. A teacher walks into the room, and they immediately stop what they are doing and sit obediently in their seats. The signal for appropriate behavior is the teacher walking into the room. This signal is nonverbal, and meaningless to the NLD child who may continue to do what the other children were doing, not understanding that the time for fun has ended.

Example no. 2

The students are in class, and a teacher is present. While her back is turned, other students are passing notes, making faces, and whispering. The teacher turns to face the class, hands on hips, and simply stares at them. Again this signal for obedience is nonverbal, and again, meaningless to the NLD child, who may continue to copy what the other students were just doing behind the teacher's back.

Example no. 3

During class instruction, the teacher moves from one subject to another by simply putting one book away, and picking up another. The other students note this nonverbal signal, and follow her actions. The NLD child misses this cue, is confused, and unable to follow the transition.

Unfortunately, in all three of these examples, a teacher who does not understand the implications of nonverbal communication for this child may reprimand her for what appears to be disobedience or lack of compliance. The reprimand, and any resulting disciplinary action, is lost on this student. It will only increase her anxiety and confusion because she does not understand what she did wrong. It is absolutely imperative that teachers avoid the use of nonverbal communication when dealing with this student. She will not process it, any more than a blind child would, and cannot be held responsible for her inability to understand what is not verbalized. If a teacher perceives that the child is being disobedient, disrespectful, or noncompliant, he/she should reconsider the circumstances to see where the communication breakdown occurred, for it surely did. Once the breakdown is identified, it is important to gently and kindly explain to the NLD child what she did that was unacceptable. It is best to do this away from the other students so that she is not embarrassed by her mistake.

Verbal Communication

Although this child may be highly verbal, and have a sophisticated vocabulary, it is very important that the teacher understand the significance of her communication deficits, in spite of her apparent strength in this area. This student is very literal and concrete in her processing of information. When you speak to her, she will process exactly what you say, and is unable to interpret what you meant but did not specifically state.

Concrete and Literal

Most very young children tend to be concrete and literal in their communication with others. Therefore, the young NLD child may not stand out among her peers as being significantly more literal. However, once she reaches the middle to upper elementary grades, when teachers and adults become less direct in their communication, this deficit will become quite pronounced. No matter the child's age, it is important to be aware that this child is very literal, and will often misunderstand what you or others say to her. What may be more obvious in the younger child, is that she has tremendous difficulty with open-ended questions. This communication deficit will continue, and appear to get worse, unless there is significant intervention. The following are examples of what may occur in the classroom:

Example no. 1

If you ask the child, "how is your family?," she will likely respond with a blank stare. There are too many variables represented by the word "how" for her to formulate an answer to your question. In order for her to answer the question, the scope needs to be narrower, and more specific, such as "is everyone in your family finally over the flu?"

Example no. 2

Although this may be a child who talks a lot in some circumstances, you will find that at other times she is noticeably silent. For instance, during "show and tell" time for younger children, she may bring something from home, but seem to have little to say about it. Or, after a vacation, when prodded to share what she did, she may respond, but with few details and no apparent emotion. For example, if she and her family went to Disney World, she will state that, with little or no elaboration. However, another child who went to Disney World would clearly display excitement, tell you about the great rides, the characters, the airplane ride, and many associated details. In fact, you may have trouble bringing the child's sharing to closure so that you can move on to the next child. With the NLD child, you would find yourself trying to elicit both information and emotion. It isn't that she doesn't have a lot to share, or didn't have a good time, but rather that she has tremendous difficulty organizing her thoughts in order to verbalize them.

Because there is such a risk of the child misunderstanding what is said, it is critical that the teacher check with the student to be sure that she fully understands a task or other instructions. Do not assume that since she didn't ask for clarification that she knows what to do.

If it is a task that the teacher gives to the entire class, once they have started, he/she should go to the NLD child, check to see that she has also begun the task, and has a full understanding of what is required. Continual checks on her progress should be made, and any course correction that is necessary should be made in a clear, constructive manner, without indicating that she has done something wrong. Remember that this is likely a sensitive child who wants to follow the rules, and she will feel reprimanded if she has misunderstood the instructions.

While working with an NLD student, it may be helpful to use strategies that are appropriate for an ESL child (English as a second language). The NLD and ESL student populations share many similar traits, such as deficits in the pragmatic and cultural use of English. It would be helpful for the NLD student's teacher(s) to meet with an ESL teacher who can share his/her teaching strategies.

There are many instances in which the NLD student may appear to be uncooperative or oppositional, but are actually the result of poor communication. The following are examples of teacher/student interaction where improved communication can avoid a difficult situation:

Example no. 1

The child is scheduled to go to the resource room for additional help with math. The regular class is going to play a fun game that the child wants to participate in, but will miss if she goes to the resource room. The resource room teacher comes to collect the student, and says to her, "would you like to come with me now?" The NLD student says "no," and the teacher assumes that the child is being rude. However, from the child's perspective, the teacher asked a question, and the child responded honestly. The teacher created the communication problem by phrasing her approach as a question, rather than a statement.

Example no. 2

If the NLD child is given an assignment, and asks "Why do I have to do this?," she is not being oppositional. Her question is basic – what is the purpose for doing this? How will I use it? She needs a detailed explanation of the purpose of the assignment, how it fits into the bigger picture of the lesson, and the benefit being derived. Without a clear contextual understanding, the task will be meaningless and in all likelihood she will be unable to do it, or to benefit from it.

Example no. 3

The teacher assigns a homework exercise that is a map activity. The NLD student says that she can't do it. The teacher may respond with, "just do your best," and the child gets upset. The fact is that she really can't do the assignment, no matter how hard she tries to "do her best." This child isn't trying to avoid work, and she isn't being uncooperative. She needs understanding and an alternative assignment.

If our perception is that this student is being manipulative, difficult, resistive, rude, or uncooperative, we are doing something wrong. It is critical to look beyond the presenting behavior in order to identify the problem. A breakdown in communication is the likely culprit. It is not the child's responsibility to figure out our intent, it is our responsibility to ensure that she understands. This student is communication handicapped. Just as we would not require a blind child to see, we cannot require a communication handicapped child to understand what we mean but do not clearly state, or "get a grip" when she is confused and anxious because she does not understand.

Multiple Meanings

Words with multiple meanings pose a particular challenge for the NLD student. Although she has an excellent vocabulary, she is often derailed when one word means two very different things. It is important that multiple meanings of the same word be taught and explained.

Example

A seventh-grade NLD student is studying the United Kingdom in social studies, and families of animals in science. When she takes her mid-term social studies examination, she does very well. However, when faced with her science examination, the teacher has used the words 'animal kingdom' instead of the familiar 'animal families' and she fails the examination. She did not understand that the word 'kingdom' was being used in the same context as 'families', and was focused exclusively on its application to her social studies class, unable to apply it to her science exam. When the word was subsequently explained, and she retook the examination, she aced it.

Word substitutions, which may have a different contextual meaning for the student, are often major stumbling blocks to her educational success. It is important to continually check for understanding, rather than assume that this child's apparently sophisticated vocabulary will automatically compensate for semantic issues.

It would be *very* beneficial for the NLD student to receive pragmatic instruction from a speech and language professional (SLP) who has expertise in this area. Early intervention to improve this student's functional use of language is extremely important.

SOCIAL SKILLS

The NLD child will either be the solitary child in the classroom, or one whose behavior with other children is markedly immature. Her social skills lag considerably behind her peer group, and many NLD youngsters are content to play by themselves. If this is the case, it would be a mistake to encourage her to join a group, or have another child join her in an activity, without adult facilitation. With the young child, the primary reason for her solitary play is likely because she is not developmentally ready for shared activity. She needs to be guided in the social process so that she does not become overwhelmed or angry. It is important for the adults who interact with this child to understand that social skills do not come naturally to her, and she will not learn them through observation. Direct verbal instruction is the method of choice in teaching these children *what* to do, *when* to do it, and *how* to do it. Rules governing social interaction need to be explicitly explained to the child, *and* practiced.

Peer Interaction

During unstructured times, such as recess or independent play, the young NLD child will need adult assistance in her attempts to play with other children. If the activity level of the other children is overwhelming, remove the NLD youngster from the chaos, and allow her to enjoy a favored activity by herself.

It is most appropriate to facilitate the interaction between the NLD child and an age mate. Select a responsible peer who is sensitive and not too rambunctious to interact with the NLD child. Next, select an activity that you are sure that the NLD youngster is capable of doing, avoiding activities which require dexterity, fine-motor coordination, or pretend play. These are all activities which will likely be difficult for her. The adult facilitator should then work with the two children, verbally explaining the activity for the NLD child as it proceeds. Mediated social interactions are absolutely critical for this youngster. In time, and with enough practice, she will learn appropriate skills for interacting with her peer group.

Lunch time will be challenging for this child, especially if it is in a cafeteria. She should have an assigned seat at a table with children who are good role models. It is important that an adult monitor her during this period, providing intervention when needed. She may have difficulty eating her lunch if there is boisterous activity surrounding her. If she is clearly overwhelmed by the traditional environment, it would be beneficial to allow her to eat her lunch in a quiet place, such as the classroom, or elsewhere, as long as an adult is present to assist her.

An additional situation that is very stressful for the NLD youngster is riding on the school bus. Not only is this an unstructured time, but generally it is also unsupervised, with the exception of the bus driver. The children often become unruly, and the negative aspects of the social environment are inappropriate for the NLD child. It is best for the child to have an assigned seat that is near enough to the driver so that if the child needs assistance, he/she can provide it.

The NLD student should be monitored during all social situations, especially those that are unstructured. Unfortunately, because of her problems and social deficits, she is likely to be teased, the butt of jokes, or bullied. An adult should always be present to intercede, so that she is not subjected to abuse by her classmates. The NLD child's peer group will invariably be more socially adept, and if social situations are not monitored closely, she is apt to be blamed for problems that she did not create.

Social Acceptance

It is important to the NLD student that she be accepted, not only by her teachers and other adults, but by her peer group. It is also important that the adults act as role models for the children. If the teacher is accepting of the NLD child, it is more likely that the students will be as well.

In order to increase the likelihood that this student will be accepted by her peer group, she should fit into their culture. Her appearance should not set her apart. If all of the girls wear jeans to school, the NLD child should be encouraged to dress similarly. Parents may be unaware of what particular look is considered to be "in" or, conversely, "the kiss of death." Teachers should share with parents what is considered to be the acceptable "uniform" for a particular age group, including clothes, shoes, backpacks, lunch boxes, etc. Actually, uniforms are the ideal! They level the apparel playing field, so that the NLD child does not have to figure out what is socially appropriate to wear, or worry about being ridiculed for her choices.

BEHAVIOR

Many people working with NLD children are sometimes mystified by their behavior. They may feel that these children are defiant, rude, spoiled, lazy, and any number of other incorrect observations. None of this is true, and not only represents ignorance, but seriously damages the self-esteem of these very special kids. They want to learn, to fit in, to follow the rules – they just don't understand all those unwritten rules!

If you were to bring home a brand new puppy, clearly you would not expect it to know anything. Instead, you would teach it very patiently and concretely, using a tremendous amount of repetition before the puppy could grasp what is expected of it. NLD children need this same approach. Everyone who has contact with this child should have a clear understanding of her communication and social deficits, anticipate misunderstandings, and be as patient and concrete as they would with an innocent, because she is. Unfortunately, since the child presents an *illusion* of age-appropriate communication skills, her deficits are rarely fully understood or appreciated. Let's look at a few situations where the behavior of these children is often misunderstood.

1. Change (even with prior notice) is extremely stressful and difficult for this child to handle. When the NLD student's established routine and/or rules are changed, she may respond inappropriately. She *depends* on consistency in *all* aspects of her school experience, and unusual behavior should be an indication that she is confused and/or overwhelmed. Verbally reassure her, explain *exactly* what will take place, and at what point her schedule will return to normal.

2. A situation where the NLD student feels she is being "ambushed" with something that she is requested/required to do, but not prepared for, will likely cause anxiety, which may result in unusual behavior. For instance, if she is required to use the school library during class time to work on a research project, and her established method of doing research is by using her computer at home, she may balk at going to the library. Discuss with the child her reluctance, and find out what the underlying problem is. Rather than forcing her to use the library for her research, encourage her to use the strategy that is effective for her. When the class goes to the library, she can simply sit and read quietly while the other children do their research.

3. If this student explains how she compensates for a particular problem, or what works for her, and it is ignored or discounted, she will become frustrated, often resulting in tears or anger. This student lives with her problem on a daily basis, and should be encouraged in her efforts to self-advocate and compensate for her deficits.

4. When she asks "why" she has to do something she should not be given an answer such as "your parents want it" or "it's in your program." Her question was far more basic – what is the purpose? Without a clear contextual understanding, her ability to proceed is compromised, and an inappropriate response from an adult will likely result in agitation. When the NLD child asks "why," *always* assume that she is in need of clarification.

5. Sometimes the NLD child becomes silly for no apparent reason. No matter what type of admonishment you provide, the silliness continues. Silliness should not be perceived as the student's attempt to be funny, and contrary to how it may seem, this child is not happy. Silliness is almost always an indication that she is either overwhelmed or very anxious. Develop an agreed-upon strategy with this student for times when this occurs. At the first sign of silliness, provide her with a signal that she should use the strategy,

which may be going to the rest room, getting a drink of water, or some other appropriate means of calming herself.

Listen to this child! Her school work is vitally important to her, and she takes great pride in her work. When faced with resistance, first assume that it is a reflection of the student's frustration and confusion. Determine what is causing the resistance or behavior, and the resolution will likely be quite obvious.

ANXIETY MANAGEMENT

The NLD student is often quite anxious. This should come as no surprise. Due to her significant challenges, the world is often a frightening place for her. Just navigating the environment, dealing with the social and communication demands, and the sensory assaults is difficult at best, and that doesn't address her academic learning problems. In order for this child to function within a school setting, it is critical to provide her with a support system and safety net. There are several things that can significantly reduce this student's anxiety and stress.

Provide a Safe Place

One of the first, and simplest, things that can be done for this student is to identify a safe place where she can go whenever she is feeling anxious or overwhelmed. This may be the school nurse's office, the guidance office, or, if there is one on the premises, the school psychologist. Naturally, in addition to a safe place, there must be an identified person that she is to report to, who will assist her. Therefore, when considering the available options, it is important to remember that the selected individual needs to be available throughout the day. The younger child should be escorted to her safe place, preferably by an adult, but a responsible and compassionate classmate may suffice. The older NLD student should be provided with a permanent hall pass, and be allowed to leave class at any time in order to go to her safe place so that she can calm down or re-group. All teachers must be advised of this accommodation, and should know the location of the identified safe place, along with the individual who is to handle the NLD child in these circumstances. There may be occasions when the student becomes distraught, and rather than send her to the designated safe place, it would be more appropriate to have her identified individual come and collect her. This may be especially true for the younger child.

Procedures should be established for transitioning the NLD student from the safe place back to her class. For the older student, who may have missed her class change, someone should collect her books if they were left in her classroom, and escort her to the next class.

Once the child knows that procedures have been established, she will be far less likely to feel trapped when her anxiety catches her unaware. Without the identification of a safe place and associated individual, the NLD student may actually develop panic attacks.

Provide a Security Blanket

It is quite helpful to reassure this child by providing her with a special item from home that she is allowed to take to school with her every day. Naturally, it should be something which is quite small – a beanie animal, a lucky charm such as a rabbit's foot, or something which can be worn around the neck. The selection of just the right item may be a special activity that the parent and child can share. They may set aside a certain day and time to shop for the item, or find something that the child already owns that is associated with family and safety. The child could be told by the parent that when she takes it to school with her each day, it will remind her of home, and being safe and loved. She might be instructed to clutch or stroke the item when she feels herself getting upset, and in this way, may actually be able to self-soothe. This technique is helpful for the NLD child right through middle school, and possibly beyond. Even when this student seems to be doing quite well, showing little or no anxiety at school, you might find that she still has her special item tucked inside her backpack.

A key to successful anxiety management at school is to provide a very nurturing environment for the younger NLD child, gradually moving to a supportive one as she gets older. Do not force independence on this student, since she will need support far longer than you would expect of a neurologically typical child. However, in the upper grades, the support should be less intrusive and obvious so that the NLD student is not subjected to peer rejection or teasing as a result.

Schedules and Routines

Another important strategy for controlling the NLD child's level of anxiety is to provide her with a considerable amount of predictability. This student thrives on schedules and routine, and may become quite anxious when faced with unanticipated changes. A very simple method of avoiding potential anxiety is to inform her of scheduling changes as soon as possible. Another is to provide her with a daily schedule, so that she doesn't have to remember what will happen next, or where she has to be at a particular time. The child's schedule can be typed up, and reduced in size. Make tons of copies, so that a fresh copy of the schedule can be clipped to the child's backpack, or placed in her pocket, each morning. All teachers should be aware that this student carries a daily schedule with her, and *any* changes should be marked on her schedule *and* verbally explained to her at the *beginning* of each day.

Figure 5.1 is an example of a simple schedule for a child in the early elementary years. For the child who does not yet read, pictures may/should replace words. Be sure to circle the appropriate day of the week before providing it to the child.

Monday	Tuesday	Wednesday	Thursday	Friday
Mrs. Hanley's Classroom	Mrs. Hanley's Classroom	Mrs. Hanley's Classroom	Mrs. Hanley's Classroom	Mrs. Hanley's Classroom
Reading Spelling	Reading Spelling	Reading Spelling	Reading Spelling	Reading Spelling
Snack	Snack	Snack	Snack	Snack
Grammar Penmanship	Grammar Penmanship	Grammar Penmanship	Grammar Penmanship	Grammar Penmanship
Lunch Recess	Lunch Recess	Lunch Recess	Lunch Recess	Lunch Recess
Arithmetic Art	Arithmetic Gym	Arithmetic Library	Arithmetic Gym	Arithmetic Health
Bus for Home	Bus for Home	Bus for Home	Bus for Home	Bus for Home

Figure 5.1 School Schedule

For NLD children in the upper grades, carrying a school schedule is absolutely critical. Once the child reaches an age when students change classrooms for each subject, it will be very confusing for her to remember where she is supposed to be, and when she is supposed to be there. In addition to the "shrunk down" copy of the schedule provided to the student, she should also have a back-up, full-size copy of her schedule(s) in her organizational binder, in the event that she loses the schedule that she is carrying. Times and room locations should be included on the schedule for this age group, because they change classrooms for most subjects, so that time and location are important. Again, it is critical to make changes to the student's schedule at the beginning of each day, so that she is prepared for any change to her routine.

The following is a copy of one middle school student's schedule. This student actually had two schedules, because there was an "A

Week" schedule, and a "B Week" schedule, which alternated throughout the year. It is quite common for students in middle and high school to have schedules that change from day to day, or week to week. This particular sample is for the student's "A Week" schedule.

	Monday	Tuesday	Wednesday	Thursday	Friday
8:00–8:13	Homeroom #221 Mrs. Childress	Homeroom #221 Mrs. Childress	Homeroom #221 Mrs. Childress	Homeroom #221 Mrs. Childress	Homeroom #221 Mrs. Childress
8:15–8:55	Skills for Living #227 Mrs.Cohen	Skills for Living #227 Mrs.Cohen	Skills for Living #227 Mrs.Cohen	Skills for Living #227 Mrs.Cohen	Skills for Living #227 Mrs.Cohen
8:57-9:37	1:1 Math #224 Mrs. Woodhall	1:1 Math #224 Mrs. Woodhall	1:1 Math #224 Mrs. Woodhall	1:1 Math #224 Mrs. Woodhall	1:1 Math #224 Mrs. Woodhall
9:39–10:19	Social Studies #219 Mrs. Wyland	Social Studies #219 Mrs. Wyland	Social Studies #219 Mrs. Wyland	Social Studies #219 Mrs. Wyland	Social Studies #219 Mrs. Wyland
10:21–11:01	Lang. Arts #221 Mrs. Childress	Lang. Arts #221 Mrs. Childress	Lang. Arts #221 Mrs. Childress	Lang. Arts #221 Mrs. Childress	Lang. Arts #221 Mrs. Childress
11:03–11:43	Study Skills #221 Mrs. Childress	Study Skills #221 Mrs. Childress	Study Skills #221 Mrs. Childress	Study Skills #221 Mrs. Childress	Study Skills #221 Mrs. Childress
11:45–12:10	Lunch/Caf.	Lunch/Caf.	Lunch/Caf.	Lunch/Caf.	Lunch/Caf.
12:12–1:00	Study Period #221 Mrs. Childress	Study Period #221 Mrs. Childress	Study Period #221 Mrs. Childress	Study Period #221 Mrs. Childress	Study Period #221 Mrs. Childress
1:02–1:42	Resource Help #222 Mrs. Woodhall	Resource Help #222 Mrs. Woodhall	Resource Help #222 Mrs. Woodhall	Resource Help #222 Mrs. Woodhall	Resource Help #222 Mrs. Woodhall
1:44–2:25	Science #229 Mr. Kustigian	Science #229 Mr. Kustigian	Science #229 Mr. Kustigian	Science #229 Mr. Kustigian	Science #229 Mr. Kustigian

Figure 5.2 "A" Week – School Schedule

The level of detail required on the student's schedule will depend on the complexity of her schedule, and her specific needs. Some children may require less detail, while others may require that the schedule show only the particular day that applies, so they don't become confused.

Teacher Introductions

As you know by now, novelty or change of any kind is very stressful for this student. One of the most difficult situations for her is to spend her entire summer vacation worrying about what the next year will be like once school resumes. By the time the first day of school rolls around, this child may be so anxious that she may balk at attending school at all. With just a bit of planning, there are a few things that can be done to reduce her stress and anxiety.

The NLD student should meet her teacher for the coming school year before the summer break begins. This is best done on the last day of school, after the other students have left the building, or on the following day if the teachers attend school past the last day with students. Prior to the introduction, the receiving teacher should be briefed on the profile of the NLD student, so that she will know how best to put the child at ease. The meeting can be short, fifteen minutes or so, and the receiving teacher can explain a little bit about what the students will learn in the coming year. The NLD student and teacher should meet at least one more time a day or so before the new school year begins, again for only a few moments. It would be helpful for the teacher to assign the child her desk during this meeting, so the child knows exactly where to go when she enters the classroom on the first day of school.

For the older student, who will have several teachers, the same approach is appropriate. The middle or high school student may suffer from even more anxiety than the grammar school student, because of the demands of multiple teachers. As with the younger student, arrange a meeting for the last day of school once the other students have been dismissed. The receiving teachers should be briefed on the NLD student's profile prior to meeting her. It is important to be understanding of the teachers who are just gearing down from the current year's students, and not yet thinking about the next school year. The purpose of a meeting between the new teachers and the NLD student is simply to reduce her level of anxiety. She should meet each teacher, preferably in his/her respective classroom, and a brief five-minute chat should be sufficient. Again, as with the younger child, this student should have an opportunity to revisit her new teachers a day or so before the new school year begins. Even at this age, an assigned seat is beneficial so that the NLD student knows exactly where to go on the first day of school.

Familiar Students

It is very helpful for the younger NLD child to know what other students will be in her class. For the older student, she needs to know what students will share her class schedule. As soon as the school has finalized the class and schedule assignments, provide the NLD student with a list of her classmates and/or those who will share her schedule.

It is also very beneficial to provide the NLD student with some continuity from year to year. For the younger child, the school should arrange to have several familiar students in her class, particularly students who have been kind and understanding. For the older child, every effort should be made to identify a "buddy" who shares the NLD child's schedule. This continuity not only provides reassurance for the NLD student, but for the older child, there is the added benefit that she can follow her "buddy" from class to class, increasing the likelihood that she will be able to get where she needs to be without becoming lost.

Prevent Overload

Because it is so difficult for this student to manage her day, she may become overwhelmed and/or exhausted. Naturally, this would compromise her ability to remain attentive and focused, and to learn. It is often helpful to provide the older student with a study period twice a day – once in the morning, and again in the afternoon – so that she does not become over-stressed. This period may either be a quiet time for her to do homework, or read, or it may be time spent in the resource room to receive additional support from a special education teacher or paraprofessional. However, it should not be a time for teaching, which would defeat the purpose of providing the child with a break. How this period is used will depend on the particular needs of the NLD student.

SUMMARY

The NLD child, although developmentally younger than her peer group, may speak like an adult. She has significant communication and social deficits which compromise her learning and development. This student is quite literal and concrete, and behavioral issues generally result from misunderstandings. She typically struggles with very high levels of anxiety, and may be prone to panic attacks.

Communication Skills

This student is communication handicapped, as a result of her severe nonverbal communication deficits. Nonverbal communication should be avoided, since this child, like a blind child, is unable to process this form of communication. Say what you mean, and mean what you say. This student cannot intuit what is not specifically stated. ESL strategies may be very effective for her. Words with multiple meanings should be pointed out to this student. Misunderstandings are an ongoing problem for her, and should be anticipated and dealt with in an understanding and supportive manner.

Social Skills

The NLD student is often the solitary child in the classroom. Her social skills lag considerably behind her peer group and her interaction with other children is markedly immature. She requires social skills training, and adult facilitation when she is in an unstructured setting with other children. Unstructured situations such as the cafeteria and recess may overwhelm her. Social acceptance may be enhanced by dressing the child appropriately, and teaching her to note what her classmates wear, etc. and how appearance often plays a role in peer acceptance or rejection.

Behavior

Situations which may trigger an inappropriate behavioral response include:

- When the NLD student's established routine and/or rules are changed, she may respond inappropriately. Verbally reassure her, explain exactly what will take place, and at what point her schedule will return to normal.

- A situation where the NLD student feels that she is being "ambushed" with something which she is requested/required to do, but not prepared for, will likely cause anxiety, which may result in unusual behavior. Discuss with the child her reluctance, and find out what the underlying problem is.

° If this student explains how she compensates for a particular problem, or what works for her, and it is ignored or discounted, she will become frustrated, often resulting in tears or anger. This student lives with her problem on a daily basis, and should be encouraged in her efforts to self-advocate and compensate for her deficits.

° When the NLD child asks "why," always assume that she is in need of clarification.

° There should be a zero tolerance for teasing and bullying of the child.

Anxiety Management

The NLD student is often quite anxious. In order for this child to function within a school setting, it is critical to provide her with a support system and safety net. There are several things that can significantly reduce this student's anxiety and stress.

° Provide a safe place where she can go whenever she is feeling anxious or overwhelmed.

° Reassure her by providing her with a special item from home that she is allowed to take to school with her every day.

° Inform her of scheduling changes before they occur. Provide her with a daily copy of her schedule and mark any changes on it after verbally explaining what will occur.

° Introduce her to new teachers before the school year begins. Show her where she will sit before the first day of class.

° For the younger child, the school should arrange to have several familiar students in her class, particularly students who have been kind and understanding. For the older child, every effort should be made to identify a "buddy" who shares the NLD child's schedule.

° Prevent stress and overload by providing the older student with a study period twice per day – once in the morning, and again in the afternoon.

Chapter 6

Psychomotor and Spatial Challenges

Two of the more obvious characteristics of the NLD child is that she is often physically awkward and also gets lost easily. She has difficulty getting her body to do what she wants it to, when she wants it to – whether it is while trying to print or write, or attempting to do something more physically demanding such as climb or jump rope. In addition, she is unable to gauge where her body is in space in relation to other objects, so she may bump into things or people. Overall, she appears rather "klutzy." The NLD student has serious difficulty finding her way from place to place, which is both a nuisance and a danger. Her problems in these areas are upsetting to her, create additional situations where she may be teased, and further isolate her socially.

PSYCHOMOTOR SKILLS

It is very frustrating when your body won't cooperate. It is difficult to learn new physical tasks, but when you understand what you are supposed to do, but you just can't get your body to perform the task, it is enough to make a person want to give up. NLD children constantly face this challenge, and it is important to understand that it is a neurological problem, and to know the types of activities which may be affected.

Fine-motor Skills

The NLD youngster will almost always have impaired fine-motor skills, and difficulties with finger dexterity, so that using a pencil, drawing with crayons, using scissors, and similar tasks will all be quite difficult. The NLD child should receive support from an occupational therapist who is trained to work with youngsters who have difficulty with these skills.

In the classroom, it is important for the teacher to appreciate the child's difficulty with fine-motor tasks, and assist her or accommodate when necessary. Ideally, the student will have ongoing interaction with the occupational therapist, but if this is not the case, there are things that can be done in the classroom to help the NLD child.

Pencils, Erasers, and Manipulatives

The student will likely hold her pencil in an awkward fashion. The teacher should encourage the appropriate grasp, but without reprimand. For the youngest child, fat pencils will be easier to comfortably hold. For the slightly older child, it may be helpful to put one of those little rubber gizmos on the pencil, that have indentations for the correct positioning of the child's fingers. Soft lead is recommended because the student will likely press very hard on the paper, causing it to tear. Softer lead is not as apt to tear the paper. Once the child learns how to hold a pencil, and becomes somewhat proficient in printing, it would be helpful to introduce her to a mechanical pencil. Although the use of a mechanical pencil will initially be somewhat frustrating, it will help her determine how much pressure to place on the pencil. The reason that it may initially be frustrating is because the lead will often break. However, in time she will learn how much pressure to apply without tearing the paper or the breaking the lead. It is best that all writing instruments provided to the child be fatter than normal, or built-up in the area where she places her fingers. Many of the new mechanical pencils have a grip area that is cushioned, and these are excellent for the NLD student.

A problem similar to pressing hard when she writes with a pencil occurs when she attempts to erase. She will likely press very hard while erasing, tearing the paper. The child should be provided with a high quality eraser that she can hold in her fist, rather than using one that is on the end of a pencil. This should reduce the risk of tearing the paper, and avoid much of the child's frustration when she attempts to make corrections.

Most children with NLD have physical deficits on the left side of their body, which may or may not be noticeable. Because of this, the right-handed child will often "forget" to hold a paper stable with her left hand while she is trying to write or draw. She will need constant, gentle reminders to hold the paper stable with her free hand.

Math manipulatives will likely also be a challenge for this student. She may be unable to pick up small coins, small beads, or other similar objects, or manipulate them in any way. However, rather than avoid the use of manipulatives, simply substitute larger objects that the NLD child can manage.

Arts and Crafts

Accommodations will also be required for arts and crafts activities. The child may find it awkward to hold a crayon, stay within the lines when coloring, or hold a paint brush. Provide fatter crayons or sidewalk chalk, and allow her to draw freehand on a large piece of paper. If painting is the activity, provide a larger-handled paintbrush which will be easier for her to hold. Also provide her with non-spill paint containers so that she doesn't inadvertently knock over her paint. Again, allow free-form painting on a large piece of paper. She may not want to participate in finger-painting activities, due to her tactile defensiveness issues. Any activity that requires finger dexterity will be difficult, so she will probably be unable to string small beads or the like. Provide her with a heavy cord, and larger beads so that she can participate in the activity, and assist her if she is unable to do it on her own. Learning how to use scissors may cause this child significant difficulty. If this is the case, it is best to simply have an adult do the cutting for the child, rather than have her try and manage the use of scissors.

The older NLD student will continue to be challenged by arts and crafts activities. Classes such as sewing or woodworking will be problematic. It is important to encourage the NLD student to participate in these activities, in order to continue to develop her fine-motor skills. However, the teacher must be patient, supportive, and willing to take the time required to teach the child how to do a particular task.

With practice, and with the help of an occupational therapist, the NLD student's fine-motor skills should improve over time. Until they do, appropriate accommodations should be provided whenever the child is faced with an activity which demands finger dexterity. She should *always* be encouraged and complimented for her efforts, *never* criticized for her physical limitations, and *never* be excluded from participating in an activity because of her deficits.

Self-help Skills

Psychomotor and fine-motor deficits also affect this child's self-help skills. The young NLD child will likely be the last in her class to be able to put her jacket on unassisted, zip zippers and button buttons. A problem that is almost universal within the NLD population is the inability to tie shoe laces until the child is in the upper elementary grades. As with the NLD student's fine-motor deficits, she should receive support from an occupational therapist to assist her in learning how to perform self-help skills.

Parents should be sensitive to the NLD child's difficulties with self-help skills, and dress her in clothes that require as little assistance as possible. The young child should wear pants without zippers or buttons, so that she is able to go to the bathroom without assistance.

Jackets and shoes, if possible, should have Velcro closures, and hats that must be tied should be avoided. A raincoat with a hood should replace an umbrella, and boots should be pull-on without laces. Although the child's teacher will have to assist her, the proper selection of clothing should reduce the demand on the teacher's time *and* allow the child to be more independent.

The middle school-aged child will have new challenges with self-help skills. Lockers replace cubbies, and generally the child is required to manage a combination lock. It would be best if the child were provided with a key-lock for her locker, which is easier to manage. If a combination lock is required, it should be provided to the child at the end of the school year preceding the year when she will have to use it. She can then practice the combination over the summer so that she is proficient with its use when school starts.

In middle school, children are required to manage a gym locker in addition to their book locker, change into gym clothes for their physical education class, and are sometimes required to take showers. These requirements should be waived for the NLD student. Although her self-help skills may have improved, it is unlikely that they have improved to such a degree that she is able to shower, quickly change clothes and shoes, use a second locker and combination lock, within the time allowed. Instead, she should be allowed to wear comfortable clothes on the days that she will have physical education, and not be required to change clothes or shower. If the child is able, an option may be to have her change *only* her shirt, not her pants or shoes. She may be required to use deodorant before putting her school shirt back on, and then comb her hair. These limited tasks are far easier for this student to attempt than the unrealistic expectation of a shower and full change of clothes. Ideally, the NLD student's schedule can be developed so that her physical education class is at the end of the day, avoiding any issues related to showering or changing clothes.

Physical Education

Ideally, the NLD child should receive physical therapy, and/or occupational therapy in place of a regular physical education class, particularly in the early elementary grades. It is more appropriate to target this child's specific needs, and work on her areas of deficit, rather than place her in a regular physical education class where she will likely be limited in her ability to fully participate in all activities. In addition, she will struggle with the less structured nature of the regular class, as well as the social demands inherent in this environment.

Modified Program

If the child is required to participate in a regular physical education class, the course requirements should be modified. She should not be held to the same physical fitness standards as her age mates. The combination of her difficulty with psychomotor functioning and developmental delays will compromise her ability to be as physically adept as others of her age. Requiring that she perform certain functions could actually be dangerous for this child. It is critical that her abilities and deficits be documented so that she is not required to perform an activity that might result in injury.

Team Sports

Individual physical activities are extremely challenging, and made more difficult when other children are added to the equation. Clearly, the most challenging physical activities for NLD children are team sports. Not only is the child uncoordinated, but she is likely mystified by the rules of play. When you think about it from her perspective, the rules *are* quite puzzling. Let's use baseball as an example, and discuss the rules when you are at bat:

> If you hit the ball and it stays within the first and third base lines, it's okay to run, however if it's outside of those two lines, it's considered a foul. If someone on the other team catches it before it hits the ground, you're out, but if they don't, you're safe. You're only supposed to swing at the ball if it is inside the

batting zone. There are strikes when you swing and miss, and fouls that are considered strikes. But, since you can't strike out from fouls, the third foul isn't considered a strike. It's all so confusing! The child is trying with all of her might to use a skinny stick to hit that little white ball coming directly at her – and then she does!

Surprise, surprise, somehow she managed to hit the ball, and it stayed between those two lines. Someone tells her to run to first base, so she does. Now the next batter is up – does she run or stay? – if it isn't caught, you run, but if it is, you need to stay, or, you can be "thrown out."

All of the "if this, then that" rules have the child completely confused and overwhelmed. Add to that all the screaming and shouting, the jeering and cheering, and the child *can't think*. And then there's the absolute worst part – when she's sitting on the bench, waiting for her turn at bat, there's all that awful *socializing* going on.

To make matters worse, this child will likely be mortified if she makes a mistake, especially one that brings ridicule from her teammates. Rather than subject the NLD child to all of this stress, it may be kinder to involve her in some type of activity that makes her feel part of the team, without setting her up to fail. If she is willing, it might be more rewarding for her to act as an umpire or referee, where she can focus on a single aspect of the game.

In order for this child to benefit from team sports, she will need direct and specific verbal instruction in the rules that govern the game…on exactly what is to be done, how, and when. If the children are to participate in teams, the physical education teacher should select the members of each team. Most children, left to their own devices, will naturally pick their friends and those who will strengthen their team. It is all too common for the physically and socially awkward child to be excluded, or the last one picked for a team. This is devastating for the NLD child, and undermines the concept of teaching children the important concept of teamwork. As adults, we all know that physical fitness alone does not make a winning team. Rather, it is the ability of the individual members to work as one, with a common goal, that makes winning teams. This is a valuable lesson to be taught to youngsters in their physical education classes, with the added benefit to the NLD child that she is treated as an equal member of a team. Therefore, the physical education teacher should manage the selection of team members, and encourage the philosophy of teamwork.

SPATIAL DEFICITS

One of the most frustrating and potentially dangerous aspects of NLD is the child's spatial problem. Most NLD youngsters have a tremendous amount of difficulty gauging how near or far they are to another person or object, and how to get from one place to another, or find their way home. Keeping appropriate physical distance between oneself and another individual is an issue that can effectively be taught through social skills training. However, that leaves two other problems that are more difficult to address: the child's inability to gauge the distance between where she is in space, and where another object is, *and* her inability to physically navigate an environment without becoming hopelessly lost.

Gauging Distance

Individuals with NLD generally have difficulty determining where they are in space, and how close they are to other objects. Combined with their physical awkwardness, this puts them at risk for injury, and for being reprimanded for breaking things that they bump into.

The physical danger arises from the NLD child's inability to gauge where to place a knife when cutting, how close her arm may be to the hot racks when removing an item from the oven, or how close she may be to an oncoming vehicle. Although most of these issues are generally dealt with in the home, it is important for teachers to be aware of the child's problem in this area, in order to protect her from physical harm. She needs active supervision in order to prevent accidents.

What is most common in the school environment is that the child may continually bump into things, which causes a myriad of problems. Common unfortunate situations include:

- ° bumping or falling against a table where there is electronic equipment, knocking it to the floor, resulting in significant damage

- ° bumping into other students or their desks, annoying other children, resulting in more problems with social relationships

- ° knocking over paint containers during arts and crafts activities, likely damaging other students' projects.

Simple solutions, such as storing fragile electronic equipment out of harm's way, providing maximum space between desks, and spill-proof paint containers for youngsters, can avoid unfortunate situations. However, not all problems can be anticipated. Although teachers and students will naturally be frustrated with the NLD student's "bumping" and "knocking over" problem, it is important to remember that she should not be reprimanded for something that she is unable to control.

Getting Lost

One of the hallmarks of NLD is that these kids invariably get lost. This may not be as apparent in a school setting for the youngest children, because they are allowed little or no independence. In most schools, children in the early grades move from place to place as a class, so that there is little opportunity for the NLD child to become lost. However, in the middle to upper elementary grades, when the child is allowed more independence to move about the school unassisted, her problem will likely become quite pronounced. Although it may appear that the student's spatial problem has become more severe, this is probably not the case. What has likely happened is that adults have an expectation that "at her age," the child *should* be able to move from place to place on her own, when, in fact, she can't. Too often, she will either get lost, or arrive late at her destination. Field trips pose a significant risk for this child becoming separated from her group, and consequently lost. There are many things that can be done to assist the NLD child with her spatial difficulties.

A traditional physical environment is extremely important for this child. She needs "markers" that she can refer to in order to learn how to navigate through the building on her own – a concrete road map so that she can find her way to and from various locations. She needs to be taught verbally how to move about within the school…"go out the door, turn right, and count three doors on the right – the third door, which is red, is the girl's bathroom."

Finding Her Way

Prior to the start of school each year, parents of NLD children should be provided with a simple map of the school, along with their child's schedule. All pertinent locations should be noted on the map, and if the building is more than a single floor, the layout for each floor should be clearly marked. Arrangements should be made for the child to visit the school on several occasions over the summer break in order to practice "walking through" her schedule when the building is quiet. Remember, this isn't a tour, it is a learning experience. Sufficient time should be allowed not only to walk the child from point of origin (getting off of the bus) through her schedule, but also to verbally script the process by noting things such as room numbers, permanent fixtures that the student can use as directional cues, and so forth. For the middle school child, who will change classrooms for each period, it will likely take several months to learn how to find her way to classes, the bathroom, cafeteria, etc. It would be helpful to arrange for another student to share the NLD student's schedule, and act as a buddy to help her get from place to place.

There are a couple of very important points to keep in mind when accommodating this child's spatial deficits:

° This student's spatial challenges generally do not improve over time. She will continue to need the same level of support, or more as demands increase, in each subsequent year of school.

° This student will not be able to find her way to a specific place within the school if her reference point is changed. After several months, the NLD child may be able to find her way from her classroom to other locations within the school without assistance. However, the next year, when she is in a different homeroom, resulting in a different reference point and sequence of schedule, she will have to learn all over again how to navigate throughout the school.

° This student's spatial problems may be quite severe. If so, she should be assigned a paraprofessional to continue the work that was begun during the summer break, teaching the child how to get from place to place. Initially, the paraprofessional may have to physically collect the child at the end of each class, and escort her to her next class. With instruction, and over time, the role of the paraprofessional may shift to one of "shadowing" the student from location to location. If the student needs to be excused during class, and the paraprofessional is unavailable, the teacher should assign a buddy to escort the NLD child to her destination.

The NLD student should never be disciplined for being tardy to class. Discipline is designed for a situation where you are trying to correct *behavior*. This child's reason for arriving late to class is not because of poor planning, or disrespect, but because of her spatial difficulties.

Transportation and Field Trips

There is a significant danger of the NLD child getting lost on her way to and/or from the assigned school bus stop. Combined with her social naiveté, she is at increased risk of being targeted by a predator. For both of these reasons, she should always be picked up directly in front of her own house, where a parent or caregiver can be sure that she gets on and off the bus safely. Arrangements for this accommodation should be handled by a school official.

For most children, school field trips are great fun, and eagerly anticipated. However, the parents of NLD children are likely to dread the thought of their spatially challenged youngster participating in these activities. Handling the NLD child on a field trip as you would another of her age, whatever the NLD child's age, is irresponsible. The risk of this child becoming separated from her group is *very* real, and she probably does not have the skill to either figure out where to go, what to do, or who to ask for help. If the child is assigned a paraprofessional at school to assist with spatial difficulties, the paraprofessional should accompany her on all field trips. If there is no paraprofessional support, then it is *strongly* recommended that one of the child's parents, grandparents, or another caregiver, act as chaperone for all field trips. Since students are allowed more independence on field trips with each successive year, the necessity for supervision of the NLD child will continue throughout her education. Although it would be humiliating for the older NLD student to have an adult hovering over her, she will continue to need someone who is specifically responsible for her safety. The adult chaperone of a first-grade child will likely hold her hand, but by middle or high school should probably stay in the background, available only as the need warrants.

SUMMARY

Two of the more obvious characteristics of the NLD child is that she is often physically awkward and she gets lost easily. Her psychomotor deficits cause problems with fine-motor skills, self-help skills, and physical education.

Fine-motor Skills

In addition to benefiting from an intervention program with an occupational therapist, the following can and should be done in the classroom:

- Provide the most comfortable writing instrument, and teach the correct pressure to use when writing and erasing. Supply appropriate aids such as finger grips and high quality erasers. Mechanical pencils are beneficial for the older student.

- Use larger paintbrushes, as well as fatter crayons and chalk, and allow free-form painting. Assist with scissor activities, or do cutting for the child.

- Replace small manipulatives, such as coins and beads, with larger ones that are easier to handle.

- Supervise sewing, woodworking activities, and the like, for middle school students, and teach her with patience rather than avoiding these activities.

Self-help Skills

The young NLD child will likely be the last in her class to be able to put her jacket on unassisted, zip zippers and button buttons. The requirement for the older student to change clothes or shower for physical education class is unrealistic. She should receive support from an occupational therapist to assist her in learning how to perform self-help skills. In addition, the following is recommended:

- Parents should dress the child in clothes that require as little assistance as possible. The NLD student should be allowed to wear comfortable clothes on the days that she will have physical education, and not be required to change or shower.

- If a combination lock is required for the older student's locker, it should be provided to the child at the end of the school year preceding the year when she will have to use it, so that she can practice the combination over the summer.

Physical Education

The NLD child should receive physical therapy and/or occupational therapy in place of a regular physical education class, in order to work on her areas of deficit. However, if she is required to participate in a physical education class, her program should be modified. She should not be held to the same physical fitness standards as her age mates, due to her psychomotor deficits and developmental delays.

Provide direct and specific verbal instruction in the rules that govern team sports – on exactly what is to be done, how, and when. The physical education teacher should manage the selection of team members, and encourage the philosophy of teamwork.

Gauging Distance

Determining the appropriate physical proximity to another individual is best dealt with through social skills training. However, the classroom teacher can use a simple technique with the NLD student if she has difficulty in this area. It is called the "arm's length rule," which simply means that the general distance between people is an arm's length – closer may crowd another child, and further away signals a lack of involvement.

Simple solutions, such as storing fragile electronic equipment out of harm's way, providing maximum space between desks and spill-proof paint containers for youngsters, can avoid unfortunate situations.

Getting Lost/Finding Her Way

A concrete roadmap with "markers" should be provided so that she can find her way to and from various locations. She needs to be taught verbally how to move about within the school…"go out the door, turn right, and count three doors on the right – the third door, which is red, is the girl's bathroom."

Arrange for the child to practice "walking through" her schedule before the start of each school year. Remember that when the student's reference point changes, she will have to relearn how to find locations within the building.

A paraprofessional to assist her from class to class, or shadow her, will be necessary if the NLD student's spatial problems are severe.

Transportation and Field Trips

School bus transportation should be arranged so that the NLD child is picked up and dropped off in front of her home.

Close supervision is critical on field trips so that the student doesn't become separated from her group. If possible, the child's parent should chaperone all field trips, or, if the student is assigned a paraprofessional, he/she should accompany the child on all field trips.

Chapter 7

Arithmetic and Math

NLD students will almost certainly have difficulty with at least some aspects of arithmetic and math. Several problems contribute to deficits in this area. The child has poor fine-motor skills, which make it hard for her to form numbers correctly, and properly align them on the page. Her visual organization and processing problems cause difficulty with both recognizing mathematical symbols that govern the required operation, and identifying which numbers to work on at what point. The requirement to shift mental set between various basic skills, while performing activities such as multiplication and division, further compromises her arithmetic skills. As math becomes more abstract, this student's ability to compensate for her deficits may become almost impossible.

Many NLD children may be able to learn math facts and basic arithmetic skills in a regular education classroom. This is because these students have very strong rote memory skills, and as a result, do not have significant difficulty learning basic math skills. However, as the demands become more difficult – generally beginning in the upper elementary grades – this student will likely need direct, one-on-one instruction for math. Teaching strategies will demand creativity and verbal instruction. Arithmetic and math require strong visual and spatial skills, which are major areas of disability for this child. Traditional methods for teaching arithmetic and math will, in most cases, not work.

NLD students are, more often than not, unimodal learners – meaning that they do not benefit from hearing and seeing something at the same time. Although this strategy often enhances the learning process for other students, it can cause major difficulties for the NLD youngster. Therefore, it is important to verbally explain, *in detail*, the concept you are teaching, and *then* illustrate it on the blackboard.

Math textbooks may be a hindrance rather than a help to the NLD student. Many of today's math textbooks are highly visual, and for the NLD student, highly distracting. Black on white presentations in a very simple style will work best for this student. Workbooks are more effective for this student than textbooks. Not only do they tend to be black on white, but the student writes directly in the book.

This student should *never* be encouraged to guess what the answer may be. Although this is a common practice when teaching arithmetic and math, it assumes that the child will consider all of the variables and then make an educated guess. The NLD child, when encouraged to guess at the answer, does not understand what the purpose of a guess is, and given the situation, will probably come up with something that is not remotely realistic. Unfortunately, what likely follows is that the child is reprimanded for acting like the class clown, when she did exactly what you asked her to do – guess!

The NLD child will have tremendous difficulty learning to tell time, and will struggle significantly with any math problems that are related to time. Eventually, she *will* be able to tell time based on an analog clock, however until she can, it would be useful for her to use a digital watch. Once she reaches a developmental level where she can understand time, which may lag well behind her age mates, it would be helpful to teach concepts such as elapsed time. However, any exercise should be quite simple and straightforward. Concepts such as rounding, estimating, and place values will be challenging, and will likely require one-on-one instruction in order for the student to learn these concepts, as will place values and many other math concepts.

The remainder of this chapter will deal primarily with specific teaching strategies for basic arithmetic skills, multiplication, division, and word problems. Fractions, algebra, geometry and higher-level math will also be addressed.

BASIC ARITHMETIC SKILLS

The first problem that must be addressed is the child's inability to form her numbers both clearly and correctly. She should not be required to copy problems from the blackboard or book. Copying requires strong visual organization and discrimination skills, which this student lacks. The likelihood of making copying mistakes is significant. Because of the child's disability in this area, the teacher should provide arithmetic problems on paper, allowing enough space for this particular student to complete the exercise.

In order to assist this student in aligning numbers correctly, math problems should be presented and performed on graph paper. The technique of folding a paper in order to make "squares" in order to define the work area for each math problem is not effective for the NLD student. She needs far more demarcation of the space in which to complete her work. For the young child, large scale graph paper is recommended, moving to smaller scale paper as the child's handwriting and visual discrimination skills improve – *if* they improve. She should not be handicapped by her graphomotor and visual discrimination skills while doing math exercises. Providing the assigned problems on graph paper allows the student to focus her attention on the correct activity, which is working on math skills. The use of graph paper when doing math should continue for as long as this student benefits from its use.

For the younger student, there should be no more than three problems per page – and ideally only one. All problems should be of the same type in order to compensate for the child's difficulty with noting the appropriate operational symbol. Addition problems would be on one page, subtraction on another, and so forth. As the child advances through middle elementary grades, depending on her handwriting and visual discrimination skills, additional problems may be added to the page. However, there should never be more than 8 to 10 problems per page. Drill exercises with 25 to 100 math facts per page should *never, ever* be assigned to this student. This type of presentation will not reflect the child's ability to perform a particular arithmetic exercise. Figure 7.1 below represents an inappropriate presentation of addition math problems for the NLD student. It is followed by Figure 7.2, an appropriate presentation of the same material.

Math Facts			
2+2=	3+9=	6+9=	3+8=
3+5=	4+7=	5+1=	6+7=
7+2=	3+4=	7+6=	8+4=
6+6=	4+5=	5+8=	7+4=
9+1=	8+7=	8+1=	1+5=
7+1=	8+5=	5+5=	4+3=
8+3=	5+5=	3+6=	9+4=
9+5=	7+7=	4+2=	5+4=
5+3=	6+4=	5+7=	9+3=
7+5=	8+2=	9+2=	7+8=
8+6=	2+8=	7+9=	8+8=
3+3=	5+9=	5+6=	6+8=
6+5=	4+1=	6+1=	7+3=
4+9=	8+9=	5+2=	6+3=
4+4=	6+2=	3+7=	4+8=

Figure 7.1 Addition Math Facts – 60 Problems per Page

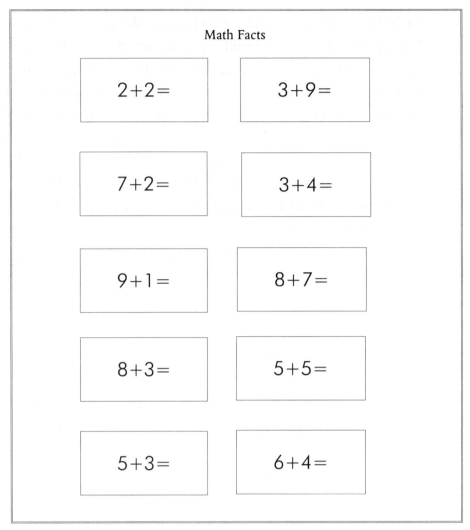

Figure 7.2 Addition Math Facts – 10 Problems Per Page

The NLD student will be more able to complete the majority of the 60 problems within the assigned time, as long as they are presented as 10 problems per page (even though there are 6 pages to complete), rather than presenting all 60 problems on a single page. However, what is more important is that the percentage of correct answers improves *dramatically* when the presentation of the material is appropriate to the student's needs.

Flashcards, which are often used to develop more rapid recall of math facts, are generally ineffective for this student. She is not a visual learner, and this technique is only appropriate for visual learners. Since this student is an auditory learner, drill of math facts should be performed auditorily. If the math facts can be taught to a rhyme, it will likely improve her recall even more.

A major problem for these youngsters is moving from a vertical presentation of math facts and arithmetic problems to a horizontal presentation. Many NLD students are unable to make this switch, recognizing that the information is the same, simply presented in a different format. They do not "get" that whether the math problem is presented vertically or horizontally, if the numbers remain the same, the exercise remains unchanged, and both presentations will result in the same answer. Different presentations of the same mathematical information is a major stumbling block for most NLD youngsters, and may actually require that they learn their math facts all over again in a horizontal format.

The NLD student will not make the "automatic" connections that her peer group makes. She will not realize that $5 + 3$ is the same as $3 + 5$, or that 4×6 is the same as 6×4, unless it is specifically pointed out to her. Tips such as these, which may seem obvious to others, must be specifically taught to this student.

The concepts of carrying and regrouping numbers is difficult for the NLD student to comprehend. She will need very specific instruction in these operations, and a teacher or aid should sit with her and watch her complete each step of the problem, stopping and correcting her when she makes a mistake.

When teaching new concepts to the NLD student, provide as much context as possible. For example, when subtraction is introduced, explain that subtraction is the opposite of addition. Rather than adding numbers together to come up with a total, you are removing numbers to come up with a remainder. It would be effective to show the concept using manipulatives. For example, demonstrate the concept of adding five pennies and five pennies to make ten pennies. Then show the opposite operation, taking five pennies away from the ten pennies, and the remainder is five pennies.

MULTIPLICATION

As this child moves into the areas of multiplication and division, she is likely to struggle, particularly as the problems become more complex. Proper number alignment is absolutely critical if the child is to have any hope of correctly answering the problem. Visual organization and discrimination become far more demanding, and the child may actually shut down – refusing to even attempt to do her math assignments. Continued use of graph paper, and one to three problems per page, are critical as the child learns to do multiplication. It is important to remember that this child will learn her multiplication facts auditorily far more quickly than if she is forced to use visual aids such as flashcards. Remember to explain that the concept of multiplication is a more efficient way to add multiple or large numbers. Again, use a manipulative such as pennies, first demonstrating addition, followed by multiplication so that the child understands the connection between the two concepts. For example, add 5 pennies, then 5 more pennies, then 5 more pennies, totaling 15 pennies. Illustrate the problem on paper: $5 + 5 + 5 = 15$. Next show her the manipulatives again with three groups of five, and explain that multiplication is simply counting the number of groups, in this case it is three, and multiplying the number of groups by the number within each group. Again illustrate the problem on paper: $3 \times 5 = 15$. Point out that the answer to both problems is the same. You may need to explain that although addition of this particular problem might be just as easy as multiplication, as the numbers get larger, that will not be the case.

Remember that this student will have the same difficulty recognizing that vertical and horizontal presentation of multiplication problems is simply a different way of looking at the same information, which will result in the same answer. She will have difficulty with changes in presentation, regardless of what the concept is. Remember, this student does not generalize information, so she will not make the connection on her own.

When multiplication problems move beyond facts to multi-digit numbers, some students benefit from doing these more complex problems with colored pencils. The concept is to multiply each digit in a separate color so that the child doesn't get confused. For other students, however, this method has created greater confusion. If the student is taught math in a regular education classroom, it would be very beneficial for the teacher to enlist the help of either the math specialist or a special education teacher in order to expand his/her repertoire of teaching strategies, particularly as they relate to non-visual learners.

DIVISION

Division, and particularly long division, are the most complex and challenging of the arithmetic functions. The first stumbling block is that the child is required to "guess" how many times one number may "go into" another number. This child cannot, and does not, guess! When asked to do so, she will likely look at you with a blank expression and do absolutely nothing, or provide an answer that is grossly unrealistic. She is then expected to multiply the number that she "guessed" by the divisor and identify whether the resulting number is smaller or larger than the dividend, and whether or not it can be subtracted from the dividend. The result...TILT, OVERLOAD, OVERLOAD!!!!...and all systems shut down. In order to teach division, it must be broken down into its component parts.

First, the child should have already mastered her multiplication math facts before being assigned long-division problems. Since division is the task, and not multiplication, provide the child with a multiplication sheet so that she will not have to continue to shift mental set between the various arithmetic operations that are needed in order to perform division problems. She should be allowed to look on the multiplication sheet rather than "guess" what number should "go into" the dividend. The sheet should resemble Figure 7.3.

Multiplication Facts										
x	0	1	2	3	4	5	6	7	8	9
0	0	0	0	0	0	0	0	0	0	0
1	0	1	2	3	4	5	6	7	8	9
2	0	2	4	6	8	10	12	14	16	18
3	0	3	6	9	12	15	18	21	24	27
4	0	4	8	12	16	20	24	28	32	36
5	0	5	10	15	20	25	30	35	40	45
6	0	6	12	18	24	30	36	42	48	54
7	0	7	14	21	28	35	42	49	56	63
8	0	8	16	24	32	40	48	56	64	72
9	0	9	18	27	36	45	54	63	72	81

Figure 7.3 Multiplication Math Facts

It would be helpful to either laminate the multiplication facts sheet, or slip it into a plastic sleeve so that it does not get dog-eared with use by the student. The reason that this particular format was used for the multiplication facts is so that the tracking of sliding the student's finger down and over is the same mental process of down and over that will be used with the division card that follows.

The next tool that is suggested is a division card. This is simply an index card, or some material of similar weight, with a corner cut out, which will be used as a "window" for the student as she works through division problems. It should look something like Figure 7.4.

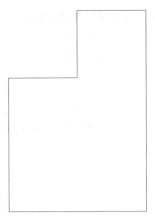

Figure 7.4 Sample Division Card

The student should also be provided with a calculator, assuming that she has been taught how to use one. The calculator may be used as she chooses, either to perform arithmetic calculations, or to check her answer for accuracy.

The purpose of the division card is to block extraneous information, so that the child can focus on the specific part of the problem that she is to work on. Also, it is sequentially shifted down one line, and then over one column, until each step of the process is completed. The following illustrates how the division card would be used in a simple division exercise:

Problem 5 | 2 5

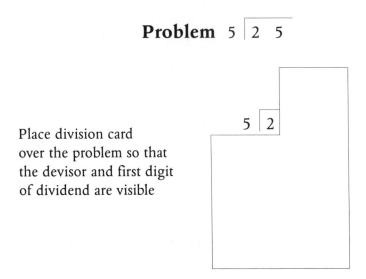

Place division card
over the problem so that
the devisor and first digit
of dividend are visible

Question 1:   Is there a number which can be multiplied by 5, and be equal to or less than 2?

Answer: The answer is no, so zero is placed above the 2 and the card is shifted to the right to get a bigger number.

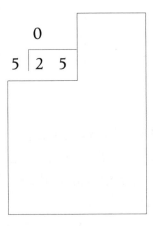

Question 2:   Is there a number which can be multiplied by 5, and be equal to or less than 25?

Answer: The answer is yes, and the number is 5, so a 5 is placed above the dividend.

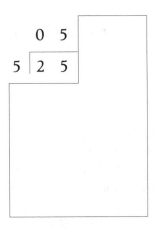

Slide the division card down.

Question 3: What is 5x5?
If necessary, check math facts sheet for answer.

Answer: The answer is 25, which is equal to the dividend, so it is the answer we will use.

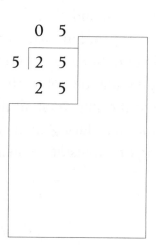

Enter the multiplication answer on the line which has been revealed by sliding the division card down.

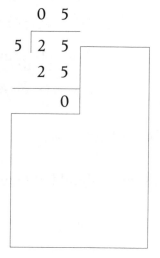

Slide the division card down one more line, subtract and enter the answer.

This method of teaching may seem very tedious and time-consuming, but it has proven to be an effective strategy in teaching NLD children how to do long division. Although it was designed specifically for NLD students, it has proven to be very effective in teaching long division to many other children who have math difficulties. *All math concepts need to be taught to NLD children in this step-by-step fashion, breaking a problem down into each step, no matter how small it might seem.*

Even after the child has learned a concept, she will often "forget to remember" when called upon to perform a problem. Therefore, for each math concept/operation taught, the NLD student should be provided with an index card on which is listed the steps necessary to complete a problem for that particular concept/operation. Depending on the student's preference, this may be either an icon or word representation for each specific step. The cards should be available to the student at all times, during class, when completing homework, *and* during math quizzes and tests. Figure 7.5 is an illustration of a division sequence card.

Division Sequence

1. Divide

2. Multiply

3. Subtract

4. Shift Right

5. Slide Down

Figure 7.5 Division Sequence Card

The NLD student should be taught how to use a calculator as early as possible. Although the calculator should not replace the learning process, the use of a calculator should be encouraged when calculation is not the objective of the exercise. For instance, it may be appropriate to modify the student's assignments so that she shows her work for the first two or three problems, and is then allowed to use a calculator for the remaining exercise.

WORD PROBLEMS

The NLD student will likely have considerable difficulty with word problems. Therefore, it is critical to approach teaching word problems in a very direct and simple manner. It will take this student a very long time to be able to determine what information contained within a word problem is relevant, and what is extraneous. Not only will the child need to be taught how to determine what information to use in solving the math problem, but she will also need to understand what the problem is. Words that should signify the operation called for may not be enough of a cue for this child. Before she attempts to do the actual math, the teacher should review her work to determine if she has selected the appropriate and relevant information, *and* has correctly identified what operation(s) is being called for – addition, subtraction, etc. It would be prudent to wait until the NLD child is very proficient with basic word problems, where she uses all of the facts presented, before introducing non-relevant information.

Teach the child that certain words and phrases represent a specific operation, and provide lists of words with the operation which correlates to it. A math vocabulary chart (see Figure 7.6) should be provided to the student, explained, and she should be allowed to use it when she is working on math problems.

Math Vocabulary	
Operation	**Vocabulary**
Addition	Together, altogether, sum, in all, both, gained, won, saved, received, etc.
Subtraction	Difference between, from, left, how many (more or less), how much (taller, heavier, farther), withdrawal, spend, lost, remain, etc.
Multiplication	Area, times, product, double, triple, twice, etc.
Division	Into, share, each, average, monthly, daily, weekly, yearly, quotient, half as many, etc.

Figure 7.6 Math Vocabulary Chart

As the NLD student is being taught to identify the information within the problem that is needed in order to answer the question, it would be extremely helpful to highlight both the information, and the word, or words, that indicate what operation is called for. Either underlining, circling, or more effectively using a colored highlighter, will allow the child to focus on the necessary information. It is important to explain to her that questions are often implied, rather than specifically stated. Initially, it would be best if she were allowed to "walk through" the steps, while someone else writes down the information for her. Then she should complete the operation(s).

In some situations, it might be helpful to translate word problems into icon representations to help simplify the information that is being provided, so she can more readily solve the problem. Although NLD students are not visual learners, a simple icon representation can sometimes be quite effective, especially in the area of math. Complex visual material, on the other hand, will not enhance their ability to process information. An example of converting a word problem to a visual representation follows:

Question: *Mary is taller than Suzie, but shorter than Holly. Who is the tallest?*

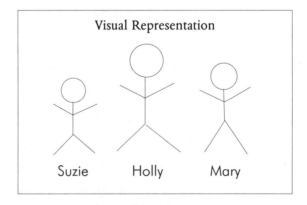

Answer: *Holly is tallest*

FRACTIONS

As math instruction moves into the area of fractions, decimals, and other less concrete material, the NLD student will continue to struggle. Again, simple icon representations may be effective in teaching the basic concept of fractions. However, once the instruction moves into activities such as converting improper fractions to mixed numbers, and adding, subtracting, or other manipulations of fractions, the NLD child will likely become frustrated. Converting fractions to percentages and decimals will also be very challenging. She may actually reach her plateau with fractions, percentages, and decimals rather quickly, on a rather basic level, and not be able to move forward. Continued instruction may not result in appreciable gain and will likely cause considerable frustration for the student. If this occurs, it would be wise to move to the next math concept rather than run the risk of having the child completely shut down in the area of math.

Although this apparent "block" happens quite frequently with fractions, it can happen at any point during the math curriculum. However, it generally occurs at some point when the concept becomes less concrete and more abstract. Periodically the student should be reintroduced to fractions (or wherever the "block" occurred) in an attempt to make further progress. If, after a year or two, it doesn't appear that the student will be able to manually perform the required operation(s), then a calculator should be provided for these situations.

NLD students should not be expected to complete the same number of math exercises as children who do not have a math disability. It takes far longer, and uses far more energy for her to complete a math problem. Therefore, their assignments should be cut by half to three quarters. Assigning the "odd" or "even" problems is a simple accommodation. If this is not possible, then the student should be graded only on what she was able to complete.

ALGEBRA, GEOMETRY AND BEYOND

During middle school, the NLD student will be introduced to simple geometry and pre-algebra. Some NLD students can learn algebra, some may be able to handle geometry, a very few of them may be able to do both, while the majority will have severe difficulty or be unable to do either one. Regardless of how a particular NLD student responds to these higher-level math concepts and skills, at some point, almost all of them will require one-on-one instruction in order to make meaningful progress.

It is strongly recommended that NLD students complete a course in consumer math. Most of them seem to struggle with handling cash, managing a checkbook, as well as a budget, and other math life skills. However, with proper instruction, they can learn how to manage these activities, and the most effective way to begin the process is to have them take a class while they are still in high school.

Although arithmetic and math is very difficult for this child, it is important not to give up on her prematurely. She can learn many concepts, and become proficient in many areas, if she is taught with patience and creativity. If she is to continue her education beyond high school, it is important that she have as much college preparatory math as possible in order to increase the likelihood that she will be admitted to the college of her choice.

SUMMARY

NLD students will almost certainly have difficulty with at least some aspects of arithmetic and math. Several problems contribute to deficits in this area. As math becomes more abstract, this student's ability to compensate for her deficits may become almost impossible. Traditional methods for teaching arithmetic and math will, in most cases, not work for this child. The following strategies should prove beneficial in teaching the NLD student arithmetic and math:

Teaching Strategies

- These students are unimodal learners, meaning that they do not process visual and auditory simultaneously. Teach verbally, and follow with a visual presentation.

- Math textbooks may be too visually distracting for the student. Use black-on-white presentation. Workbooks, where the student can write in the book, are best.

- Do not encourage this student to guess at an answer, because it will not be an educated guess.

- Flashcards will not generally benefit this child in developing proficiency with math facts. Use verbal/auditory strategies instead.

- Provide context for the child when introducing new concepts, e.g. subtraction is the opposite of addition. Use manipulatives to demonstrate.

- Teach all math concepts in a very direct, step-by-step manner, breaking the problem down into its smallest steps.

° Provide a division card and multiplication math facts for the child when she is taught long division.

° Provide the student with operations cards which illustrate the sequence of each operation. Use either words or icon representations, whichever is easier for the child.

° The vocabulary of word problems may confuse this child. Point out words that are operational cues, and provide the student with a math vocabulary card.

° Teach the child to highlight the information which will be used to solve the problem. Ensure that she is proficient before introducing word problems with extraneous information.

° Teach the student how to convert word problems to icon representations of the information necessary to solve the problem.

° If the student plateaus, or develops a "block," move to the next concept. Continue to return to the operation that caused difficulty until the student either masters it, or it becomes apparent that she never will.

° Have the NLD student take a consumer math class while she is in high school in order to improve her independent living skills.

° At some point, she will likely require one-on-one math instruction in order to make meaningful progress.

Accommodations

○ Time concepts will be very difficult for this student. Encourage a digital watch or clock, and introduce analog when the student is developmentally ready.

○ Teach the use of a calculator early, and encourage its use when calculation is not the objective.

○ Reduce the number of assigned math problems, e.g. have the child do either the "odds" or "evens."

Presentation

○ The student should not copy from the board or book. Problems should be provided to the student.

○ Graph paper is helpful for the student in aligning numbers of math problems.

○ Significantly limit the number of problems per page, and do not mix math operations on a page.

Chapter 8

Reading, Spelling, and Vocabulary

Much of the literature on NLD indicates that these students are early and efficient readers. Although it is true that a large percentage of NLD children are early readers, others have initial difficulty acquiring decoding skills, regardless of their fascination with letters and words, and their well-developed vocabulary. Youngsters are taught reading skills at an age when research indicates that the brain has developed fully in the areas that enable the child to understand the written word. With NLD youngsters, this development may occur somewhat earlier or later than the expected chronological age. Regardless of age, once the child is able to process basic decoding skills, her ability develops remarkably well. Whether the NLD student is an early or late reader, comprehension is almost always a weakness, although this may not be readily apparent until fourth or fifth grade as textbooks become a more integral part of the curriculum. For both groups of NLD children, the early and later readers, spelling is almost always a strength.

READING

All young children love to be read to, but the NLD youngster has a particular fascination with listening to a story, and may often sit quietly for extended periods of time, as a parent reads stories to her. As toddlers, books may be among her favorite "toys," bringing one to an adult to be read to, or sitting with a book in her lap, turning the pages, and giving the illusion that she is reading. Some of these children *are* reading. It is not unusual for an NLD child to read by age three or four. But for those who don't read at this tender age she may also sit with a book in her lap, "reading" the pages, and turning to the next page at just the right time, so that she appears to be able to read. In actuality, she has memorized the story that she has heard read to her, along with the cues as to when the "script" calls for her to turn to the next page in the book. Since the area of strength for NLD children is auditory, this skill of memorizing a story may not be at all difficult for her. Whether the child is reading, or has memorized favorite stories, she has a pronounced fascination with words.

Decoding

When young children begin their formal education in school, they are first taught the alphabet, and that various letters of the alphabet are combined to represent a word. They are then taught to identify and spell words, to understand that words can be put together to form a sentence, a paragraph, or a story. NLD youngsters don't generally follow the same developmental path as their age mates. There is the group of NLD children who are precocious readers, and may already be reading when they enter school. And there is the smaller group of NLD youngsters who are unable to learn the skills necessary to decode along with their classmates. It is the rare case when an NLD child is "on track" with her early reading skills, neither significantly ahead or behind other children of the same age.

For the precocious NLD reader, it is tempting to target her as a gifted child, who would benefit from an accelerated or enriched program. If the child has not yet been diagnosed with NLD, it is even more likely that she will be identified as gifted. Unfortunately, what is not being recognized is that, through words, she is compensating for deficits in other areas. Although she may seem to be a gifted reader at this point, early identification as a gifted student may do more harm than good. If she is placed in an enrichment program, she will likely have significant difficulty in areas that do not relate to reading. However, it would make sense to allow this child to read at her own level, even if that is significantly beyond the level of her age mates.

For the NLD youngster who is unable to grasp the written word at a typical age, the premise is that, based on the natural history of the disorder, she will develop reading skills at a certain point without special intervention. Although that may well be true, it would seem irresponsible to just sit back and wait for this to occur. What would the child do in the meantime? Sit in her class while her classmates are reading, becoming more and more frustrated with her inability to do so? It would be more appropriate for this child to be in a "pull out" program for reading and other language arts curricula, and develop an individualized program that may facilitate her acquiring decoding skills. The NLD student may or may not respond to a phonics-based approach. Or, she may need to understand the use of long and short vowels in order to make sense of words and their meanings. Rather than teaching words associated with a particular letter of the alphabet, for example "A" words such as apple, ant, and alligator, she may learn best by a word families strategy, for example "at" words such as cat, sat, fat, hat, etc., which can then be strung together to form a sentence…The fat cat sat on the hat. Whatever method is selected, clearly a special educator or reading specialist should work with the NLD child to determine what teaching approach would be most appropriate.

All NLD youngsters are likely to have visual processing deficits, and would benefit from reading with a "marker" in order to hold her place on the line and page. This can be an index card, a ruler, or some other simple device that allows the child to more effectively track the words on a straight line, rather than lose her place, or pick up words from the lines above or below the one that she is attempting to read.

Comprehension

The word "comprehension," in its simplest terms, is defined as: "The act or ability of understanding – to get the meaning." In terms of reading, comprehension is then defined as constructing meaning through an individual's interaction with written language. Clearly, this is a far more demanding skill than simple decoding. It involves a myriad of sub-skills, such as an understanding of the vocabulary contained within the text, the story line or main idea, the direct or inferred message of the author, the ability to identify relevant versus irrelevant information, the type of medium (fact or fiction), the application of what is already known to what is being read, and much more.

A deficit in the area of reading comprehension is often missed by educators. Tests that are used to measure reading comprehension actually fail to do so. These testing instruments require that the student read and process the information contained within a short passage. In actuality, all this really measures is the student's ability to decode, recall a very limited amount of information, and possibly the level of the student's vocabulary. Considering the complexity of skills needed for good reading comprehension, how then can the level of a student's reading comprehension be determined by reading a brief passage? The short answer is that it can't. In order to accurately assess a student's reading comprehension ability, an evaluation should be based on the child's ability to effectively process several pages of text, of both fiction and nonfiction material.

In the early school years, reading demands are quite direct and generally fiction-based. Therefore, a comprehension deficit is less pronounced in the younger student. The storyline is rather simple, and the NLD child has little difficulty extracting direct meaning from what she reads. As fiction becomes more complex, and as the child is required to read textbook material, she is no longer able to keep pace with her peers. Even NLD students who may have been targeted as gifted readers, because of their strong decoding skills, begin to have reading comprehension problems.

This breakdown in the child's ability to read often confuses educators and parents alike. The student has previously demonstrated strong decoding skills and a well developed vocabulary, so that when her difficulty with reading comprehension begins to surface, it may erroneously be attributed to a motivational issue. This is definitely *not* the case! Her disability in this area is significant, and *seriously* impedes her ability to learn in the upper elementary grades, middle and high school, and beyond.

To better understand what is causing the breakdown in this child's reading, it is important to realize that early reading, which is primarily a decoding exercise, uses the student's rote strength, and is over-learned behavior – a left hemisphere activity. Reading *comprehension*, on the other hand, is a right hemisphere and whole-brain activity – the areas of deficit for this child. To fully appreciate the demands of reading comprehension, it is important to understand the required cognitive competencies.

At a very basic level, the student must have the ability to:

° observe and recall information

° remember dates, events, and places

° understand major ideas.

In actuality, at this basic level, the NLD student is dependent on her memory skills. Since she has fairly intact memory skills, it is not surprising that she is able to function at this basic level. She will have far less difficulty understanding fiction material, which generally has common components, such as plot, setting, characters, and so forth, than nonfiction material, which is riddled with novelty. However, as reading becomes more abstract, the message less clearly stated, or worse yet, merely inferred, the NLD child is unable to process the information contained within the material.

Although we refer to reading textbook material as a reading comprehension skill, it is far more than that. The expectation is that the student is able to *learn* through reading. In order to do so, the student needs to possess proficiency with a complex set of cognitive competencies. In addition to the three mentioned above – observe and recall information, remember dates, events, and places, as well as understand major ideas – there are a host of higher-level cognitive skills, which include the ability to:

- translate understanding into new context
- interpret facts, compare, contrast
- infer causes, and predict consequences
- use acquired knowledge
- use concepts/theories in new situations
- solve problems using required skills and knowledge
- observe patterns
- organize parts
- recognize hidden meanings
- identify components
- use old ideas to create new ones
- generalize from given facts
- integrate knowledge from several areas
- predict, draw conclusions
- compare/discriminate between ideas
- assess value of theories
- make choices based on reasoned argument
- verify value of evidence
- recognize subjectivity.

The NLD student has significant deficits in these higher-level cognitive skills. As a result, her ability to process textbook material which she is required to read is seriously compromised. She is unable to identify what information is relevant and important enough to remember, and what is not. So, although rote tasks such as recall are generally a strength, when left to identify pertinent information on her own, she is unable to do so.

As a result of the NLD student's deficits in cognitive skills, specifically those that are required to process textbook material, most will not have even the basic skills necessary to manage such a reading assignment.

To further complicate the child's reading disability, she has visual processing deficits. She will have difficulty visually "tracking" a line of text. The smaller the type, and the less black-on-white contrast, the more difficult the task of simply reading the words on a page. If required to read material that is presented in a small typeface, with narrow margins (reduced "white space"), and poor contrast between print and paper, she will likely shut down. She is unable to process material presented in this fashion, whether it is fiction or nonfiction.

It is absolutely imperative that educators understand the magnitude of this child's reading disability. Intervention should start early, and be intense. Regardless of what part of the child's curriculum covers instruction of specific cognitive skills, these skills must be *specifically taught* to this child in a direct, step-by-step manner. She will *not* develop them on her own, and they are absolutely critical to her academic success. At all times, the NLD student's visual processing deficits must be accommodated.

Literature

The following are some teaching strategies that will be helpful in improving the NLD student's reading comprehension of literature. This is not to be considered a complete list, but should provide the child's teacher with direction on how best to attack this area of deficit.

° The student should be encouraged to use a marker – a ruler, index card, or some other similar aid – to help her maintain her place on a page. This strategy should alleviate, at least somewhat, the difficulty she has with visual tracking.

° Reading material should be presented with good black-on-white contrast, and significant "white space" on the page. Book chapters can be reproduced on a copying machine, using the enlarge feature to increase the size of the type. Large-print books will also accomplish this objective.

° Directly teach concepts such as plot, setting, main idea, characterization, and so forth. To teach these concepts to her seventh and eighth graders, a middle school language arts teacher uses beautifully illustrated picture books (designed for very young children), which she reads to the class. Each book is carefully selected to teach the students one or more of these concepts. The students absolutely love this, and not surprisingly, learn a lot. It is a very creative and effective strategy.

° For all reading requirements, frontload the assignment. Frontloading means "setting the stage" for the material to be read. If a particular assignment calls for the student to read The Diary of Anne Frank, there should first be class instruction on the Holocaust, and the concept of 'ethnic cleansing.' This will provide the NLD student with a context for her reading, significantly increasing her likelihood of extracting information and meaning from what she reads.

° Always provide a purpose for a specific reading assignment *before* the child begins to read. If a short story is assigned, the teacher may say something like, "This story is about a group of special needs children who go to camp. When you are finished reading the story, I want you to be able to tell me what you think was the most important thing that the children learned from their camp experience."

○ When assigning a novel, the same technique of assigning a purpose should be provided, but it also needs to be broken down into manageable chunks with associated due dates. A guided reading worksheet with assigned segments and pertinent questions should be provided to the NLD student. Depending on the ability of the student, the questions may all relate to plot, or may include questions on setting, characterization, predicting, etc. The important point is that, by breaking the task down for the child with interim due dates, and through the use of guided questions, she will more likely be able to complete the assignment on time *and* understand the novel. Figure 8.1 illustrates what a worksheet for guided reading might look like.

○ Always provide assignment expectations before the child begins to read. For instance, if there will be a test, or a book report, explain exactly what the expectations are. The use of rubrics, checklists, and models will significantly increase the NLD student's success with these types of assignments.

○ The technique, often used by classroom teachers, of having students take turns reading out loud in class is not effective for this child. Although her learning style is auditory, youngsters do not generally read with the cadence and inflection of an adult, thereby compromising the NLD student's ability to make sense of the reading passage. It is critical for her to hear the appropriate verbal cues that enhance the meaning of material she processes auditorily. Text that is read out loud in class should always be read by an adult who is familiar with the material.

○ As reading demands become more complex, the NLD child's reading rate may deteriorate. Allow plenty of time for her to complete her reading assignments.

Book	Nothing To Fear
Date Due	Assignment
9/11	Read to page 33 to find out how Danny gets into trouble and what his father wants to do about it.
9/14	Read to page 69 to find out what kind of a person Mr. Weissman is.
9/16	Read to page 104 to learn what Mama is like and who Maggie is.
9/18	Read to page 154 to learn why Mr. Weissman finally decides that Danny is a good boy.
9/21	Read to page 181 to learn what Danny's Depression Christmas was like.
9/23	Read to page 216 to learn about Maggie and her guilt.
9/25	Read to page 235 to find out how a man named Hank came into Danny's life and what Hank was like.
9/28	Read to page 244 to learn more about Hank's Sadness.
9/30	Read to page 270 to learn what happened to Pa.
10/2	Read to the end of the book to find out what happened to Ma.
10/15	Write a one-and-a-half page essay on what you learned from the book about the Great Depression.

Figure 8.1 Guided Reading Worksheet

It is important to understand that if the child *hears* rather than reads more complex material, her deficits, although significant, are somewhat less severe. Every effort should be made to accommodate this student's learning style by providing auditory instruction.

- ° It is very, *very* helpful for the NLD student to "read" novels by listening to them on audiotape. Because of her reading disability, visual processing deficits, and compromised reading speed for new and complex material, she can easily fall behind the other students when reading an assigned book. However, when using a medium compatible with her learning style, she is able to keep up with her classmates, and be more successful in the process. Audiotapes of fiction and literary selections are available through the Reading for the Blind and Dyslexic organization, most local libraries (or through their lending arrangements with other libraries), as well as through bookstores, if the parent chooses to purchase the book on tape.

○ If an audiotape is not available for a particular book that a teacher feels is critical to the curriculum, then consideration *must* be given to the quality of the presentation. As children enter the middle school years, many of the outside reading requirements are of paperback books. These books tend to have poorer contrast of ink to paper than hardcover books, smaller type, and significantly less "white space" on the page. There are two alternatives to paperback books. One is to obtain a hardcover book from the school or local library, and arrange for it to be checked out for the duration of the assignment, rather than for the normal period of one to two weeks. The second option is to arrange for a large-print copy of the book. Large-print books have all of the advantages of hardcover books, but the type is larger. Implementing either of these options may require a bit of preplanning, but are absolutely necessary in order to accommodate the NLD student's disability.

Textbooks

Reading textbook material can be an overwhelming challenge for the NLD student. She will need intense, and in all likelihood, prolonged instruction in order to learn the skills necessary to process textbook material.

The following are strategies that will benefit this student when she is required to read nonfiction, specifically in subjects such as social studies, history, and science. However, it is strongly recommended that the school reading specialist be consulted to develop a specific program for this student in order to address her reading comprehension disability in the content areas.

- The student should be encouraged to use a marker – a ruler, index card, or some other similar aid – to help her maintain her place on a page. This strategy should alleviate, at least somewhat, the difficulty she has with visual tracking.

- Never, *ever* require the NLD student to read a segment or chapter of a textbook before the material has been covered in class. The reading assignment should be a *review* of what has already been taught. If the review reading is more than a few pages, an alternative strategy will be necessary. Either the material should be read to the student by an adult, or, preferably, provided on audiotape so that she can listen to it.

- Although textbooks on tape are available through Reading for the Blind and Dyslexic (RFBD), they are not ideal for this student. Many teachers do not follow a textbook from beginning to end, but rather assign reading in various sections of the book that relate specifically to their lesson plan. It is difficult for the student to find the appropriate place on a particular RFBD tape in order to begin listening. Based on the reading selection that is assigned, an adult would have to set the tape to the proper starting point each day. Also, since these tapes are designed for blind as well as reading disabled individuals, every illustration is described in minute detail and is quite tedious for the student to listen to, disrupting her learning process. Many RFBD readers speak in an articulate, but rather monotone style, not providing the appropriate cadence and auditory cues that this student requires. For these reasons, even though the

NLD student is an auditory learner, she will likely find textbooks on tape from RFBD more of a nuisance than a benefit. An alternative to RFBD tapes is to have a paraprofessional, or some other school staff member, record the textbook reading assignment on an audiotape and provide it to the child at the appropriate time. This approach would take a bit of planning and coordination with the classroom teacher, but can work quite effectively.

○ As with literature, if there will be a test, or some other activity, subsequent to a textbook reading assignment, inform the student what it will be *before* she begins to read. Be specific in what she will need to know or do, using checklists, rubrics, models, a skeleton study guide, etc. to clarify the expectation.

○ There will likely be times when the NLD student has no alternative but to read from a textbook. This child's reading rate will probably be quite slow for this type of material. Allow plenty of time in order for the child to complete these reading assignments, but keep the assignment short, and avoid them whenever possible.

○ To increase this student's comprehension of textbook material, follow reading assignments with class discussion, or small group discussion. She learns quite well through discussion of a topic, even if she merely listens, rather than participates.

○ Teachers should avoid having students take turns reading textbook material out loud in class. Although her learning style is auditory, youngsters do not generally read with the cadence and inflection of an adult, thereby compromising the NLD student's ability to make sense of the reading passage. For textbook or other nonfiction material, it is even *more* critical for her to hear the appropriate verbal cues that will enhance the meaning of material that she processes auditorily. Reading out loud should be performed by an adult who is familiar with the material.

° The NLD student should *always* be allowed to write and highlight in her textbooks. Teaching the child the technique of highlighting the main idea in one color, and supporting information in a second color can be very helpful.

° The NLD student will need specific instruction in the following areas in order to improve her comprehension of textbook and other nonfiction material, and enable her to answer related questions:

- The structure and organization of a textbook.

- Identifying main ideas and supporting information.

- Identifying relevant vs. irrelevant information.

- Highlighting, outlining and notetaking strategies.

- Converting what she has read into her own words.

- Answering end-of-chapter questions.

SPELLING

NLD students are generally accomplished spellers. If they spell a word incorrectly, it will generally be spelled phonetically. Due to her strength in the area of rote learning, it is possible that this student is the top speller in the class. However, these youngsters do have some difficulties with spelling that need accommodation. The following are areas of potential difficulty, along with alternative strategies of support:

° This child may not be able to spell out loud, even if she is a gifted speller. She is unable to visualize the word in her head, and likely has learned the word by storing a sequence of letters. Therefore, she may only be able to spell on paper where she can visually, and sequentially, reproduce the word. If this is true for your NLD student, she will not want to participate in spelling bees, and encouragement to do so may only create anxiety. Her strength in the area of spelling should be recognized in some other way, rather than selecting her to represent her class or grade in a spelling bee.

○ When the child is assigned words to learn how to spell, she may prefer to learn them auditorily.

○ If she is required to write her spelling words a certain amount of times, she may need to learn them by storing the sequence of letters. With this sequential method, you would print the word "clown" for her clearly as a model to follow, and rather than writing the word five or ten times, she may do better by printing the letter "c" on the correct number of lines (5 or 10), then go back and print the letter "l" on each line, followed by "o" and so forth until the word is completed for the assigned number of repetitions. This method is likely to be more compatible with her learning style than the traditional method of writing each word in its entirety before starting on the next repetition.

○ This student may be slow to generalize accurate spelling to other subjects. For instance, when she is doing a social studies assignment, she will be focused on that particular material, and may forget to generalize what she has learned in spelling. She should be graded for spelling *only* in that subject area, and *not* in other classes such as social studies, etc. However, it *is* appropriate to correct her spelling at all times. Eventually spelling will become automatic for this student, but probably not until middle school.

○ Because of her visual processing deficits, activities such as word jumbles, or other visual exercises should *not* be assigned to this student. She will likely be totally incapable of working in this medium, and will become extremely frustrated. Simple, sequential spelling instruction is the method by which this child will learn.

VOCABULARY

Vocabulary is clearly an area of strength for the NLD student. However, as with spelling, there are also accommodations that must be made due to her other areas of disability. The following are suggestions:

° It is best to avoid combining spelling and vocabulary instruction and exercises. This child needs very deliberate cues in order to shift mental set. Even if you will be covering the same words in both areas of the language arts block, it is effective to do spelling during a spelling block, and vocabulary during a vocabulary block. Once you complete the spelling block, explain to the class that now that you are finished working on spelling, you are going to work on vocabulary, or what the words mean.

° As with spelling, avoid word jumbles as well as crossword puzzles and similar exercises, since this student will likely be incapable of doing them. Writing the definition of the word is far more effective in helping this child understand its meaning. Also, having the child use the word in a sentence is effective, as long as the writing exercise doesn't cause her fatigue. She should be allowed to dictate her sentences, rather than being required to write them out.

° Disposable vocabulary workbooks are generally the most effective tool when teaching vocabulary, as long as the exercises do not include visual processing activities such as word jumbles or crossword puzzles. Fill in the blanks, or matching activities are exercises that this child should be able to perform, and reduces the demand for writing, which is an area of difficulty.

° This student will have difficulty with words that have multiple meanings. It is critical to point out all of the possible meanings of a word that is being taught. Sample sentences should be used to further illustrate how a single word can be used in a variety of situations.

○ The older student will likely use contextual cues to help her understand words that are unfamiliar, or that she may not recall the meaning of. However, do not assume that she will automatically know how to do this on her own. She should receive specific instruction in how to determine word meanings from contextual cues.

Although this child likely has, or quickly develops, a sophisticated vocabulary, this does not mean that she has competent language skills. It is important to remember that her functional understanding and use of language is impaired.

SUMMARY

NLD students develop excellent decoding skills, although some may lag behind their peer group. Where spelling and vocabulary are a relative strength for these youngsters, reading comprehension is a significant weakness. At all times, the NLD student's visual processing deficits must be accommodated.

Reading

Avoid the temptation to target the NLD youngster as gifted on the basis of early reading skills. Use alternative strategies to foster decoding skills for the NLD child who struggles with early reading instruction.

Reading comprehension is an area of significant deficit for the NLD student. It is absolutely imperative that educators understand the magnitude of this child's reading disability. Intervention should start early, and be intense.

Fiction concepts such as plot, setting, main idea, characterization, etc. must be specifically taught. For nonfiction and textbook material she will need direct instruction in:

- the structure and organization of a textbook
- identifying main ideas and supporting information
- identifying relevant vs. irrelevant information
- highlighting, outlining and notetaking strategies
- converting what she has read into her own words
- answering end-of-chapter questions.

In order for this student to learn through reading, she will need direct instruction in the cognitive skills required to process, and benefit from, nonfiction and textbook material.

Teaching strategies that are very beneficial for improving the NLD student's reading skills include the following:

- ° Using a marker to improve visual tracking.

- ° Having sharp contrast of print to paper, large print, and increased "white space."

- ° Providing context by frontloading all reading assignments.

- ° Providing a purpose for reading assignments – what it is about and why it is being assigned.

- ° Using a guided reading approach for literature assignments – provide a guided reading worksheet.

- ° Following nonfiction and textbook reading assignments with class or small group discussion.

- ° Providing post-reading assignment expectations prior to the reading assignment – rubrics, checklists, and models are very helpful.

- ° Having an adult do classroom reading out loud rather than a student.

- ° Allowing sufficient time for the slow NLD reader.

- ° Encouraging the use of books on tape.

Spelling

Although spelling is generally a relative strength, the student will need the following accommodations:

○ If the student is unable to spell out loud, avoid a traditional spelling bee.

○ Allow the child the option of learning her spelling words auditorily.

○ Allow flexibility in how the student writes her spelling repetitions.

○ Do not grade for spelling in content areas other than spelling.

○ Avoid the use of visual activities such as word jumbles and searches.

Vocabulary

Although vocabulary is also a relative strength, the student will need the following accommodations:

○ Specific instruction focused on words with multiple meanings.

○ Specific instruction in the use of contextual cues.

○ Workbooks, because they reduce the demand for writing.

○ As with spelling, avoid visual exercises such as word jumbles and crossword puzzles.

Chapter 9

Penmanship, Writing and Composition

NLD students generally have significant problems with most aspects of the writing process, from penmanship and the physical act of writing, to grammar and punctuation, organizing their thoughts and ideas, and composing their thoughts and ideas into a cohesive end product. The good news is that intervention results in meaningful improvement, which is sometimes quite significant, and technology tools allow the student to compensate for their areas of deficit.

PENMANSHIP

This student will have difficulty with the physical aspects of writing. Holding the pencil correctly, applying the correct amount of pressure, staying on the line, gauging how much space on the paper she needs in order to form a letter correctly, gauging the space to allow between letters and sentences, and recalling how a letter is to be formed, is often overwhelming for this student. When working with this child, it is important to be conscious of how complex the writing process is. The child needs to be taught each step of the process separately before bringing it all together.

Prewriting

It would be very beneficial to teach the underlying mechanics of writing before the student is taught how to write letters and numbers. This includes instruction and practice in the shapes and sizes that will be used, as well as how to hold the pencil and how much pressure to apply. She should not be taught how to do this on a blackboard or other vertical surface, but rather on a horizontal surface, since this is how she will be required to do the majority of her writing.

Provide the size and type of pencil that is comfortable for the child to hold. Experiment with a variety of pencils, from the fat ones that are often used in the early elementary grades, to a regular no. 2 pencil, to mechanical pencils with a gel or rubber grip. If a standard pencil is used, provide a cushioned grip so that the child knows where to put her fingers when she holds the instrument, and to alleviate finger fatigue, which will surely occur. The NLD student should be allowed the continued use of a pencil when the other students are introduced to a pen. This student should not be expected to switch from one writing instrument that she is comfortable with to another that further compromises her ability to write legibly. Also, since she will likely make far more mistakes than other children, she needs the ability to erase and correct.

Young children are generally taught how to make letters by looking at a representation and then copying it. Because of her visual, tactile, and psychomotor deficits, the NLD student may not be able to learn in this manner. Instead, she may need a verbal description of how to form each of the shapes, and once she has mastered them, receive the same verbal description of how to form numbers and the letters of the alphabet.

Paper Supplies

Paper supplies that are used in the early elementary grades are often quite thin, and tear very easily. The NLD child should be provided with a heavier grade of paper, or a "white board" in order to practice her shapes. When practicing her preprinting exercises, it is usually easier for the child to make large shapes rather than small. Allow her to practice making her shapes larger than she will be required to use when she later begins to write functionally. Once she has mastered the shape, she should be taught how to make each the size that will be required when printing letters and numbers. Only after the child has mastered the shapes and sizing, should she be introduced to instruction of actual numbers and letters.

It may be helpful to provide this student with graph paper when she is writing words, and forming sentences, so that she allows the correct amount of space between letters, words, and sentences. It is important to verbally explain the underlying concept…if the letters are too crowded, it will be hard to read, and if there isn't space between sentences, it will be difficult for someone to see where one sentence ends and another begins. Graph paper will provide her with the boundaries for appropriate spacing that she will not develop naturally. Make sure to explain that she needs to leave one blank between each word, and two blank squares between each sentence.

Many teachers have students fold the sides of the paper to mark where the acceptable margins should be. This student will need a more defined margin marker, such as a dark line drawn down the left and right sides of the page.

Legible and Functional

With time and practice, the NLD child will learn how to write numbers and letters, which may actually be quite legible and appropriately sized. However, there are two potential problems. The first is that although the child may print beautifully, it may be so slow and laborious that it is nonfunctional. The second is that she may have finally mastered printing, only to be faced with learning cursive writing. Some NLD children find cursive writing easier than printing, while others have significant difficulty. We must keep in mind that the student needs to learn a functional skill. The objective in teaching the child penmanship is so that she can take notes and communicate in writing. If she "draws" her letters, she will never be able to write fast enough to keep up with her work. Considering our technological environment, the future physical writing demands for this child will be quite different than for prior generations. There will be far less need for good penmanship skills. Therefore, it is wise to determine whether printing or cursive is easier for the child, and allow her to master either one or the other, but not both.

The NLD child should not be graded on her penmanship skills since she has a disability that prevents her from mastering this skill. Her writing assignments should be reduced in length to accommodate her difficulty in this area. For assignments which do require more writing, such as a book report or research paper, the NLD student should be allowed to dictate to someone acting as her scribe. The long-term goal for this child is to develop keyboarding skills to a level that allows her to do the majority of her work on a computer no later than the beginning of high school. An occupational therapist should be consulted to determine at what developmental age this student should be introduced to keyboarding, as well as the most appropriate method of instruction to use.

WRITING

As classwork moves from forming letters and words to writing sentences and paragraphs, the demands become more complex. The child has to form letters and words, use the correct grammar and punctuation, recall what she knows about the topic at hand, organize her thoughts, and express her thoughts concisely and accurately on paper. Clearly, this is a challenge for the NLD student. However, the fact that she is a "rule-driven" child will work to her benefit when learning the rules of writing.

Because this student depends on words for her primary means of communication, and likely has a well developed vocabulary, she will have an immediate advantage in this area. Coupled with her thirst for structure and operating within the rules, and her strong rote memory skills, there is every reason to believe that she can be taught to become a very effective writer. The key will be to provide her with specific instruction in all of the rules of writing. Since writing may be developed to the level of a true strength, or even talent, for this student, she should be provided with the most talented educators in this area of her education. In addition to obvious benefits of developing her talent for writing, there is the added benefit that as her writing skills increase, so will her verbal communication skills. As she learns to write about terms such as conflict, both internal and external, she will better understand what it means when she is faced with conflict in a social interaction.

COMPOSITION

The higher-order thinking skills required for expressive writing are areas of deficit for the NLD student. Depending on the assigned task, the student may need to produce original thoughts, elaborate on ideas, incorporate prior learned knowledge, think critically, apply new concepts, and be able to take the perspective of the individual(s) who will read the final product. Although it may seem like an impossible task to teach this student, who relies on rote memory skills and thinks somewhat rigidly, how to develop the necessary skills to become a good writer, it can be done. With patience, and the right strategies, she can be taught.

Models, Rubrics and Checklists

As with all students, you begin with the basics, and build from there, adding a new concept when the prior one has been mastered. Children don't develop good writing skills quickly, it takes time. What is important when working with the NLD student is to be very explicit in your instruction, and always provide her with models, rubrics, and checklists in order to reinforce the concept being taught.

The class should be provided with models of the writing exercise being taught. Models should be provided for various quality levels, and the teacher should point out the strengths and weaknesses of each. A rubric will provide the NLD student with clear expectations of what is required by the teacher, and what the grade equivalent will be for various levels of quality. The models that are provided to the students should be graded based on the rubric to further reinforce teacher expectations. Figure 9.1 is a sample of a rubric that was provided to a class of seventh grade language arts students for an argumentative writing assignment:

Childress Rubric for Scoring Argumentative Pieces

Score Point: 6 (equivalent to an A)
Well developed responses:

- A powerful opening paragraph that hooks the reader and vehemently states the writer's position.
- At least three reasons well supported with specific detail.
- Very strong organizational strategy.
- Very fluent.
- Very few misspellings, errors in punctuation, capitalization, sentence formation, and usage.
- Very sophisticated vocabulary.

Score Point: 5 (equivalent to a B)
Developed responses:

- Fairly strong opening paragraph that hooks the reader and clearly states the writer's position.
- Three reasons supported with specific detail.
- Strong organizational strategy.
- Moderately fluent.
- Few misspellings, errors in punctuation, capitalization, sentence formation, and usage.
- Sophisticated vocabulary.

Score Point: 4 (equivalent to a C)
Somewhat developed responses:

- An opening that states the writer's position fairly clearly.
- Two or three reasons supported with some specific and some general detail.
- Acceptable organizational strategy.
- Somewhat fluent, but occasionally "listy."
- Some errors in punctuation, capitalization, sentence formation, and usage.
- Less sophisticated vocabulary.

Score Point: 3 (equivalent to a D)
Undeveloped responses:

- Weak opening in which writer's position is difficult to determine.
- Reasons that show little support and are more general than specific.
- Little evidence of organizational strategy.
- Choppy and "listy."
- Many errors in punctuation, capitalization, sentence formation, and usage.
- Unsophisticated vocabulary.

Score Point: 2 (equivalent to an F)
Undeveloped responses:

- No clear position.
- Disorganized.
- Misspellings, errors in punctuation, capitalization, sentence formation, and usage.
- Childish vocabulary.

Score Point: 1
Very sparse responses:

- Vague position.
- Vague details.
- Confused.

Figure 9.1 Sample Rubric

The combination of the models and a rubric should provide the student with a very clear understanding of what is required before she begins her writing assignment.

Structured Writing

This student needs a structured approach to writing, which should be used consistently with her from one assignment to the next, and from year to year. The first thing to explain to this student is that when you write, there is a beginning, a middle, and an end. However, the NLD child needs to understand what you mean by these words. The beginning sets the stage for what you are going to write about, the middle is what you are writing about, and the end brings the piece to a close so that it doesn't end abruptly. This concept applies whether the student is writing a paragraph or a long report, and should be consistently reinforced.

Careful consideration must be given to the selection of a structured approach that will be used for instruction in composition. An example of one strategy that does not work with NLD students is sometimes called a writing web. This strategy uses a graphical representation for writing, where there is a daisy-shaped image – with a circle in the center, and spokes radiating out from the center. The concept is that the main idea should be entered in the center circle, and supporting ideas should be entered on the spokes radiating out from the circle. This type of strategy does nothing but confuse the NLD student. First, she has to determine what the main idea is, or should be – something that is quite difficult for her. Then, she has a bunch of ideas, without the slightest idea of how to group them in order to include the information in a writing assignment. This technique is too visual, and far too abstract for the NLD student.

Using a 1–3–1 Model

After the NLD youngster understands the concept of what is included in a beginning, middle, and end of a writing assignment, she will need instruction in expanding the middle, which is the bulk of the work product. Once these basic concepts are understood, the student should be introduced to a structure that she will be able to apply to all writing assignments. Figure 9.2 shows a particularly effective graphic organizer for the NLD student, which has been coined the 1–3–1 Writing Model.

Introduction – set the stage – tell what you're going to write about.	
Important Fact	Discuss or expand on the important fact
Important Fact	Discuss or expand on the important fact
Important Fact	Discuss or expand on the important fact
Conclusion/Summary – wrap it up – bring closure to your topic.	

Figure 9.2 1–3–1 Writing Model

This particular model directs the student's organization of information, and is flexible enough that it can be modified to fit a variety of different writing assignments. Although the physical format should always be consistent, some students may require different trigger words to describe what material is to be included in each section.

The student should be encouraged to write directly on this form, and then convert her notes to a prose document. The younger child, with less writing experience, and little or no keyboarding skills, should dictate her paper to someone who types it for her. As the child gets older, she should convert her own worksheet to a typed document. The following examples will illustrate how a student can use this template for a variety of writing assignments.

The first example is an essay written by a sixth grader. The assignment was to write a biography of a classmate, including information about his family, his early life, hobbies, life at present, and his future plans.

The Life of Matthew Denning

Guess who I'm writing about? Matthew Denning. He was born August 16, 1985. He lived with his mom, dad, and sister Carrie in Tolland, Connecticut. While Matthew was still small, his family moved to a house on Barstow Lane, which is also in Tolland.

Matt doesn't remember much about being little, but he does remember that he loved carrots!!! He did some funny things when he was a baby! For example, he used to fall asleep in his high chair, face first on the tray! His head almost went in his food bowl! Also, he used to take unused toilet paper and roll it on the floor all over the house! He also used to climb up the food cabinet and sit on the shelf!

Matt went to Parker Memorial School, but didn't like it much. He found "little kids" annoying. His favorite grade was kindergarten. He had Mrs. Hanley and found that it was easy. Matt's best memory at Parker was in the third grade. His teacher was Mrs. Bauman, and his fourth report card was great! He loved soccer, and played it all the time. He also liked building things with Legos. He went to Disney World in first grade and loved the rides. Who wouldn't? Matt always wanted a puppy, so he begged his parents until they finally got him a Golden Retriever. He named her Cedar.

Matt is now 11 years old and a student at Tolland Middle School. His favorite grade in the middle school is the grade he is in now – sixth. His friends are Joey Lutz, Chris King, and Mark Richardson. He went to Nature's Classroom this year and had a great time. Matt thinks it was worth all the money his parents paid! He is still playing soccer and one of his new hobbies is baseball. He went to Disney World again in fourth grade and his favorite ride was Space Mountain.

Matt's future plans include going to college at UConn. His goal in life is to be a rich and successful architect. He also wants to get married, have three dogs, and live in the country.

Figure 9.3 Sample Biographical Essay

The student effectively used the 1–3–1 format by explaining in the first paragraph who she would be writing about, using the three middle paragraphs to explain Matt's life when he was young, during his elementary years, and then during middle school. The fifth and closing paragraph was used to explain Matt's future plans.

The next example of a 1–3–1 application was written by a seventh- grade student. The assignment was to write a recommendation letter to a group of judges. The student was required to recommend a character from a story that the class had read, for recognition as a hero. Figure 9.3 shows a slightly modified 1–3–1 worksheet that applies specifically to this assignment.

Introduction – set the stage – tell what you're going to write about.	
Fact or Reason no. 1	Why do you feel this way? – support your no. 1 statement with a couple of sentences.
Fact or Reason no. 2	Why do you feel this way? – support your no. 2 statement with a couple of sentences.
Fact or Reason no. 3	Why do you feel this way? – support your no. 3 statement with a couple of sentences.
Conclusion/Summary – wrap it up – sell your recommendation to the judges	

Figure 9.4 1–3–1 Worksheet: Letter of Recommendation

By making slight modifications, the 1–3–1 worksheet can be tailored to a particular assignment. Adapting the worksheet to the specific assignment is particularly beneficial for the young or inexperienced writer. The following is the student's final work product:

Letter of Recommendation

Dear Judges,

A man, who risked his life, just to make other lives better. A man, who taught his people how to read and write, even when he knew he could be beaten and killed by doing so. A man, who admitted teaching his people, and had his finger chopped off, just for educating others. This is the kind of man who deserves the Hero Award. This man, is Night John.

First, he taught his people to read. It is illegal for a Negro to even know the alphabet, let alone know how to write a sentence and be able to read it! He risked his life by teaching people how to read and write. That's real courage right there, judges. Would you risk your life, just for the benefit of others? Many people these days wouldn't. Night John decided to take a stand, and be stronger than the average human being. He made the decision to risk his life for his people. This is what a Hero Award winner should be, and Night John suits that perfectly.

Second, he admitted to teaching his people the alphabet, and how to read and write. There was a woman who tried to take the blame for him, but he wouldn't let her pay for something that she didn't do. When the slave master found out about his teaching to the other Negroes, they punished him, of course. They chopped off his right index finger with an axe.

How many of us today are brave enough to admit what we've done wrong? Whether it be who stole a pack of gum at a drug store, or who killed an innocent victim while they were taking a walk in a park at night, we deny it all to save ourselves from punishment. Night John didn't believe in blaming it on someone else. He took the blame, and saved someone's finger from being chopped off.

Finally, he kept others spirits high when they were feeling down. His first day at the new plantation, he started singing as he was working in the fields, with no fear of the master getting mad and beating him. Others working near him started to join in. Before you knew it, all of the slaves were singing as they were working. Don't you want to hand over the award to a man who can make others happy? That is the most important characteristic the Hero Award winner should have. Face it, judges, would you hand over the award to someone who couldn't make others happy? I know that if I were an intelligent judge like yourself, I wouldn't give the award to anyone who couldn't put a smile across my face.

So as you can see, a brave slave, Night John, should receive the Hero Award. Do you want someone who can make others happy? Who can lift others' spirits? Who can take the blame of what they have done wrong? Who can risk his life to teach others to improve their lives? If so, then Night John is your award winner this year. Give the award to a deserving man. Give the Hero Award to Night John.

Thank you for your time,

Student's name

Figure 9.5 Persuasive Writing Sample

By using the 1–3–1 strategy, the student explained her purpose for writing the letter in the first paragraph, provided three arguments for why the individual should receive recognition, with supporting data provided for each, and used the final paragraph to summarize her arguments, and "sell" her recommendation. Clearly, this is a very different assignment from the previous one, which was a biographical essay, but the 1-3-1 model works equally well for both.

The sample rubric, 1-3-1 model worksheets, and completed writing assignments used in this chapter are for a middle school student who has been exposed to this process for several years. When the student is first introduced to these tools in the earlier grades, the rubric, models, and associated assignments should naturally be quite simple and age appropriate.

Proofing and Editing

Clearly, there is significant work which is required between completion of the 1-3-1 worksheet and the final product. The student will need to proof and edit her work. It is helpful to provide the NLD student with a sequence of tasks to perform during the proofing and editing process. This sequence of tasks should be listed on an index card for the student to refer back to when necessary. The sequence may go something like…Did you include all of the parts that are required for the assignment? Is the content complete? Did you check and correct your spelling? Did you check and correct your grammar? Did you check and correct your punctuation? Did you capitalize where necessary?

Proof and Edit Checklist

Are required parts included?

Is content complete?

Did you check & correct:

- Spelling?
- Grammar?
- Punctuation?
- Capitalization?

Figure 9.6 Proof and Edit Checklist

Once the student has developed keyboarding skills, and is doing her own writing on a computer, she should be encouraged to use the spelling and grammar checker in the word-processing program.

Final Thoughts

There are two additional points that need to be addressed regarding the NLD student's unique writing needs. She will have tremendous difficulty selecting a topic on her own, and needs guidance in doing so. Where possible, assign a topic for this student. Abstract material is often beyond her ability. When assigning a topic, avoid abstract topics.

With early and ongoing quality instruction in writing, the NLD student will likely develop excellent skills, especially in the area of expressive writing. This strength may result in beneficial opportunities for this child, such as:

- awards and other recognition of her writing talent
- social opportunities in high school and/or college, such as working on the school newspaper
- future career opportunities.

SUMMARY

NLD students generally have significant problems with most aspects of the writing process, however appropriate intervention results in improvement that may be quite significant.

Penmanship

Holding a pencil correctly, applying the correct amount of pressure, staying on the line, gauging how much space on the paper she needs in order to form a letter correctly, gauging the space to allow between letters and sentences, and recalling how a letter is to be formed is often overwhelming for this student.

- ° Develop prewriting skills by practicing shapes before teaching her how to write the alphabet or numbers.

- ° Select a pencil that will avoid finger fatigue, and encourage proper finger placement. Continue with pencil rather than changing to pen.

- ° Verbally describe how to make letters, rather than providing only a visual representation.

- ° Provide paper that won't tear easily. Graph paper is excellent at teaching spacing.

- ° Keep the objective in mind – to develop functional writing skills with speed and legibility. If the student draws her cursive letters, revert to printing.

- ° Do not grade penmanship.

- ° Introduce keyboarding at developmentally appropriate age.

Writing

Moving from the basic level of forming letters and words to the complexity of writing sentences and paragraphs will be difficult for this student.

- ○ She thrives on structure and rules. Provide her with specific instruction in all of the rules of writing.

- ○ Her well developed vocabulary will be an immediate advantage in this area.

- ○ Writing may be developed to the level of a true strength, or even talent, for this student

- ○ Writing helps improve this student's communication skills.

- ○ Verbal mnemonics for the rules of grammar are exceptionally helpful to this student.

Composition

Higher-order thinking skills required for expressive writing include the ability to produce original thoughts, elaborate on ideas, incorporate prior learned knowledge, think critically, apply new concepts, and be able to take the perspective of the individual(s) who will read the final product. Although it may seem like an impossible task to teach this student, who relies on rote memory skills and thinks somewhat rigidly, how to develop the necessary skills to become a good writer, it *can* be done. With the right intervention, she may actually become a gifted writer.

○ Begin with the basics, and build from there, adding a new concept when the prior one has been mastered.

○ Provide models, rubrics, and checklists in order to reinforce the concept being taught.

○ Provide a structured approach to writing, and use consistently from one assignment to the next, and from year to year.

○ Consider using a 1-3-1 Writing Model as a graphic organizer, and modify trigger words depending on the assignment.

○ The younger student should dictate to someone who can type her prose. The child who has developed keyboarding skills should type her own, and be encouraged to use the word-processing spelling and grammar checker.

○ Provide a sequence of tasks for the proofing and editing process. List on an index card for the student to refer back to when necessary.

○ Assign a writing topic, and avoid abstract material.

Chapter 10

Organization, Study Skills, and Homework

It is probably safe to say that most parents find that, for a variety of reasons, their child struggles with organization, study skills, and/or homework. Parents of NLD youngsters will find that the child struggles in all of these areas, with significant difficulty surfacing in the late elementary and middle school grades as the student is expected to do more work independently. In order for the NLD child to be successful, she will need considerably more specific instruction in how to organize herself and her work, what and how to study, and how to complete homework assignments. Intervention in all three of these areas should begin very early. Otherwise, the likelihood that this student will "hit the wall" by fifth or sixth grade is almost a certainty. Although she may always have difficulty in one or more of these areas, there are numerous strategies that can be implemented at an early age to help her, particularly in the area of organization.

ORGANIZATION

The objective in teaching organizational skills is to empower the child to have control over her work and her environment. If adults provide organizational consistency for this student over an extended period of time, eventually she will begin to recreate it, because it works for her and she needs it.

Classroom

There should be clearly marked schedules in prominent locations. In addition to schedules posted on the wall, the very young child should be provided with a schedule at her "cubbie" (where she keeps her personal possessions) as well as at her desk. If she does not yet read, simple pictorial representations of each activity should be used. Any changes to the daily routine should be marked on these schedules, and explained to the student. By the age of eight or nine years old, the desk schedule should be replaced with one that the student carries with her each day, and any changes to her routine should be explained to her and marked on her schedule. (Refer to Chapter 5 for more information on schedules.)

Classroom rules can be confusing for this child, and punitive measures should never be used. Teachers often have a system in their classroom where young students are expected to put their completed assignments in a particular place. A reward system is implemented for students who always remember to do so, and punitive measures are used to encourage those who fail to. This type of system will only serve to make the NLD child anxious, since she wants to follow the rules, but has difficulty understanding them and following through. She will need continual verbal reinforcement and reminders. If her work has not been turned in, she should be quietly reminded to do so. This applies to the older student as well, who may have finished all assignments, but forgotten the nonverbal task of handing them in. A verbal reminder is likely all that is necessary.

It is very beneficial for the NLD student to be able to anticipate what will occur, and when. For example:

° If there will be a weekly spelling test, it should always be conducted on the same day of the week.

- ° If notebooks of older students are to be reviewed, a schedule should be established for when they will be collected for review.

- ° If there will consistently be an end-of-chapter quiz, it should always be "x" number of days following the completion of that segment of study.

- ° If student journals will be reviewed, a schedule should be established such as collecting them on Friday, and returned to the students on the following Monday.

The structure that these routines provide makes school far easier for the NLD child to manage. The less novelty she is required to deal with, the more successful she will be in school.

Folders and Books

This student should be provided with a backpack and folders with double-facing inside pockets from the very first day that she begins school. Although it may require tweaking over time, a system should be implemented that can be consistently used by the student for the remainder of her education. The very young child may have only a single folder for her papers. Papers placed in the left pocket are those that are being worked on, or must go home, and those on the right are completed assignments, ready to be turned in. As the child gets older, there should be a separate folder for each subject area, using the left and right pockets in the same way as for the younger child – work in progress, or papers for home in the left pocket, and completed assignments, ready to be turned in, inside the right pocket. Each should be three-hole punched, and kept together in a large three ring binder – preferably one that zips closed. It is recommended that each folder be a separate color, and of a heavy gauge material so that it doesn't rip, tear, or fall apart. If the selected folder does not already come three-hole punched, you can use a heavy gauge display punch at the supply store to punch them all before leaving the store.

Workbooks and textbooks should all be covered and easily identifiable for the child. If she has selected green as the folder color for science, then either a green cover on her book, or some form of prominent green marking should be on the cover. Each subject should be identified by a unique color, and the same color scheme used from one year to the next.

The NLD student should be introduced to an agenda book as early as possible. For the young child, all assignments should be entered in the agenda by an adult, with enough detail that the parent will understand the assignment without requiring that the student provide clarification. As the student reaches the mid to late elementary grades, she can be required to make the agenda entries with direct supervision by a teacher. By middle school, the student should be required to make her own agenda entries, however they should be reviewed by a teacher or paraprofessional on a daily basis. The child should be encouraged to make non-school entries in her agenda book. For example, if she takes music lessons, or religious classes, she should enter them in the agenda book. Doctor, dentist, and orthodontist appointments should also be entered. This will allow her to see in one place everything that she is required to do on a particular day.

Once the student is at the point of using multiple folders, it is helpful to keep everything organized together in a large three-hole binder. Included within the binder should be her agenda book, the color-coded subject folders, a supply of three-hole paper, a three-hole ruler, and a three-hole zippered pouch for her pencils, erasers, and so forth. The student and either a parent or teacher should be required to go through the binder at least once each week to keep it organized, and handle anything that did not reach its proper destination.

It is very helpful for the parent and teacher to have frequent and ongoing communication. Many schools have implemented various forms of electronic communication, which are wonderful. Some have a phone number that the parent or older student can call in order to get a forgotten homework assignment. Others have e-mail capability so that the parent and teacher can effectively communicate without having to make a telephone call, which is often difficult to schedule.

Many NLD youngsters who are initially very disorganized can become exceptionally well organized when consistent strategies are applied over an extended period of time.

STUDY SKILLS

Effective study skills are based primarily on a set of thinking skills that are necessary in order to acquire knowledge. If the student does not possess the appropriate thinking skills, no matter how much time is spent "studying" a topic, she will not be able to benefit from the activity.

The NLD student generally has excellent rote memory skills, which she quickly learns to depend on, and serve her well in the early to middle elementary grades. Unfortunately, she will likely rely on her rote memory when it is no longer appropriate. By late elementary school, and clearly by middle school, thinking skills are required which the NLD youngster may not possess. Her rote memory skills fail her, and she becomes frustrated, unable to understand what she is supposed to do. Thinking skills must be taught to this student in a very direct, step-by-step manner. It isn't that she can't learn, but that she needs direct instruction in all aspects of learning.

5-D Learning Model

Although there are a variety of ways to teach thinking skills to the NLD student, one method has been developed specifically for use with this student population. This method is called the 5-D learning model. Within this Model, there are five competency levels of thinking skills, each building on the prior level as follows: Define, describe, differentiate, demonstrate, and discuss. In the earliest educational grades, students are instructed at the "define" level, where knowledge is based primarily on rote memory. During this phase of learning, the child should be taught the language associated with how she might be required to demonstrate what she has learned, such as: Define, list, tell, identify, show, label, and name. Figure 10.1 illustrates the 5-D learning model, showing each "D" phase and demonstrated competency, as well as the associated trigger words.

Competence	Skills demonstrated	Trigger Words
Define	Ability to observe and recall information – memory of dates, events and places.	Define, list, tell, identify, show, label, and name.
Describe	Grasp meaning – interpret facts, compare, and contrast.	Describe, summarize, contrast, and associate.
Differentiate	Identification of components – organize parts and observe patterns.	Differentiate, analyze, separate, order, connect, arrange, compare, and select.
Demonstrate	Use of acquired knowledge – solve problems using required skills and knowledge.	Demonstrate, apply, explain, illustrate, and classify.
Discuss	Discriminate between ideas, recognize subjectivity, assess value of theories, and make choices based on reasoned argument.	Discuss, assess, rank, grade, recommend, convince, judge, explain, discriminate, and conclude.

Figure 10.1 5-D Learning Model

Each teacher who works with the NLD student should be familiar with this model, and apply it wherever possible in the student's curriculum. It is unrealistic to expect that the NLD student will understand the use of the model until she is in late middle school. Therefore, when she is learning new material, or studying learned material, it is important for the teacher and parent to reinforce the concepts at each level, along with the associated language of a particular level.

By middle school, the student should be involved with the 5-D process, and understand what each phase represents. This will allow her to better understand both the concept and language of different levels of knowledge, as well as teacher expectations associated with an assignment or test.

To reiterate, there are a variety of models that can be used to teach NLD youngsters thinking skills. The important points to consider in selecting one are that the model should be very simple and easy to remember, be used consistently throughout the student's education, and the language associated with different levels of thinking must be specifically taught.

Study Strategies

Study strategies should be introduced that complement the student's level of thinking skills and learning style. For example, applying the model outlined above, if the child is operating at the first level, which is defined as "describe," she would be responsible for reciting factual information. For the NLD student, simple verbal mnemonics would be very effective, while flashcards would not.

The topic of distinguishing relevant from irrelevant information was covered in both the reading comprehension and math sections of this book. However, it is also a major stumbling block in study skills. Since this student has difficulty distinguishing between what is relevant and irrelevant, it is often impossible for her to identify what it is that she should study. There are several things that can be done for and with this child in order to help her:

- ° Allow the student to write and highlight in all of her books. When something is identified as important, she can make some kind of notation in the book, rather than have to keep separate notes. This will also foster better reading comprehension.

- ° Provide a second set of books for this child at home. She should only be required to bring home her binder, including her agenda and work folders, rather than remembering what books she will need in order to do homework or study for a test. The added benefit is that if the books are at home, an involved parent can provide assistance in an area that the child is struggling with. The student should be allowed to write and highlight in this set of books as well as those she uses in class.

○ Rather than require that the older student take notes in class, she should be provided with notes at the beginning of each unit of instruction. The notes can either be complete, or a skeleton outline for the child to fill in. Providing notes for the student at the beginning of each unit of instruction serves two purposes – first, it allows her to listen, which is her primary learning modality, rather than write, and second, it accommodates her inability to distinguish between relevant and irrelevant information.

○ Do not assign end-of-chapter questions as homework. An assignment such as this will be quite difficult for the NLD student and will not reinforce learning. A class discussion of each question is far more effective in reinforcing the learning process for this youngster. Since the NLD student is very literal and concrete, she may only be able to answer the question at some future time if phrased exactly as it was presented in the book and discussed in class. It would be very helpful to discuss a question exactly as presented in the book, and then rephrase it so that the child understands the information in more than one context.

Study Guides

The NLD student will always need a study guide in order to prepare for any test. These guides should be provided for the younger NLD student. The older student should complete the guide with *significant* adult assistance. Guides should be typed, not handwritten, in order to compensate for the student's visual processing deficits. A consistent format should be used, throughout her education, in order to teach the student how to develop a study guide when she is required to do so on her own. A consistent prose process is recommended to facilitate learning, and transfer the skill of developing a study guide to the student. The following is one example of how a study guide might be developed. Note that there is a good amount of "white space" on the page, and each question is typed in a normal font. Each answer is indented and italicized.

Social Studies Chapter Review

1. What were the first New England Colonies?

    Massachusetts, Rhode Island, Connecticut, and New Hampshire

2. Why did the Puritans build their early towns close together?

    Easier for people to join together to protect themselves in case of war with the Indians. Also easier for the leaders to watch the people to make sure they followed the laws of the Puritan Church.

3. Why did Roger Williams leave Massachusetts?

    He was ordered to leave by the Puritan leaders of the colony because he didn't agree with a lot of the church rules.

What colony did he start?

    Colony: Rhode Island

    Settlement: Providence

4. Why did Anne Hutchinson leave Massachusetts?

    She was ordered to leave by the Puritan leaders of the colony because she didn't agree with some of the church rules.

Where did she go?

Colony: *Rhode Island*

Settlement: *Portsmouth*

5.   Why did Thomas Hooker leave Massachusetts?

He disagreed with the Puritan leaders.

What colony did he start?

Colony: *Connecticut*

Settlement: *Hartford*

6.   What are the Fundamental Orders of Connecticut?

The rules the settlers wrote to govern themselves

Why are they important?

They were the first written plan of government in an English colony. The rules said that all people should have the right to rule themselves.

7.   Why did people go to New Hampshire?

To get away from the strict Puritan rules

To find better farm land and fishing

To work in the fur trade

When did New Hampshire become a separate colony?

In 1679

8.   Who are elders?

Leaders of the colony

Figure 10.2 Sample Prose Sudy Guide

Graphic organizers are exceptional study aides for all students, but particularly for NLD students. A substantial, and seemingly overwhelming, amount of information can be presented in graphic organizer format, as presented in the following illustration:

Explorers Study Guide

Country	Who	When	What
Portugal	Dias	1487–1488	Sailed around tip of Africa
	Da Gama	1497–1498	Around Africa to India
	Cabral	1500	Reached Brazil
Spain	Columbus	1492–1504	Explored W. Indies and Caribbean
	Ponce de Leon	1508–1509	Explored Puerto Rico
	Ponce de Leon	1513	Explored Florida
	Balboa	1513	Sighted Pacific Ocean
	De Soto	1516–1520	Explored Central America
	Magallan	1519–1522	First around the world
	Naryaez and de Vacaand Estevaico	1528–1536	Spanish borderlands
	DeSoto	1539–1542	Expedition to Mississippi River
	Coronado	1540–1542	Explored SW North America
	Cabrillo	1542–1543	Explored West Coast N. America
England	Cabot	1497–1501	Explored East Coast N. America
	Hudson	1610–1611	Explored Hudson Bay
Netherlands	Hudson	1609	Explored East Coast N. America and Hudson Bay
France	da Verrazano	1524	Explored East Coast N. America and New York harbor

Cartier	1534–1542	Explored St. Lawrence River
de Champlain	1603–1615	Explored St. Lawrence River valley and founded Quebec
Marquette and Joliet	1673	Explored along the Mississippi River
La Salle	1679–1692	Explored Great Lakes and reached mouth of Mississippi River.

Figure 10.3 Sample Graphic Organizer Study Guide

A combination of prose and graphic organizer study guides will significantly improve this student's ability to succeed in elementary and middle school. There are many different prose and graphic organizer formats that can be used. However, once a format is selected, and it works for the student, it should be used consistently so that the student can eventually learn how to create them on her own. It is critical to transfer these skills to the student by early high school so that she can become a more independent learner. This is particularly important if the student is planning to attend college.

HOMEWORK

Considering how exhausting it is for the NLD child to get through a full school day, it seems like cruel and unusual punishment for her to be expected to do homework at the end of her day. Although there is considerable debate as to whether or not this student should be assigned homework at all, the following guidelines should prove helpful for those situations where homework is required.

○ The NLD student should always have adult assistance available to her when she is doing homework. The adult should make sure that the child understands what the requirements of the assignment are, and checks frequently to make sure that she is performing it correctly. The adult should also be available to answer the student's questions and provide her with necessary assistance.

° This student should never be given an assignment related to a concept or unit of study that has not first been taught in school. The purpose for homework should be to review and practice previously learned information. If she does not understand a concept and is therefore unable to do a particular task, she should not be required to do so. A parent should note on the assignment that the work was attempted, but the child needs additional instruction in the concept.

° It is extremely beneficial to have resource or study periods included in the student's schedule. By middle school, this student will need at least one morning *and* one afternoon study or resource period *every* day. This will prevent the child from becoming overwhelmed, reduce her level of stress, and help her to more effectively manage the demands of middle school. An additional benefit to incorporating these two study periods into the student's schedule is that she should be able to complete her homework while she is still at school, *before* she forgets what was covered in class, *and* she has immediate access to an adult for assistance. This approach works exceptionally well for NLD students, and is highly recommended. Every attempt should be made to accommodate a morning and afternoon study or resource period for this student.

There will likely be times when home assignments are required. Hopefully, this won't be often. However, when these situations arise, the following recommendations should lessen the stress for both parent and child:

° Determine the best time of day for the child to do her homework. For many, it is helpful to provide the child with a snack when she returns home, and begin to do her homework immediately. Unfortunately, this is not always possible, and not all children respond to this schedule.

However, it is important to avoid working with this child when she is tired.

° When a homework assignment is entered into the student's agenda book at school, there should be enough detail so that the parent will understand the assignment. It is likely that the child will not remember details that occurred earlier in the day, and/or be able to explain them to a parent who is trying to assist her.

° Limit the amount of time that is required of the child. Assignments will often take her considerably longer to complete than for other students her age. The teacher should advise the parent of how much time is expected of a student for a particular assignment, and a timer should be set for that length of time. If she is expected to spend 20 minutes on spelling, the timer would be set for 20 minutes, and the child should then be graded only for the work that she was able to complete within the established timeframe. This approach should be used throughout the student's education. An accommodation such as this is very reasonable for an NLD student, and most teachers should be very receptive to this request.

° It is often beneficial for the NLD student to listen to music while she is doing homework. However, she should wear headphones. Simply listening to music without headphones can be a distraction. Because of this student's auditory acuity, listening to music through headphones blocks out extraneous auditory distractions. The type of music is not a major consideration. Many of these students seem to be able to concentrate on their assignment while listening to loud, and what we might consider obnoxious music. Somehow it allows them to stay focused on task, and pace themselves. Whatever works!

There are numerous horror stories about what NLD students, and their families, have faced regarding homework. As common as it may be, it is outrageous. These children have a significant disability that must be addressed. Homework accommodations should be the easiest to address. In defense of teachers, many are unaware of the homework hardship. Often, a meeting with the child's teacher is all it will take to work out a reasonable plan. If not, then parents should feel comfortable escalating the problem within the school until the situation is properly addressed.

Long-term Projects

Long-term projects are very challenging for the NLD student. She has poor organizational and planning skills, an impaired sense of time, difficulty distinguishing between relevant and irrelevant information, a reading disability, and graphomotor deficits. All of these problems compromise her ability to manage a long-term assignment on her own.

Large assignments should be broken down into small increments and dates established for each, with an end product required for each step. Each mini assignment should be entered into the student's agenda book. There should also be an established time in her schedule when she and the teacher meet to check on her progress, and make sure that she is still moving toward her goal. The final mini assignment should be to put all of the incremental parts together to complete the whole project. Because of the enormity of the task, this student will likely need considerable assistance throughout the process, and in putting all of the pieces together at the end.

It is very helpful for the NLD student to have a report format that can be used consistently, or as consistently as possible. For example, there should be a format for book reports. After doing several reports with assistance using the same format, she will likely be able to complete them on her own, as long as they are straightforward. As the child moves through her late elementary and middle school grades, the report requirements may be modified to include additional information, but should retain a similar format. This same concept should be applied to other reports and research papers. A format should be developed and provided to the student so that she will eventually be able to do them without assistance.

This student probably has very poor research skills. She should be encouraged to use a computer for her research whenever possible. It is far easier for her to develop internet search techniques than to manage the spatial and organizational demands of a library.

SUMMARY

In order for the NLD child to be successful, she will need considerable direct instruction in how to organize herself and her work, *what* and *how* to study, and how to complete homework assignments.

Organization

The objective in teaching organizational skills is to empower the child to have control over her work and her environment.

- Provide clearly marked schedules in prominent locations.

- Teach the child classroom rules. Provide verbal reminders and avoid reward systems.

- Use folders to organize the student's work. Color-code folders and books.

- Introduce the use of an agenda very early. Enter all commitments, so that she learns to depend on it.

Study Skills

The NLD student generally has excellent rote memory skills. Thinking skills must be taught to this student in a very direct, step-by-step manner.

° Use a structured approach to teach the NLD youngster thinking skills.

° Allow the student to write and highlight in all of her books. Provide a second set of books for this child at home.

° Provide notes at the beginning of each unit of instruction. Do not assign end-of-chapter questions as homework.

° The NLD student will always need a study guide. A combination of prose and graphic organizer study guides will significantly improve this student's ability to succeed.

Homework

The following guidelines should prove helpful for those situations where homework is required of the NLD student.

° The NLD student should always have adult assistance when she is doing homework.

° She should never be assigned homework related to a concept that has not been taught in school.

° Resource or study periods should be included in the student's schedule – by middle school, at least one morning and one afternoon study or resource period every day.

° Allow the NLD student to listen to music through headphones while she is doing homework.

° Limit the amount of homework time that is required of the child. Use a timer to set the appropriate time limit.

- ° Provide a report format that can be used consistently.

- ° Encourage the use of a computer for research whenever possible.

- ° Large assignments should be broken down into small increments, with dates and an end product required for each. Each should be entered into an agenda book and regular meetings arranged with the teacher to see if she is still moving toward her goal. The final assignment brings parts together to complete the whole. This student will need considerable assistance throughout the process, and in putting all of the pieces together at the end.

Chapter 11

Quizzes, Exams, and Standardized Testing

Testing, of any kind, creates a significant problem for NLD students. Although these children may learn a great deal, being able to retrieve what they have learned, at the right time, and in the appropriate context, is often quite difficult. Further complicating the situation is the youngster's challenge with the physical act of writing. Putting it all together at test-time may be completely overwhelming for this student. Ideally, the NLD student is tested verbally, so that she does not have to cope with her dysgraphia, and can ask for clarification if she does not understand the context of the question. It is not unusual for these students to fail a written quiz or test, only to get an excellent grade if retested verbally. However, for those times when verbal testing is not possible, this chapter will deal with issues related to pencil and paper testing.

QUIZZES AND EXAMS

Frontloading quizzes and exams is as important to the NLD student as frontloading instructional material. This child will respond quite poorly to insufficient notice, limited "white space" on the paper and essay questions, and should be provided with the tools that she needs in order to compensate for her disability.

Provide Prior Notice

Insufficient notice for tests of any kind puts this child at a serious disadvantage. She needs clear expectations of what is expected of her at all times, and needs sufficient notice to prepare herself academically and emotionally for a test of any kind. The most difficult situation for this student is clearly no notice, or what is often called a "pop quiz." A "pop quiz" clearly throws her off stride because it was not anticipated, and she becomes anxious when she is caught by surprise. Her anxiety will almost certainly compromise her ability to respond at her level of knowledge. There should be appropriate prior notice, in writing, with sufficient time for the student to prepare for any quiz, test, or examination.

Provide a Study Guide

This student is unable to distinguish between relevant and irrelevant information. Therefore, telling her to "study Chapter 8" does not provide her with the information that she needs in order to prepare for a test. She will need a study guide covering the material that she will be responsible for knowing. Many people consider this to be "cheating," since it "gives" the student the answers. This is not so. The study guide should cover all of the material that is pertinent from the chapter, which she *may* be tested on. This will reinforce the learning process, and prepare the student for the test. The test questions should be a subset of the material contained within the study guide.

Compensate for Visual Perception Problems

In order for this child to be able to accurately process the information on a test page, there should be a limited number of problems or questions per page. The increased amount of "white space" increases the child's ability to visually focus on the material. It may also be helpful to teach the child how to block the problems or questions on the page that she is not working on, in order to increase her ability to focus her attention on what she is working on. Math tests should not have mixed concepts on the same page, since this student has difficulty shifting from one set of operational rules to another. She may not "see" the operational sign that is indicated. Placing different concepts on separate pages provides her with a cue to shift from one operation to another.

Quizzes and exams should always be typed. This student has enough trouble with visual processing without having the additional challenge of attempting to decipher the teacher's printing, or worse yet, handwriting!

Provide the Student with Appropriate Tools

Encourage the student to use the aids that allow her to demonstrate her knowledge, e.g., a division card, multiplication facts sheet, calculator, and concept cards for math tests. Accommodate the child's fine-motor difficulty by allowing plenty of space on the page for her work, and use graph paper for math tests. If the student would benefit from access to a computer, then arrange for her to have access to one during test taking.

Test Format

As you read in the first paragraph of this chapter, although these children may learn a great deal, being able to retrieve what they have learned, at the right time and in the appropriate context, is often quite challenging. NLD students do not have the ability to infer, or read between the lines, so tests should be very direct and straightforward. Also, the presentation of the material can be a help or hindrance. For example, matching exercises may be difficult for this child, because she is unable to focus on a select portion of the page in order to process the information. Matching exercises require the student to move back and forth between columns of information, which creates visual confusion for the NLD student.

The following is an illustration of a test which is *inappropriately* formatted for an NLD student. This particular format is commonly used in schools throughout the United States. It happens to be an actual test administered to an NLD child who received a failing grade, although she knew the material.

Explorers

A. Matching

1.	_____	main part of a continent	a. empire
2.	_____	to appoint a person or group to do something	b. slavery
3.	_____	to gain something by force, defeat	c. America
4.	_____	Spanish word for "flower"	d. Fountain of Youth
5.	_____	found the water route around the New World	e. Jacques Cartier
6.	_____	made people young again	f. mainland
7.	_____	the New World	g. conquer
8.	_____	explored the St. Lawrence River in Canada	h. Florida
9.	_____	a large amount of territory under one ruler	i. commission
10.	_____	forcing a person or group to work without pay	j. Ferdinand Magellan

B. Multiple Choice

1. Ponce de Leon named the southeastern tip of North America

_____

a. California   b. New Jersey
c. Florida   d. North Carolina

2. Pizarro wanted to conquer the empire of the _____

a. Incas   b. Aztecs   c. Romans   d. Greeks

3. The Incas were forced to remove gold and silver from the_____

a. Blue Ridge Mountains   b. Andes Mountains
c. Himalayan Mountainsd.   Allegheny Mountains

4. _____ never completed his journey to the Far East because he was killed in the Phillipines.

a. Columbus   b. Sir Francis Drake
c. Marco Polo   d. Magellan

5. Sir Francis Drake's expedition was the _____ to sail around the world.

a. second   c. third   b. first   d. fourth

C. True or False

_____ 1. Spain sent John Cabot to explore because he thought he could reach the East Indies by sailing east.

_____ 2. Ponce de Leon led a group in search of gold and the Fountain of Youth.

_____ 3. Francisco Pizarro was determined to conquer the Incas and take their land and riches for France.

_____ 4. It took Magellan's men four years to complete the trip around the world.

_____ 5. Magellan's voyage proved that the Earth was really flat.

_____ 6. Giovanni da Verrazano defeated the Aztec king Montezuma.

_____ 7. Some people in Europe believed there was a northern route to the Far East.

_____ 8. Columbus and Cabot were sure they had reached Asia.

_____ 9. From North Carolina, Verrazano sailed north to Mexico.

_____10. America is named after Amerigo Vespucci.

Figure 11.1 Inappropriately Formatted Test

Let's look at this test from the perspective of the NLD student, and determine what types of problems she might encounter:

- There is not enough "white space" for the child to visually process the information.

- There are no specific directions for the child to follow. For example, in the first section: Is the student to insert the lower case letter in the blank that precedes the statement? Is she to circle the correct answer? Is she to draw a line between the statement in the first column to the corresponding answer in the second column?

- The upper-case letters, numbers, and lower-case letters are confusing. For example, in the first section titled "A. Matching," what is the purpose of the "A," and how do the numbers in the first column relate to the lower-case letters in the second column?

- In the second section, titled "B. Multiple Choice," again there are no instructions. Is the student to write the correct answer on the line, or circle the correct answer?

- The formatting in the "B" section switches back and forth between choices of two and two, to four choices strung across the line. Is there a purpose for this?

- In the third section, titled "C. True or False," again there are no instructions. Apparently, the child is supposed to write a "T" or an "F" in the spaces provided, but that is not indicated.

- The student is required to retrieve the correct information in various ways, from matching words with sentence fragments, to true and false. These are very different mental processes for the NLD student, who has difficulty shifting mental set.

Other students may be unaffected by this testing format, but the NLD student will struggle with the requirements of the test and try to recall what she has learned, putting her at a distinct disadvantage.

The following is an illustration of an *appropriately* formatted test of the same subject matter. Changes have been made to accommodate the NLD student's needs.

Explorers

Multiple Choice – Circle the correct answer for each question

1. Who explored the St. Lawrence River in Canada?

    a.   Hernando Cortes
    b.   Magellan
    c.   Amerigo Vespucci
    d.   Jacques Cartier

2. Who was America named after?

    a.   Christopher Columbus
    b.   Sir Francis Drake
    c.   John Cabot
    d.   Amerigo Vespucci

3. Why did Magellan never make the trip to the Far East?

    a.   He was sick and had to return home
    b.   He jumped overboard
    c.   He was killed in the Philippines
    d.   He went west

4. What did Ponce de Leon name the southeastern tip of North America?

    a.   Florida
    b.   New Jersey
    c.   North Carolina
    d.   California

5.   Who's expedition was the second to sail around the world?

   a.   Christopher Columbus
   b.   Juan Ponce de Leon
   c.   Ferdinand Magellan
   d.   Sir Francis Drake

6.   Which group of people did Pizarro conquer?

   a.   Aztecs
   b.   Incas
   c.   Romans
   d.   Greeks

Fill In The Blanks – Write the correct answer on the line below each question

7.   How many years did it take Magellan to complete the trip around the world?

_____

8.   Who defeated the Aztec king Montezuma?

_____

9.   Which explorers were sure they had reached Asia when they found the New World?

_____ and _____

10. Where did Verrazano sail to?

_____

11. What country did John Cabot come from?

_____

12. What group of people did Pizarro conquer and take riches (steal) from?

_____

Vocabulary – Circle the correct answer

13. Another name for a large amount of territory (land) under one ruler?

     a.   colony
     b.   continent
     c.   empire
     d.   voyage

14. Another name for the word continent

     a.   mainland
     b.   conquer
     c.   slavery
     d.   communism

15. Which word means: to gain something by force or to defeat?

     a.   loot
     b.   conquer
     c.   slavery
     d.   commission

Figure 11.2 Appropriately Formatted Test

Let's look at what changes have been made, and how they benefit the NLD child:

- ° There are no section letters, strictly names indicating the task to be performed.

- ° There aren't multiple columns, with numbers in one column and letters in another, simply a number for each question.

- ° There are specific instructions at the beginning of each section, so that the student will know what is required of her, without having to figure it out.

- ° There is significantly more "white space" on the page, allowing the student to more easily process the information.

- ° Where there are answer choices presented, they are all formatted vertically.

- ° In question no. 13, the word "territory" is also defined in parenthesis as "land," since the textbook and class instruction used both words to represent the same thing. This avoids the child's confusion over what the word "territory" represents.

- ° Although there are three sections – multiple choice, fill in the blanks, and vocabulary – each question is very direct in its presentation, facilitating the student's ability to recall the correct information.

Figure 11.3 is an illustration of a simple science quiz administered to an NLD student who had the highest grade average in the class, and *knew* the material *very* well. Unfortunately, the absence of specific instructions as to how to complete the exercise, combined with the visual component of this quiz was too much for this student, who failed the quiz miserably.

Looking at this quiz, it is immediately apparent to most of us that the task is to answer questions 1–8 at the bottom of the page, and insert the correct word into each of the appropriate spots on the top half of the page. The key to which word to insert is the number of letters in the word, which is represented by the dashes, and the correct position of the corresponding letter within the word, also cued by the dashes. What seems to be an apparently simple exercise to many, totally derailed this NLD student. However, upon being

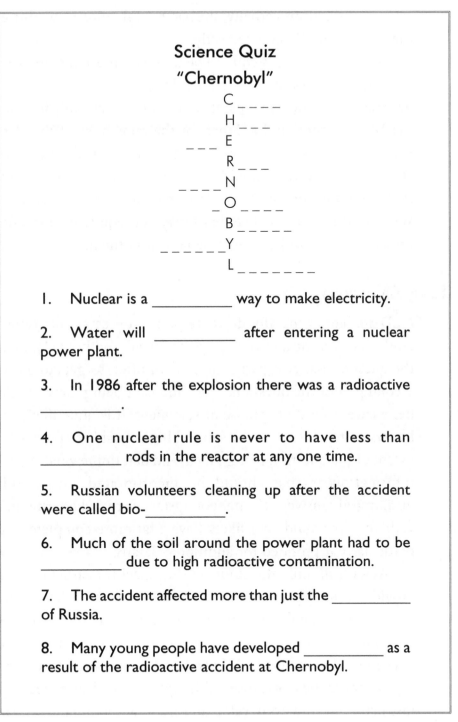

Science Quiz
"Chernobyl"

```
        C _ _ _ _
        H _ _ _
    _ _ _ E
        R _ _ _
  _ _ _ _ N
      _ O _ _ _ _
        B _ _ _ _ _
 _ _ _ _ _ _ Y
        L _ _ _ _ _ _ _
```

1.   Nuclear is a _____ way to make electricity.

2.   Water will _____ after entering a nuclear power plant.

3.   In 1986 after the explosion there was a radioactive _____.

4.   One nuclear rule is never to have less than _____ rods in the reactor at any one time.

5.   Russian volunteers cleaning up after the accident were called bio-_____.

6.   Much of the soil around the power plant had to be _____ due to high radioactive contamination.

7.   The accident affected more than just the _____ of Russia.

8.   Many young people have developed _____ as a result of the radioactive accident at Chernobyl.

Figure 11.3 Inappropriately Formatted Quiz

asked the questions verbally, she had no difficulty answering each of them quite rapidly and correctly.

It is critical for this child to be tested on the assigned material in a manner that doesn't create a hardship for her. However, it is not necessary to create two separate tests – one specifically formatted for the NLD student, and another for the remainder of the class. Nor should she be singled out as having a test that is different from her classmates. One test should be prepared for all of the students, incorporating the modifications that are needed for the NLD student. Although other students may not require the modifications presented, they will certainly benefit from them.

Essay Questions

NLD students generally do quite poorly on essay questions. They tend to answer the question quite specifically, without elaboration. If the question has two parts, the student often forgets to answer the second part of the question. The child isn't being "lazy" by limiting her answer to a short phrase or statement. It is quite likely that she knows quite a bit about the subject, but is unable to process the full extent of the question being asked, and determine what the relevant information is that should be incorporated into a full and meaningful answer. If the youngster were asked the question verbally, she would very likely have a far more complete response, particularly if prodded for additional details.

As with all skills, this student needs specific instruction in how to provide an appropriate answer to an essay question. This will likely take a considerable amount of time. Until she has developed the necessary skills to provide a complete and thorough answer to essay questions, she should be allowed and encouraged to use graphic organizers in lieu of prose. Although she will also need specific instruction in how to develop and use graphic organizers, she will learn how to do this far more quickly than she will develop the skills necessary for composing a prose answer to an essay question. Clearly, the intent of testing is to determine whether or not the child has learned the material, and encouraging the use of graphic organizers will allow this student to demonstrate her knowledge of the subject matter.

Let's take a look at a typical essay question, what the teacher expectation is for a full-credit prose answer, and how it can be converted to a graphic organizer. The following is an essay question from a social studies test administered to a fifth-grade class.

Question:

New Amsterdam was growing, but the other settlements of New Netherland were not. What were two ways the Dutch West India Company tried to get people to come? Were they a success or failure?

There was a small amount of blank space provided, where the student was expected to write her answer. The following is what the teacher was looking for in the student's answer in order to allow full credit.

Answer:

The Dutch West India Company offered large parcels of land along the Hudson River to anyone who brought 50 new people to the colony. This didn't work because most of the new colonists left the settlements to start their own farms in another area. Since this was a failure, they then changed their plan to offer land, or the right to work in the fur trade, to anyone willing to come to the colony. This new plan was successful because the people coming to the colony received a direct benefit.

We could certainly debate whether or not this question would be appropriate for a fifth-grade student, but that is not the purpose in providing this example. This type of question is a classic illustration of what the NLD student will have significant difficulty with. First, because her writing is awkward and large, there was not enough space provided for the child to write any form of answer. Also, the question calls for two answers, with a subpart to each. The NLD student would likely answer what she could of the "two ways" portion of the question, but would probably forget that there was a second part – to indicate the success or failure of each. If she did remember to answer the second part of each question, the question asked was whether or not the plan was a success or a failure, but the teacher expected the student to provide a reason for the success or failure. We can hear the NLD student now, "but you didn't say you wanted to know why it was a success or failure…you only asked if it was a success or failure!" This student will clearly not intuit what is not specifically stated.

Now let's look at how the student might have fully demonstrated her knowledge of the subject by answering the question in a graphic organizer format.

Answer:	
Plan	*Success/Failure*
I person + 50 more = land	*Failure*
I person = land or work	*Success*

The use of a graphic organizer allows the NLD student to retrieve and organize the information that is needed in order to answer the question, without becoming confused by the task requirement of composing her answer using complete sentences. Also, remember that the second part of the asked was whether or not the plan was a success or failure. The student was not asked to elaborate on her answer, therefore she answered the question that was asked.

As the student becomes more able to answer essay questions with prose, she should be graded on her accuracy, rather than elaboration. It will be quite some time before this student is proficient at providing a comprehensive traditional response to essay questions – probably not until she is well into high school.

Other Considerations

It is extremely beneficial to provide consistent quiz and test formats for the NLD student, who needs a lot of predictability. She has a tremendous amount of difficulty anticipating what a test might consist of, and has trouble figuring out the requirements of the task. If all quizzes and tests are formatted in the same manner, she will quickly become accustomed to the teacher's expectation, which will significantly reduce her anxiety and increase her level of performance.

Open-book tests are pure torture for the NLD student, who finds a textbook a complete mystery. She does not readily understand the use of a table of contents, index, chapter and sub-chapter headings, or section headings. Therefore, finding information in a textbook is an exercise in frustration for her. Also, if told to use the book to find the answers, she will probably do exactly as she is told – find the answers in the book – and not think to use an alternative strategy such as referring to her notes, or answering the questions from memory. For these reasons, open-book tests should be avoided.

Finally, it should be remembered that this student will generally do best when tests are administered verbally, and she is prompted for elaboration if necessary. A teacher may be quite surprised at the amount of information that this child has learned, but has been unable to share in written form.

STANDARDIZED TESTING

Students all over the country are faced with standardized testing, whether they are state mastery tests, or other forms of testing to determine whether or not the students are learning. Considering the federal government's interest in improving the education of students in the United States, we are sure to see an increase in standardized testing. The question of how, or whether, to accommodate the NLD student for standardized testing is a difficult one to answer.

Should the Student be Exempt?

Although some parents may agree to a school recommendation to have their child exempted from standardized testing, this may hurt rather than help the child. It is important for parents to understand that often the purpose of administering these tests is to determine how effective the teachers are at teaching. However, the results will also be an objective measure of whether or not the child is actually learning, and if she is struggling in a particular area. School grades are often subjective rather than objective in nature, and therefore may not accurately reflect how a child is performing in school. At some point, parents of an NLD student may find themselves at odds with school personnel over the progress of their child. The only objective measure may be the results of standardized testing. Therefore, it is in the NLD child's best interest to be included in all standardized testing.

There is no guarantee that the student will always qualify for an exempt status. If she is suddenly required to take standardized testing, and has no prior experience, she will likely do poorly. This will be a novel task for her, and we know that this student has significant difficulty with novelty. Consequently, it is wise for the NLD student to participate in all standardized testing.

Should the Student Receive Accommodations?

Another consideration is whether or not this student will receive accommodations for standardized testing. Will she have extended time? Will the test be administered in a quiet place? Will the questions be read to her? At first blush, it may seem that all of these would be beneficial. However, there are advantages and disadvantages to having these accommodations. If the child will always have these accommodations, then it would make sense to have them. Unfortunately, this may not be the case. The child may not consistently qualify for accommodations during her primary and secondary education.

An additional consideration is the impact on the child's schedule during the days that the testing is being done. If provided with extended time for testing, she will be missing a portion of her other classes over a period of several days. The implications of missing classroom instruction may have more serious learning consequences than the benefits derived from the extended time for standardized testing.

A new form of standardized testing is gaining in popularity and will have significant impact on all students, but particularly for NLD students. Some states have instituted a state-mandated examination in order for students to graduate from high school. There is currently significant debate over whether or not student accommodations will be allowed, and if they are, what they may consist of. Even if the NLD student has received consistent accommodations in the past, there is no guarantee that she will receive them if required to pass an examination in order to graduate from high school.

It is wise to consider having the NLD student participate in all standardized testing, *without* accommodations so that she becomes accustomed to taking them within the normal time limit, before she is faced with a situation where she may not be allowed accommodations. Granted, in the lower grades she will not do as well as she might if she had accommodations, but with practice, and over time, she should become more proficient. It is far more prudent to prepare this child for standardized testing by repeated exposure so that the task becomes less novel, than have her faced with a situation at some point where she is required to take a standardized test within time constraints, but has no prior experience with the task.

SUMMARY

Although NLD students may learn a great deal, being able to retrieve what they have learned, at the right time, and in the appropriate context, is often quite difficult. To further complicate the situation is the youngster's challenge with the physical act of writing. It is not unusual for these students to fail a written quiz or test, only to get an excellent grade if retested verbally.

Quizzes and Exams

Frontloading quizzes and exams is as important to the NLD student as frontloading instructional material. Strategies that will improve this youngster's ability to perform on tests include:

- Giving prior notice, allowing sufficient time for the student to prepare.

- Using a consistent format for all tests and exams.

- Providing a study guide covering all of the material that is pertinent from the chapter (or segment), which she may be tested on.

- Compensating for visual processing deficits by providing sufficient "white space" on the page, avoiding mixed math concepts on the same page, and typing all tests.

- Providing the student with the appropriate tools, such as concept cards, a calculator, graph paper, etc. for a math test.

- Insuring that tests are direct and straightforward, with specific instructions, and in an appropriate format. All visual activities should be avoided.

- Teaching the use of graphic organizers, and then allowing and encouraging the use of graphic organizers in lieu of prose responses to essay questions.

- Providing specific instruction in how to respond to an essay question with prose, but do not expect proficiency until high school. While learning, grading for accuracy rather than elaboration.

- Avoiding "open book" tests!

- Testing verbally!!!

Standardized Testing

The major questions related to standardized testing are whether to exempt the student, or to allow accommodations if she participates in standardized testing.

- The benefit derived from accommodations such as extended time may create learning consequences from missed classroom instruction.

- Repeated exposure to standardized testing makes the task less novel, and increases the likelihood that the student may perform well over an extended period of time and exposure.

○ Results of standardized tests may be the only objective measure of whether or not the child is learning.

○ It is wise to consider having the NLD student participate in all standardized testing, without accommodations.

Afterword

The most commonly asked question by the parent of an NLD child is, "what is the long-term prognosis for a child with NLD?" Unfortunately, there is no easy answer. But then again, there is no easy answer to this question for any child. We might know that a youngster of eight is determined to be neurologically typical, having no identifiable cognitive or physical disabilities. She may have an average intellect, be physically coordinated, and socially adept. Will these gifts guarantee adult success? There is no way to know. She may be faced with the loss of a parent, a medical condition such as diabetes, or any one of a number of challenges that derail her during the formative years, and force the youngster to travel a different path than the one which was anticipated. Or, she may have a superior intellect, but have parents and teachers who are preoccupied, so that she fails to thrive, or makes poor choices, because she feels unloved.

Clearly, the NLD child faces significant challenges. However, the earlier the child is diagnosed, the more time there is for intervention, the better the likelihood for a successful future. It won't be an easy road, and parents must make a significant commitment to their child in order to ensure that she receives the appropriate services and support. But parents can't travel this road alone. Teachers can make a world of difference for this child. The NLD student will need the best – dedicated, creative, and supportive teachers who *know* what impact they can have on the lives of children placed in their care. Teachers who have selected their profession because they love children, and draw out the best in each and every student. These professionals know that teaching is more than simply instilling knowledge, it is helping the student develop confidence, to believe in herself, and to become an independent individual who will one day be a contributing member of society. Teachers are aware of the power they hold over these youngsters and adolescents – through their efforts they can watch a child blossom under their care, or wither on the vine. In order for the NLD student to succeed, parents and teachers will need to work as partners in educating this child. Communication must be ongoing, open, and honest. If a problem develops, either party should feel comfortable raising the issue in a constructive manner.

There are additional considerations. We are not all cut out to be surgeons, astronauts, or professional athletes. We each have our own unique strengths, and the child with NLD has hers. The point is for the parent and child to develop a solid understanding of the youngster's abilities as she develops, so that good choices can be made. If she has her heart set on being an attorney, and continues to be socially awkward when she enters college, it doesn't rule out law school. However, it probably does mean that she should select an area of law that does not require the heavy social contact of family law or trial work. If the NLD student dreams of becoming a surgeon or veterinarian, but has significant difficulty with math and science, it's time for a reality check. Is her goal realistic? Can she compensate for her deficits enough to accomplish her objective? Maybe yes, and maybe no, but it *must* be determined before pursuing this career. It is often said that NLD adults are under-employed for their level of education. This may be a reflection of a poor match between the individual's choice of major in college or career, and the actual skills required in order to do the job. Good planning, and careful choices should increase the likelihood for a successful career for the individual with NLD.

Just as the child needs to develop an understanding of her strengths and weaknesses as they relate to educational and career planning, she also needs to understand how her strengths and weaknesses will affect relationships. She needs to know how to compensate for her deficits. For example, intuition is not a skill that can be learned, but she *can* learn to be understanding, compassionate, and considerate. Since she will probably always be somewhat naive, it would be wise for her to select a significant other who has more than their fare share of common sense, and maybe just a dash of cynicism. Social skills training and careful choices should increase the likelihood of successful adult relationships for the individual with NLD.

So, to answer the question, "what is the long-term prognosis for a child with NLD?" Personally, I think that the prognosis can be very good with significant intervention, careful planning, and appropriate choices. However, the more important point is whether or not the NLD child has a happy childhood, and becomes a content and fulfilled adult. As parents we can become so involved in trying to "fix" the child's problems that we forget to let her be a kid. We sometimes fail to see all of her special qualities, because of our focus on the daily stresses and problems. Make time to blow bubbles with your youngster on a bright summer day, to make angels in the snow in winter, to go for a walk. Enjoy your child and make memories with her, show her how much she is loved. These special times will be warm memories for both of you, and may help her more than a missed session with an occupational therapist or tutor.

Appendix I

Glossary of Terms

Ability Grouping
A common instructional practice of clustering students according to their academic skills. Ability grouping allows a teacher to provide the same level of instruction to the entire group.

Abstract Thinking
The ability to think in terms of ideas or concepts rather than facts.

Acceleration Programs
Rapid promotion through advanced studies for students who are gifted or talented.

Accommodations
Adaptations or adjustments provided to fit the particular needs of an individual because of his/her disability.

Achievement Batteries
Standardized tests that include several subtests that are designed to measure knowledge of particular subjects.

Achievement Motivation
The desire to experience success and to participate in activities in which success is dependent on personal effort and abilities.

Achievement Test
A test in core curriculum areas, such as reading or mathematics, to determine a student's level of academic achievement.

Adaptation
The process of adjusting individual strategies in response to the environment.

Advance Organizers
Activities and techniques that provide context of material before reading or classroom instruction.

Advanced Placement
A series of courses administered by the College Board that high school students can take to earn college credit. Students must master a generally higher level of coursework and pass an accompanying test.

Agenesis of Corpus Callosum
Agenesis of Corpus Callosum (ACC) is a rare disorder that is present at birth. It is characterized by a partial or complete absence (agenesis) of an area of the brain that connects the two cerebral hemispheres. This part of the brain is normally composed of transverse fibers. Agenesis of Corpus Callosum is usually inherited as either an autosomal recessive trait or an X-linked dominant trait. It can also be caused by an infection during the twelfth to the twenty-second week of pregnancy (intrauterine) leading to developmental disturbance of the fetal brain. In some cases mental retardation may result, but in other cases, no evident symptoms may appear and intelligence may not be impaired.

Alternate Assessment
An evaluation process that uses non-traditional testing methods to asses a student's ability and/or knowledge, which is appropriate to their specific needs and accommodates their disability.

Alternative Schools
This term generally refers to public schools governed by states or school districts that serve populations of students who are not succeeding in the traditional public school environment. Alternative schools offer students who may be failing academically, or have learning disabilities or behavioral problems, an opportunity to achieve in a different setting. While there are many different types of alternative schools, they are often characterized by smaller teacher-student ratios, modified curricula and flexible schedules.

Amygdala
A region in the forebrain involved in integrating and coordinating emotional behaviors.

Anosognosia
A lack of an individual's comprehension or awareness of the extent of their disabilities and limitations.

Aptitude Test
A test designed to measure an individual's general abilities in an attempt to predict future performance.

Asperger's Syndrome (AS)
A developmental disability characterized by normal intelligence, motor clumsiness, eccentric interests, and a limited ability to appreciate social nuances.

Assessment

An exercise, such as a written test, portfolio, or experiment, that seeks to measure a student's skills or knowledge in a subject area.

Assistive Technology Device

Any item, piece of equipment, or other device, which is acquired commercially off the shelf, modified, or customized, that is used to increase, maintain, or improve the functional capabilities of a child with a disability.

Assistive Technology Service

Any service that directly assists a child with a disability in the selection, acquisition, or use of an assistive technology device.

Association Areas

Regions of the cerebral cortex concerned with higher levels of processing.

Association Neurons

Cells that mediate interactions between neurons.

Associative Play

Much like parallel play but with increased levels of interaction in the form of sharing, turn-taking, and general interest in what another is doing.

Attention

The process of focusing on certain stimuli while screening others out.

Attention Deficit Disorder (ADD)

A neurologically based condition that is characterized by distractibility, short attention span, and impulsiveness.

Autism

A developmental disability, with onset in infancy or early childhood, characterized by severe deficits in social responsiveness and interpersonal relationships, abnormal speech and language development, and repetitive or stereotyped behaviors.

Automaticity

Process by which thoroughly learned tasks can be performed with little mental effort.

Autoreceptors

Receptors found on synaptic terminals that are activated by substances released by the terminals.

Axon

That part of the neuron that sends information away from the cell body.

Axon Terminals

Branches of an axon near its site of termination. Synapses are typically made by axon terminals.

Basic Skills

The traditional building blocks of a curriculum that are most commonly associated with explicit instruction in early elementary language arts and mathematics. Basic skills have historically been taught in isolation. Basic skills include teaching the letters of the alphabet, how to sound-out words, spelling, grammar, counting, adding, subtracting, and multiplying.

Behavioral Intervention Plan (BIP)

A written intervention plan for a student whose behavior significantly interferes with his/her learning and/or the other students' opportunity to learn.

Behavior Modification

The systematic application of consequences to change behavior.

Bilateral Integration

The harmonious working relationship between the two sides of the body.

Body Image

An abstract internal representation of spatial and physical-mechanical properties of one's body (including muscle, skeleton, organs, and so on).

Broca's Area

An area (usually found in the left frontal lobe of the cerebral cortex) critical for the production of language.

Central Nervous System

Consists of the brain and spinal cord.

Cerebellum

A prominent hindbrain structure, important for coordinating and integrating motor activity.

Cerebral Cortex

A layer of cells that covers the forebrain. Highly in-folded in humans, the cortex is divided into two hemispheres that are further subdivided into four lobes – frontal, parietal, occipital, and temporal.

Character Education

Deliberate instruction in basic virtues or morals, as opposed to weaving these values into every lesson. Because of the current deficit in children's values, there is a national movement underway to include character education in school curricula as one means of alleviating this problem.

Charter Schools

Charter schools run separately from the traditional public school system but receive public funding. They are run by groups such as teachers, parents, or foundations.

Charter schools are free of many district regulations and are often tailored to community needs.

Closure
Bringing together to form a conclusion – or the "whole" as it relates to the "parts" of a concept or situation.

Cognition
Thinking skills such as knowing, awareness, perceiving objects, remembering ideas, understanding and reasoning.

Cognitive Behavior Modification
Strategy based on behavioral and cognitive learning principles for changing behavior by using self-talk and explicit instruction.

Cognitive Sciences
A field of study that focuses on how people think and learn. Research within this field covers a wide range of disciplines, including computer science, linguistics, anthropology, sociology, and psychology. Cognitive scientists believe that children actively construct or make meaning of their world based on interactions with their environment rather than from the traditional model of schooling in which teachers lecture and drill students.

Compensations
Alternative solutions or strategies to accommodate a disability in order to remove barriers created by the disability.

Comprehension
The act or ability of understanding – getting the meaning.

Comprehensive Evaluation
A series of tests and observations, formal and informal, conducted for the purpose of determining eligibility for special education and related services, and for determining the current level of education performance.

Computer-based Instruction (CBA)
Individualized instruction administered on a computer.

Concept
An abstract idea that is generalized from specific examples.

Congenital Hypothyroidism
Congenital Hypothyroidism is a condition characterized by abnormally decreased activity of the thyroid gland and deficient production of thyroid hormones present at birth. The thyroid gland secretes hormones that play an essential role in regulating growth, maturation, and the rate of metabolism.

Constructivism

A theory which claims that children build new information onto pre-existing notions and modify their understanding in light of the new data. In the process, their ideas gain in depth and breadth. Constructivist theorists do not believe that students learn by absorbing information through lectures or repeated rote practice.

Cooperative Learning

A teaching strategy whereby small groups of students work together on an assignment in order to maximize their own and each other's learning.

Cooperative Play

Play in which children join together to achieve a common goal.

Coordination (physical)

The harmonious working together of muscle groups in performing complex movements.

Cornelia de Lange Syndrome (CdLS)

A rare genetic disorder that is apparent at birth. Associated symptoms and findings typically include delays in physical development before and after birth. There are characteristic abnormalities of the head and facial area that result in a distinctive facial appearance. In addition, there are malformations of the hands and arms, with mild to severe mental retardation.

Corpus Callosum

A thick band of axons found in the middle of the brain that carries information from one side of the brain to the other.

Critical Reading

Using the ability to analyze, evaluate, and synthesize what one reads, as well as to see relationships of ideas, as an aid in reading.

Critical Thinking

Evaluating conclusions by logically and systematically examining the problem, the evidence, and the solution. Increasingly, educators believe that schools should focus more on critical thinking than on memorization of facts.

Crystallized Intelligence

Storehouse of general information/knowledge; over-learned skills; rote "old" learning; information based on past learning.

Culture

The language, attitudes, ways of behaving, and other aspects of life that characterize a group of people.

Decode
To analyze spoken or graphic symbols of a familiar language to ascertain their intended meaning. The term is commonly used within the field of education to refer to a student's ability to identify words.

Dendrites
Bushy branch-like structures that extend from the cell body of a neuron and receive the synaptic input to the cell.

Development
The process of maturational growth.

Diagnostic Test
A measurement that provides specific information, such as whether a student can multiply, or the extent of his/her word comprehension skills. These diagnostic tests help determine a student's weaknesses and strengths so that an individual learning program can be planned.

Directionality
The projection of laterality (developed within oneself) to outside oneself.

Discovery Learning
Teaching methods in which students are encouraged to discover principles for themselves.

Discrimination
The ability to differentiate between two or more sensory stimuli.

Diskinesia
An impairment of voluntary movement, resulting in fragmented or incomplete movements; poor coordination.

Distance Learning
The use of telecommunications technologies, including satellites, telephones and cable-television systems, to broadcast instruction from one central site to one or more remote locations. Typically, a television image of a teacher is broadcast to students at other locations. This may also be done using interactive videoconferencing, so that the student is able to interact with the teacher.

DSM-IV
Diagnostic and Statistical Manual, fourth edition (American Psychiatric Association).

Dyscalculia
A specific learning difficulty – the inability to perform operations in math or arithmetic.

Dysgraphia
A disability in the physical act of printing or cursive handwriting.

Dyslexia
A developmental reading disability, which may vary in degree from mild to severe, that affects up to 10% of the nation's school children. Children born to parents with dyslexia may be eight times as likely to have the condition.

Dyssemia
Difficulty in using and understanding nonverbal signs and signals; a nonverbal communication deficit.

Echolalia
The apparent meaningless repetition of exact words or phrases spoken by another, then used in place of original speech.

Egocentric
An individual's belief that everyone views the world as they do.

Encephalopathy
A brain disorder, especially one involving alterations of brain structure.

Enrichment
A type of program designed primarily for gifted students that is intended to supplement the regular academic curriculum for students who might otherwise be bored with their class work. Whether it is an in-class or pull-out program, enrichment programs are an alternative to creating entirely separate gifted classrooms.

ESL (English as a Second Language)
A term that refers to non-English speaking students or programs pertaining to the teaching of non-English speaking students.

Etiology
The cause or source of a syndrome or disease.

Exceptional Learners
Students who have abilities or problems significant enough to require special education or other services in order to reach their potential.

Experiential Education
A style of education that stresses hands-on experience, accomplished by field trips, internships, or activity-oriented projects, as opposed to traditional classroom learning.

Eye-hand Coordination
The integration of visual and tactile systems that enables the hand to be used as a tool of the visual processes.

Fetal Alcohol Syndrome (FAS)
A characteristic pattern of birth defects that results from maternal use of alcohol during pregnancy. The range and severity of associated symptoms and findings varies widely from case to case. Affected infants and children may have learning and behavioral

abnormalities, such as increased irritability during infancy, mild to severe mental retardation, short attention span, poor judgment, and impulsiveness.

Fine-motor Skills
The use of small muscle groups for specific tasks such as handwriting.

Finger Agnosia
The inability to recognize and interpret sensory impressions with fingers (generally the fingertips), caused by an impairment in the brain.

Forebrain
The largest part of the brain, consisting principally of the thalamus, hypothalamus, basal ganglia, and cerebral cortex.

Frontal Lobe
The most anterior portion of the cerebral cortex, concerned primarily with movement and smell.

Fluid Intelligence
Practical, hands-on intelligence; how well a person "thinks on his/her feet;" how quickly and competently a person processes and utilizes the information at his/her disposal.

Formal Learning
The acquisition of knowledge through a structured means such as in a class, or at a seminar.

Free Appropriate Public Education
A term for special education and related services that have been provided at public expense, under public supervision and direction, and without charge; that meet the standards of the state educational agency; that include an appropriate preschool, elementary, or secondary school program in the state involved; and that are provided in conformity with the individualized education program required by federal law.

Frontloading
Providing "preview" materials to a student prior to the actual instruction of a unit or topic of study.

Frustration Reading Level
The readability or grade level of material that is too difficult (either word identification or comprehension) to be read successfully by a student, even with normal classroom instruction and support.

Full Inclusion
A placement in which a special education student receives instruction within the regular classroom setting for the entire school day.

Generalization
Carry-over of behaviors, skills, or concepts from one setting or task to another.

Gestalt Perception
Deriving meaning from the "whole picture," without breaking it down into parts; "putting it all together;" a holistic view.

Giftedness
Category of student exceptionality characterized by being very bright, creative, or talented.

Glia
Supporting cells in the brain that help maintain neurons, regulate the environment, and form the myelin around axons.

Grade Equivalent Score
A score showing the grade level at which a student scored on a test. For example, a student who has a grade equivalent score of 4.3 is reading as well as the average student in the nation who has been in the fourth grade for three months.

Graphic Organizer
A method of presenting information in a simplified, organized, visual manner. Examples of graphic organizers are charts, venn diagrams, flow charts, grids, and a family tree.

Gray Matter
Those regions of the brain and spinal cord where neuronal cell bodies and dendrites are abundant.

Guidepost Neurons
Specialized cells found in the developing brain that guide axonal growth.

Hard Signs (neurological)
Unequivocal, medically documented signs of brain damage, such as brain surgery, cerebral bleeding, hemiplegia, brain tumor or penetrating head injury (see also soft signs).

Hearing Impairment
A permanent or fluctuating hearing loss that significantly hinders educational performance.

Hemisphere (cortical)
Half of the cerebral cortex. The two cortical hemispheres are each subdivided into four lobes.

Heterogeneous Grouping
The grouping of students, for instruction purposes, of differing levels of intelligence or achievement in one or more skills or subjects.

Homeschooling
The practice of parents' teaching their children at home rather than sending them to public school.

Homogenous Grouping
The grouping of students according to one or more selected criteria, such as age, ability, achievement, interests, etc.

Hydrocephalus
A condition in which abnormally widened (dilated) cerebral spaces in the brain (ventricles) inhibit the normal flow of cerebrospinal fluid (CSF). The cerebrospinal fluid accumulates in the skull and puts pressure on the brain tissue.

Hyperactivity
Condition characterized by extreme restlessness and short attention span relative to peers.

Hyperlexia
A syndrome that interferes with speech, language, and social interaction. It may be accompanied by unusual or "different" behaviors. Children exhibit an intense fascination with letters, numbers, patterns, logos, etc., and a very precocious ability to read, spell, write and/or compute from as early as 18 months to before the age of five.

Hypothalamus
A forebrain region that contains nuclei concerned with basic acts and drives such as eating, drinking, and sexual activity. The hypothalamus also regulates the release of pituitary gland hormones and the autonomic nervous system, and plays an important role in emotional behavior.

Hypotonia
A condition characterized by decreased muscle tone that is manifested as muscle weakness or "floppiness." The condition can occur as a disorder of unknown cause, or as a symptom of other neuromuscular diseases.

IDEA (PL 92-142)
A United States federal law, which was originally known as the Education for All Handicapped Children Act. In exchange for federal money, schools must guarantee that all children with disabilities receive a "free, appropriate public education."

Impairment
A neurological blockage or barrier to expected development.

Impulsivity
Cognitive style of responding quickly but often without regard for accuracy.

In-Service Training

Training, generally through workshops and lectures, that is designed to keep teachers abreast of the latest developments in their field.

Inclusive Schooling

Educating all children, with and without disabilities, together in heterogeneous classrooms. Materials are adapted, modified and changed to accommodate the needs of individual students. Inclusive schooling allows disabled students to exercise their basic right to be educated in the same educational environment as their peers.

Independent Educational Evaluation

An evaluation conducted by a qualified examiner who is not employed by the public agency responsible for the education of the student. A contracted agent, for the purpose of conducting an independent evaluation, is not considered an employee of the public agency.

Independent Reading Level

An Independent Reading Level is the readability or grade level of material , which the student is able to read with good comprehension and few word-identification problems.

Independent School

A private or nonpublic school that is not part of a school system. An independent school is governed by a board of trustees instead of by the state board of education. It is funded by tuition fees, private donations and grants.

Individualized Education Plan (IEP)

A written document stating a student's present level of performance, disability, educational goals, modifications, and kind and level of services to be provided. Every IEP must be approved by a pupil planning team consisting of several members, including a school administrator, a special education teacher, and the student's parent.

Individualized Transition Plan (ITP)

A specific and formalized plan that addresses the issues necessary for a student's transition from high school to work, college or university, or community living, and who qualify for special education services under PL 92-142 (IDEA).

Inference

Going beyond available evidence to form a conclusion.

Informal Knowledge

Knowledge about a particular subject that children learn through experience outside of school. For example, a child may learn to count by using their fingers or objects for counting.

Instructional Reading Level

Instructional Reading Level is the grade level of material, which the student finds challenging, but not frustrating, to read successfully with normal classroom instruction and support.

Integration

A placement in which a special education student receives instruction within the regular classroom setting for the entire school day.

Intelligence

General aptitude for learning.

Interdisciplinary Curriculum

A curriculum that consciously applies the methodology and language from more than one discipline to examine a central theme, issue, problem, topic, or experience. An example might be the study of space travel, where class material is designed to cover the history, science, and mathematics related to space travel, and the student is required to read outside material, and develop compositions based on the same central theme.

Intervention

The therapeutic and/or educational methods employed to aid a child once a disability has been diagnosed.

Intervention-Based Multifactored Evaluation

A collaborative, problem-solving process that focuses upon concerns that affect the learner's education progress within a learning environment.

IQ

The abbreviation for "intelligence quotient," which is a person's purported mental capacity.

Kinesthesia

The sensory knowledge and awareness of the body and body parts in space; includes awareness of balance and motion.

Laterality

The internal awareness an individual has of the two sides of his/her body.

Learned Helplessness

An individual's belief that their actions will ultimately lead to failure.

Learning Disabilities

Disorders that impede the learning process that are not the result of mental retardation or emotional disturbance.

Least Restrictive Environment

A term from PL92-142 (IDEA) requiring that, to the greatest extent possible, students with disabilities have the right to be educated with their non-disabled peers.

Literal Comprehension
The act or process of understanding what is explicitly stated or clearly implied in text or speech.

Long-term Memory
A type of memory function that enables people to retain memories for long periods – weeks, months, or longer.

Low-incidence Disability
A severely disabling condition with an expected incidence rate of less than 1% of the total statewide enrollment for kindergarten through grade-12 students.

Magnet School
A school that generally places special emphasis on overall academic achievement or on a particular field such as science, the arts, or technology. The concept of a magnet school was designed to attract students from elsewhere in the school district.

Mainstreaming
Placing students with special needs in regular classroom settings with support services for all or part of the day.

Manipulative
Any physical object that can be used to represent a problem situation, or develop a mathematical concept, such as marbles, blocks, coins, etc.

Math Specialist
A person in the field of education who has advanced training in math instruction. This may be the individual who is most capable of identifying the unique math difficulties of NLD students, and suggesting appropriate intervention strategies.

Meaningful Learning
Mental processing of new information that leads to connections with previously learned knowledge.

Mediated Learning
A teaching method in which the teacher guides instruction so that the student will master and internalize the skills that permit higher cognitive functioning.

Mentoring
The process whereby a professional, in consultation with the teacher, works closely with a student, instructing and motivating him or her.

Metacognition
The process of planning, assessing, and monitoring one's own thinking.

Midline
An invisible line marking the middle of the body, running from head to toe, separating the right from the left side of the body.

Mind Blindness
An inability to take the perspective of another.

Mnemonic
Something that aids an individual's ability to remember.

Modality
A sensory mode used by an individual to process information (i.e. auditory, visual, tactile, kinesthetic).

Modeling
Demonstrating to a student how to do a task, with the expectation that the student will be able to copy the steps that are demonstrated (modeled). Modeling often involves talking about how to work through a task, or thinking aloud.

Monoamine
A type of substance released at synapses that functions mainly as a neuromodulator.

Multiple Intelligence
A theory presented by Gardner (1983) that there are at least seven distinct "intelligences:" verbal/linguistic, logical/mathematical, visual/spatial, kinesthetic, musical, interpersonal, and intrapersonal.

Multi-sensory Approach
An instructional strategy that uses a combination of several senses.

Myelin
An insulating layer of membrane formed around axons – much like insulation around electrical wires.

Neuromodulator
Substance released at a synapse that causes biochemical changes in a neuron.

Neurons
Cells in the brain involved in the reception, integration, and transmission of signals.

Neurotransmitter
Substance released at a synapse that causes fast electrical excitation or inhibition of a neuron.

Nonverbal Communication
The use of facial expression, tone of voice, gesture, eye contact, physical proximity, touch, expressive movement, cultural differences, and other "nonverbal" acts. Nonverbal communication comprises at least 65% of all human communication.

Notetaking
A study strategy that requires decisions about what to write in order to remember key points of presented material.

Object Permanence
The knowledge that an object exists even when it is out of sight.

Observational Learning
Learning a task through the observation and imitation of others.

Obsess
To fill the mind with (focus solely on) one thought to an unreasonable or unhealthy extent.

Obsessive Compulsive Disorder
A mental disorder characterized by recurrent habitual obsessive or compulsive thoughts or actions. These obsessions and compulsions may become very distressing and time-consuming. In severe cases they can significantly interfere with a person's normal routine, occupational functioning, usual social activities or relationships with others.

Occipital Lobe
The most posterior portion of the cerebral cortex, concerned with visual processing.

Occupational Therapy
A type of therapy designed to improve, develop or restore functions impaired or lost through either illness, injury or deprivation; to improve an individual's ability to perform tasks for independent functioning if those functions are lost or impaired; through early intervention, to prevent the initial or further impairment or loss of function.

Orbitofrontal Cortex
An area found in the lower part of the frontal lobes, important for the expression of emotional behaviors.

Parallel Play
Play in which children engage in the same or similar activity side by side, but with very little interaction or mutual influence.

Paraprofessional
An individual who is employed by the school district for the purpose of assisting assigned students with individual or small group academics under the direction of a teacher. They may also assist with monitoring students as they access building facilities and services.

Parietal Lobe
That region of the cerebral cortex between the frontal and occipital lobes concerned primarily with somatosensory information processing.

Parochial School

A school that is church-related, most commonly to the Roman Catholic Church, but also to other Protestant denominations. Hebrew day schools can also be termed parochial.

Percentile Rank Scores

A score that compares a person's result with all others who took the same test. Percentile scores start at 1 and go to 99, so a percentile score of 80 means that the individual scored higher than 79%, and lower than 19%, of all other individuals who took the test.

Perception

The process by which patterns of environmental energies become known as objects, events, people, and other aspects of the world. Also known as insight, comprehension.

Perceptual Motor Disability

Difficulty in using a utensil. It causes problems with clarity of handwriting, letter formation, pencil pressure, etc.

Performance-based Assessment

Assessment that requires students to perform hands-on tasks, such as writing an essay or conducting a science experiment. Such assessments are becoming increasingly common as alternatives to multiple-choice, machine-scored tests.

Peripheral Nervous System

Parts of the nervous system outside of the brain and spinal cord.

Perseverate

The continuation of an action (commonly a thought) usually to an exceptional degree, or beyond an appropriate point.

Phonics

The most common strategy used to teach letter–sound relationships to beginning readers by having them "sound out" words.

Physical Therapy

A health specialty which aims to prevent physical disability as well as to habilitate or rehabilitate those with physical disabilities that are either congenital or acquired, resulting from, or secondary to, injury or disease.

Positron Emission Tomography (PET) Scanning

A method for detecting increases in activity of a part of the brain.

Pragmatics

The relation between signs or linguistic expressions and their users (functional use of language).

Prereading
Activities engaged in immediately before the act of reading, such as learning the background of a story or identifying purposes for reading the assigned material.

Prewriting
The initial creative stage of writing, prior to drafting, in which the student formulates ideas, gathers information, and considers ways to organize them.

Primary Motor Area
The region of the cerebral cortex where fine movements are initiated. Found in the frontal lobes adjacent to the central sulcus.

Primary Sensory Area
Regions where sensory information is first processed in the cerebral cortex.

Private Speech
Children's self-talk, which guides their thinking and action. Generally these verbalizations are eventually internalized as silent inner speech.

Proprioceptive Information
Sensory information from muscles, joints, and tendons that we are not conscious of.

Prosody
Tone, accent, modulation and all other characteristics of speech.

Psycholinguistics
The interdisciplinary field of psychology and linguistics in which language behavior is examined. Psycholinguistics includes such topics as language acquisition, conversational analysis, and the sequencing of themes and topics in discourse.

Psychomotor
Muscular activity which is directly related to, or resulting from, mental processes – the brain controlling movement.

Pull-out Programs
Compensatory education programs in which students are placed in separate classes for remediation or enrichment.

Pyramidal Cell
A prominent neuron found in all areas of the cerebral cortex.

Raw Test Score
A score that represents the number of correct answers a student gets on a test.

Reading Flexibility
The adjustment of one's reading speed, purpose, or strategies to the prevailing contextual conditions.

Related Services
Non-academic services that a child requires in order to receive a free appropriate public education. Examples of these services may be special transportation, speech-language pathology and audiology services, counseling services, and others that are determined to be necessary by the pupil planning team of the disabled student.

Reading Specialist
A person in the field of education who has advanced training in reading education. This may be the individual who is most capable of identifying the unique reading difficulties of NLD students, and suggesting appropriate intervention strategies.

Recreational Reading
Reading that is initiated for personal satisfaction during leisure time at any age.

Rote Learning
Memorization of facts or associations.

Scaffolding
The process of support provided to a student for learning and problem solving. The support may include clues, reminders, encouragement, breaking the problem down into steps, providing an example, or anything else that allows the student to develop learning independence.

Schizophrenia
A severe mental disease characterized by thought and mood disorders, hallucinations, etc.

Scoring Rubric (Scoring Guide)
An established set of guidelines developed to rate student work that describes what is being assessed, and provides a scoring scale. It is helpful for the teacher/rater in assessing a student's relative standard, and for the student in understanding how their work will be evaluated.

Semantic Pragmatic Disorder
A communication disorder with mild autistic symptoms and problems generalizing information.

Semantics
The study of meanings in language – connotative meaning.

Sensory Integration
The brain's ability to take in and synthesize multi-modality experiences perceived by the senses (vision, hearing, smell, taste, touch, motion, and temperature).

Sensory Integration Therapy (SIT)
An occupational therapy treatment program consisting of exercises that encourage the individual to use as many nerve-cell connections as possible.

Sensorimotor
Having to do with both sensory and motor activity in the body.

Serotonin
A substance released at synapses that most often acts as a neuromodulator. Decreased levels of serotonin in the brain have been linked to depression.

Short-term Memory
A type of memory function that involves the initial storage of information. Short-term memories are unstable and easily disrupted.

Social Perceptual Disability
A disability characterized by the inability to effectively use nonverbal cues in a social setting.

Soft Signs (neurological)
Behavioral deviations identified by a neurologist, where a traditional neurological examination does not reveal hard signs of brain damage or dysfunction. These indications (including poor directional sense, neuromuscular clumsiness, and others) are strongly suggestive of abnormal functioning of the central nervous system.

Soto's Syndrome
A rare genetic disorder characterized by excessive growth prior to and after birth. Children affected by Sotos syndrome may exhibit characteristic facial differences and developmental delays. The syndrome is also called Cerebral Gigantism.

Special Education
Specially designed instruction, at no cost to the parents, to meet the unique educational needs of the special education student, and develop his/her maximum potential.

Specific Learning Disability
As defined in the Individuals with Disabilities Education Act (IDEA), this is a disorder in one or more of the basic psychological processes involved in understanding or in using language (spoken or written), which may manifest itself in an imperfect ability to listen, think, speak, read, write, spell, or to do mathematical calculations.

Speech-language Pathologist (SLP)
A professional educated and trained in the study of human communication, its development, and its disorders.

Speech-language Therapy
The treatment of speech and language disorders (not limited to articulation problems), including deficits in pragmatic language.

Standardized Test
Generally, those tests that are prepared and published by specialized organizations, and administered to students in school districts across the nation for comparison

purposes. The information is helpful in determining how a particular student is doing in various curriculum areas versus his/her peer group, how the school as a whole compares to other similar schools, and how an entire district compares to similar districts.

State Achievement Test

Standardized tests that are administered to all students attending a public school in a particular state. The appropriate level of mastery is determined at the state level, and the results are used in a variety of ways. The information is helpful in determining how a particular student is doing in various curriculum areas versus his/her peer group, how the school as a whole compares to other similar schools, and how an entire district compares to similar districts. In addition, the results provide information that can help the state make appropriate educational decisions by comparing groups of test scores.

Stimuli

Environmental conditions that activate the senses.

Strategies

Defined plans or methods employed towards a goal.

Student Portfolio

An organized collection of a student's work throughout a course or class year. The purpose of the portfolio is to measure the student's knowledge and skills, and often includes some form of self-reflection by the student.

Synapse

The site of functional contact between two neurons or a neuron and muscle cell.

Syndrome

A cluster of signs and symptoms that considered together, are characteristic of a particular disease or disorder.

Tactile

Of or having to do with the sense of touch.

Tactile Perception

How an individual interprets the things he/she feels or touches.

Tactile-kinesthetic

Relating to the sense of touch and the feeling of movement – touching and doing.

Teaching for Understanding

A strategy that focuses on the process of understanding – grasping the relationship among facts, procedures, concepts, and principles and forming connections between prior knowledge and new knowledge. This strategy opposes the concept that learning is merely the development of specific skills, such as adding or multiplying figures.

Temporal Lobe
The lateral-most part of the cerebral cortex, concerned with hearing and memory.

Test Norms
A set of standards against which individual student performance on a test can be measured.

Thalamus
A forebrain region that relays sensory information to the cerebral cortex.

Tourette Syndrome
A neurological movement disorder that is characterized by repetitive motor and vocal tics. Symptoms may include involuntary movements of the extremities, shoulders, and face accompanied by uncontrollable sounds and, in some cases, inappropriate words.

Turner Syndrome
A rare chromosomal disorder of females characterized by short stature and the lack of sexual development at puberty. Other physical features may include a webbed neck, heart defects, kidney abnormalities, and/or various other malformations.

Velocardiofacial Syndrome
A rare genetic disorder characterized by abnormalities of the head and facial area, heart defects that are present at birth, diminished muscle tone, mental retardation, slight delays in the acquisition of skills requiring the coordination of mental and muscular activities (psychomotor retardation), and/or learning disabilities.

Visual Discrimination
Visual adeptness at perceiving similarities and differences in geometric figures, symbols, pictures, and words.

Visualization
The ability to picture and manipulate visual images within one's mind.

Visual-motor
The relationship between visual input and motoric output, as in copying text.

Visual-motor Integration
The coordination of visual information with motor processes.

Visual Perception
How an individual interprets the things he/she sees.

Visuospatial
Of the field of vision, especially as it involves the relationships of space and configuration of the object seen.

Vocational Education

Instruction that prepares a student for employment immediately after the completion of high school. Although often thought of in terms of auto-shop or carpentry courses, these programs also frequently include a strong academic component and teach such current skills as computer-aided design.

Webbing

A strategy used during the prewriting process that uses diagrams or maps to show the relationships among the ideas to be included.

Wernicke's Area

An area in the left temporal lobe concerned with the comprehension of language, reading and writing.

Whole Language

An instructional strategy that emphasizes the wholeness of words and text, thereby reading for meaning, and in context.

Williams Syndrome

A developmental disorder affecting connective tissue and the central nervous system. Characteristics of this disorder include heart disease, dysmorphic facial features, and poor visual-motor integration.

WISC-III

Wechsler Intelligence Scale for Children (third edition). Five subtests make up the verbal scale, and five subtests make up the performance scale. The WISC-III provides three IQ scores: verbal, performance, and full scale.

White Matter

Areas of the brain where there is an abundance of myelinated axons. The myelin sheath consists of a light-colored fatty substance, which gives the tissue its whitish appearance.

Working Memory

A type of short-term memory whereby information is maintained for only the length of time needed to enable a specific task to be accomplished, such as remembering a telephone number until it is dialed.

Writing Process

A process defined by the many aspects of the complex act of producing a written communication; specifically, planning or prewriting, drafting, revising, editing, and publishing.

504 Plan

A required document, under Section 504 of PL 93-112 (the Rehabilitation Act of 1973) as it applies to an individual's right to education The Act states that a 504 Plan or an IEP must be developed to remove the barriers to learning. All students who qualify under IDEA also qualify under 504. However, the reverse is not always true. Not all students who qualify under 504 also qualify under IDEA.

Appendix II

Annotated Bibliography

Anatomy Coloring Workbook. I. Edward Alcamo, PhD, 1997, Princeton Review Publishing, NJ (ISBN 0-679-77849-87)

   The author presents a unique approach to learning the human anatomy, using a step-by-step instructional strategy, requiring the reader to use a coloring process as they learn. The section on the nervous system is particularly valuable to anyone who wants to develop a better understanding of disease or dysfunction affecting the brain. This is a fun way to tackle a complex topic.

Asperger Syndrome: A Guide for Parents and Professionals. Tony Attwood, 1998, Jessica Kingsley Publishers, London (ISBN 1-85302-577-1)

   This is an excellent book on Asperger Syndrome that would also be very interesting to the NLD population. As you read the book, at times you will forget that you are reading about Asperger Syndrome since much of what the author covers relates incredibly well to NLD. This is an easy, quick read, and you'll enjoy the author's compassion and wit.

Asperger Syndrome in the Family: Redefining Normal. Liane Holliday Willey, 2001, Jessica Kingsley Publishers, London. (ISBN 1-85302-873-8)

   This is a wonderfully inspiring story, and all the more powerful because it is true. The author provides tremendous insight into what AS adult life might be like for our children, and how to prepare them for independence and intimacy. AS and NLD are very similar disorders, and the parents of NLD children will see much that is familiar in this author's story. A great resource.

Attention Deficit Disorder and Learning Disabilities: Realities, Myths and Controversial Treatments. Barbara D. Ingersoll and Sam Goldstein, 1993, Doubleday, NY (ISBN 0-38546-931-4)

   This is a readable and informative overview of ADD and learning disabilities, with a section on NLD (referred to as "visual-motor learning disability"). This book is treatment-oriented, including alternative therapies which the authors largely disapprove of.

The Blackwell Dictionary of Cognitive Psychology. Michael W. Eysenck (editor), Andrew Ellis, Earl Hunt, and Philip Johnson-Laird (advisory editors), 1990, Blackwell Publishers, Oxford. (ISBN 0-631-15682-8 and paperback ISBN # 0-631-19257-3)

> This book contains 140 encyclopedia-style entries on topics in contemporary cognitive psychology. There are also suggestions for further reading on each topic, and a comprehensive and helpful index. This is an easy-to-use book that would be helpful for individuals looking for "thumbnail sketch" descriptions on topics ranging from body image to the pragmatics of language to nonverbal communication. An excellent resource.

Brain Repair. Donald G. Stein, Simon Brailowsky, and Bruno Will, 1995, Oxford University Press, NY (ISBN 0-19-511918-5)

> The authors of this book are neuroscientists who present in lay terms the advances being made in brain research. They discuss the concept of brain plasticity, and explain how the brain manufactures a number of chemicals that foster growth and repair of damaged neurons.

Child Neuropsychology: Assessment and Interventions for Neuropsychiatric and Neurodevelopmental Disorders of Childhood. Phyllis Anne Teeter and Margaret Semrud-Clikeman, 1997, Allyn and Bacon, MA (ISBN 0-20516-331-9)

> The authors present the most current information regarding the influences of brain function on the cognitive-perceptual, learning, behavioral, and psychosocial adjustment of children and adolescents. The intended audience is professionals working in the field of child/adolescent psychology.

Comic Strip Conversations. Carol Gray, 1994, Future Horizons
(ISBN 1-885-47722-8 – call 800-489-0727)

> The creator of "Social Stories" has expanded the concept through the use of what she refers to as "Comic Strip Conversations." This concept uses a simple, but effective, illustrative process to teach social and communication skills to children with developmental disabilities.

Communication Disorders and Interventions in Low Incidence Pediatric Populations. Lisa Schoenbrodt, EdD and Romayne A. Smith, 1995, Singular Publishing Group, CA. (ISBN 1-565932-20-X)

> In this book, the authors present the medical background, etiology, characteristics, assessment, and intervention of various neurological conditions. Specific conditions addressed include traumatic brain injury, fragile X syndrome, autism and pervasive developmental disorders.

A Compendium of Neuropsychological Tests: Administration, Norms, and Commentary. (second edition) Otfried Spreed (editor), 1998, Oxford University Press (ISBN 0-195100-19-0)

The second edition of *A Compendium of Neuropsychological Tests* incorporates the major developments in neuropyschology and new research findings about brain-behavior relations in the 1990s. Written for professionals, it has been considerably expanded and contains new chapters on test selection, administration, report writing, the informing interview, executive functions, and occupational interest and aptitude.

Cooking Made Easy. Eileen Laird, 1996, Cookbook Publishers, P. O. Box 2117, Boone, NC 28607 (or purchase through author's website at http://www.cookingmadeeasy.org)

This book is a great resource for teaching individuals with NLD how to cook. The author assumes no cooking knowledge, and the directions are incredibly specific, including information such as size of bowl needed, what utensil to use, what part of vegetables to keep and which to throw away, etc.

Creating Mind: How the Brain Works. John E. Dowling, 1998, W. W. Norton and Co., NY. (ISBN 0-393-02746-5)

The first half of this book covers the nuts and bolts necessary for an up-to-date understanding of the brain. The remainder of the book examines aspects of brain function – vision, perception, language, memory, emotion, and consciousness – that are more directly relevant to how the brain creates mind. It is an excellent handbook for the layperson who wants to develop a better understanding of the brain.

Day-To-Day Dyslexia In The Classroom. Joy Pollock and Elisabeth Waller, 1997, Routledge, London (ISBN 0-415-11132-3)

This book covers a variety of topics as they relate to reading, such as learning styles, speech and language processing, ADD, and dyspraxia, as well as sequencing and orientation difficulties. There is an excellent chapter on the language of math, as well as chapters on study skills, and classroom management.

Developmental Dyspraxia: A Practical Manual for Parents and Professionals. Madeleine Portwood, 1996, Durham County Council (ISBN 1-897585-21-7)

The topic of this book is developmental dyspraxia, which is a neurological disorder bearing a striking resemblance to characteristics of NLD. There is a very interesting and easy-to-understand chapter on the development and function of the brain, as well as suggested intervention strategies for both the early years as well as the older student.

Diagnosing Learning Disorders: A Neuropsychological Framework. Bruce F. Pennington, 1991, Guilford Press, NY (ISBN 0-89862-563-7)

Although written primarily for professionals, and therefore somewhat technical, others would benefit from the material covered in this book. There is a comprehensive section on "right hemisphere LD," which covers many of the academic characteristics of NLD, most notably math and handwriting.

DSM-IV Diagnosis in the Schools. Alvin E. House, 1999, Guilford Press, NY (ISBN 1-57230-346-8)

This is a wonderful handbook for educators and school psychologists who are required to provide appropriate support for children with an identified neurologically based disability. Although NLD is not specifically listed in the DSM-IV, the author addresses the topic under Learning Disorder NOS, and references Dr. Rourke's work in this area.

Eating an Artichoke: A Mother's Perspective on Asperger Syndrome. Echo R. Fling, 2000, Jessica Kingsley Publishers, London (ISBN 1-85302-711-1)

This is a mother's story about her young son Jimmy, diagnosed with Asperger Syndrome (AS). Parents of NLD children will relate to many of Jimmy's difficulties, such as his inability to make friends or cope with change. You will find the author's Afterword, *"The Politics of it All,"* particularly interesting as it addresses the NLD/AS connection.

Emotional Intelligence: Why It Can Matter More Than IQ. Daniel Goleman, 1995, Bantam Books, NY (ISBN 0-553-09503-X)

The author challenges the current emphasis on cognitive and academic intelligence, and suggests that emotional maturity, social judgment, etc. (deficit areas for individuals with NLD) may play a greater role in determining success in life.

The Explosive Child : A New Approach for Understanding and Parenting Easily Frustrated, 'Chronically Inflexible' Children. Ross W. Greene (editor), 1998, HarperCollins, NY (ISBN 0-06017-534-6)

The author devotes an entire chapter to describing NLD children, and points out that inflexibility and low tolerance for frustration are major issues with this disorder. He suggests that the behavior of children who are inflexible and easily frustrated is not manipulative or purposeful, but rather a result of developmental deficits.

Hearing Equals Behavior. Guy Berard, MD, Foreword by Bernard Rimland and Afterword by Annabel Stehli, 1993, Keats Publishing. (ISBN 0-87983-600-8)

The pioneer of Auditory Integration Training (AIT) clearly and simply describes the auditory system of brain function. He goes on to outline disorders that may benefit from AIT, as well as what the treatment consists of. Although this book is out of print, it is worth reading if you are able to locate it.

Helping The Child Who Doesn't Fit In. Stephen Nowicki, Jr., PhD, and Marshall P. Duke, PhD, 1992, Peachtree Publishers, GA. (ISBN 1-56145-025-1)

Nowicki and Duke explain how nonverbal behavior affects a child's social competence and acceptance. The authors describe nonverbal communication as a "language" of its own, and suggest methods of teaching children the meaning of things such as space and touch, gestures and postures, facial expressions and other necessary components of communication.

Helping Children Overcome Learning Difficulties. Jerome Rosner, 1993, Walker and Company (ISBN 0-8027-7396-6)

Although this book is not specific to a particular learning disability, it assists in the identification of particular problems that may occur with a broad range of academic difficulties. The author presents some excellent strategies for intervention and remediation.

How Brains Think. William H. Calvin, 1996, Basic Books, NY (ISBN 0-465-07278-X)

Drawing on anthropology, evolutionary biology, linguistics, and the neurosciences, Calvin considers how a more intelligent brain developed using slow biological improvements over the last few million years. Although the author is a theoretical neurophysiologist, he writes in lay language that readers will appreciate.

How To Read A Book. Mortimer J. Adler and Charles Van Doren, 1972, Simon & Schuster, NY. (ISBN 0-671-21209-5)

Although released 30 years ago, this is actually a revised edition of an earlier work, and the material continues to be relevant. The authors cover topics relating to the dimensions of reading, analytical reading, and approaches to different kinds of reading matter.

Introducing Mind & Brain. Angus Gellatly and Oscar Zarate, 1999, Totem Books (ISBN 1-84046-005-9)

The authors trace the historical development of ideas about the brain and its function, from antiquity to the age of neuro-imaging. They explain what the sciences have to say about planning and action, language, memory, attention, emotions and vision, and invite the reader to take a fresh look at the nature of mind, consciousness, and personal identity.

It's Nobody's Fault. Harold S. Koplewicz, 1996, Times Books division of Random House, NY (ISBN 0-8129-2473-8)

The author addresses the biology of childhood disorders, as well as behavioral and emotional problems, including anxiety, phobias, etc. It contains good advice on the role of medication.

Landmark Study Skills Guide. Joan Sedita, 1989, Landmark Outreach Program (ISBN 0-962-41190-6)

An excellent book with loads of practical teaching strategies to help teachers and parents work with students to improve their study skills. Topics covered include organization, notetaking, efficient use of textbooks, main idea, summarizing, and other study skills and techniques. A must read for anyone working with NLD students.

Learning Disabilities: A Family Affair. Betty B. Osman, 1979, Warner Books (ISBN 0-446-35554-2)

Although this book was written 20 years ago, it is still an excellent resource. The author explains that a learning disability affects all aspects of the individual's life, and describes the impact on both the individual and the family. The author's compassion is apparent, and parents will find this a great support book. Although this book is currently out of print, the publisher plans on a reprint. An excellent book if you are able to locate a copy.

Learning Disabilities and Psychosocial Functioning: A Neuropsychological Perspective. Byron P. Rourke and Darren R. Fuerst, 1991, The Guilford Press, NY (ISBN 0-89862-767-2)

The authors examine whether there is a cause-and-effect relationship between psychosocial dysfunction (anxiety, depression, etc.) and the pattern of neuropsychological assets and deficits of various learning disability subtypes, particularly NLD. The book presents both scientific research findings and numerous case studies, which will be of interest to researchers, clinicians, and educational specialists alike.

Learning To Learn. Carolyn Olivier and Rosemary F. Bowler, 1996, Fireside, Published by Simon and Schuster, NY (ISBN 0-684-80990-7)

The authors discuss, in easy-to-understand language, the nature of learning, how we process information, and the various learning styles of students. They share many helpful ideas, from organizational tips to test-taking strategies. The material is based on the program developed at Landmark College.

Left Brain – Right Brain: Perspectives from Cognitive Neuroscience. Sally P. Springer and Georg Deutsch, 1997, W. H. Freeman and Company, NY (ISBN 0-7167-3111-8)

A very readable, science-based overview of brain asymmetry and its implications. It is also an excellent introduction to contemporary research on brain-behavior relationships. The authors discuss topics such as developmental disabilities, the nature of hemispheric specialization, disorders of speech and language, and the role of the right hemisphere in language.

Locating and Correcting Reading Difficulties (seventh edition). James L. Shanker and Eldon E. Ekwall, 1998, Prentice-Hall, NJ (ISBN 0-13-862962-5)

The audience for this book is primarily educators and reading specialists. It is an excellent book covering 28 reading errors, and has excellent appendices. Although intended for educators, the material would be beneficial for parents.

The Misunderstood Child: Understanding and Coping With Your Child's Learning Disabilities. Larry Silver, 1998, Times Books, NY (ISBN 0-81292-987-X)
> The author of this best-selling book has a wonderful understanding of the struggles faced by parents of a special needs child. He's also an expert at providing good, solid information in a manner that is both supportive and reader-friendly.

Negotiating the Special Education Maze: A Guide for Parents and Teachers. Winifred Anderson, Stephen Chitwood, and Deidre Hayden, 1990, Woodbine House (ISBN 0-933149-30-1)
> This is a must-read book for parents of learning disabled children in the United States. It demystifies the world of special education, the legal rights of children, and the process parents may have to go through in order to secure appropriate services for their child. A great refresher book for even the veteran of the special education system.

A Neurodevelopmental Approach to Specific Learning Disorders. Kingsley Whitmore and Guy Willems (editors), 1999, Cambridge University Press (ISBN 1-898683-11-5)
> This book addresses neurodevelopmental disorders such as dyslexia, dyscalculia, dysgraphia, clumsiness, and other learning difficulties that are found within a school population. The editors present specific ideas about the causes of these disorders, along with practical information regarding clinical management.

Neuropsychological Assessment of Children: A Treatment-Oriented Approach. Byron P. Rourke, John L. Risk, and John D. Strang, 1986, Guilford Press, NY (ISBN 0-89862-676-5)
> In this book, the authors explain how neuropsychological assessment can lead to successful intervention strategies. Presenting case studies and in-depth descriptions of a range of brain-related problems, it is an essential guide for the practitioner, as well as for anyone interested in this field of study.

Neuropsychology (Handbook of Perception and Cognition). Dahlia W. Zaidel (editor), 1994, Academic Press (ISBN 0-127752-90-0)
> Following a history of neuropsychology is a discussion of brain structure, function, and evolution; the neuropsychology of perceptual functions, attention, language, and emotion; the prefrontal cortex; movement sequencing disorders and apraxia; developmental aspects; aging and dementia; the creation and perception of art; sex differences in the brain; and neuropsychological rehabilitation. A technical but comprehensive book.

The New Social Stories. Carol Gray, 1994, Future Horizons (ISBN 1-885-47720-1 - call 800-489-0727)

The author of the *Original Social Story Book,* provides 100 new "social stories" based on the concept she introduced in her first book, and includes the Social Story Kit. It is not necessary to have read the original book in order to benefit from *The New Social Stories* book.

No one to Play With: The Social Side of Learning Disabilities. Betty B. Osman, 1982, Academic Therapy Publications, Novato, CA (ISBN 0-87879-687-8)

This is a well-presented, no-nonsense book explaining that a learning disabled child's difficulties often affect his/her social skills. She refers to these difficulties as "living disabilities" and explains that some children may not acquire social skills on their own. She suggests teaching them social skills as you would an academic subject, concretely and specifically.

Nonverbal Learning Disabilities: The Syndrome and the Model. Byron P. Rourke, 1989, The Guilford Press, NY (ISBN 0-89862-378-2)

This is clearly the most quoted book on the subject of NLD. Dr. Rourke explains the premise that NLD is caused by dysfunction of white matter in the brain, and shares his extensive research and findings. He defines the disorder, outlining the characteristics, dynamics, and manifestations of NLD. Although technically written, and likely a difficult read for the layperson, it is worth the effort for anyone wanting a full understanding of this syndrome.

Nonverbal Learning Disabilities At Home: A Parent's Guide. Pamela B. Tanguay, 2001, Jessica Kingsley Publishers, London. (ISBN 1-85302-940-8)

Nonverbal Learning Disabilities at Home explores the variety of daily life problems children with NLD may face, and provides practical strategies for parents to help them cope and grow, from preschool age through their challenging adolescent years. The author, herself the parent of a child with NLD, provides solutions to the everyday challenges of the disorder, from early warning signs and self-care issues to social skills and personal safety. User-friendly and highly practical, this book is an essential guide for parents in understanding and living with NLD, and professionals working with these very special children.

Original Social Story Book. Carol Gray, 1993, Future Horizons (call 800-489-0727)

The author originally created the concept of "social stories" for children who had difficulty processing daily situations which they encountered, particularly if they had a social component. Although often referred to as an autism intervention, this concept may be particularly helpful in assisting NLD youngsters gain or improve social skills, as well as deal more appropriately with novel situations.

Parenting the Child with Learning Disabilities: The Experts Speak. Teresa Allissa Citro (editor), 1998, Learning Disabilities Association of Massachusetts. (Order through website, www.idam.org)

Several recognized experts in the field of learning disabilities, including Mel Levine, MD, and Richard D. Lavoie, MA, MEd, share information and strategies with parents of learning disabled youngsters. Topics cover issues such as the social implications of learning disabilities, strategies for fostering self-esteem, motivation and resilience, and the psychological problems associated with learning disabilities. An excellent resource.

Pervasive Developmental Disorders: Finding a Diagnosis and Getting Help. Mitzi Waltz, 1999, O'Reilly & Associates, CA (ISBN 1-56592-530-0)

The author presents an incredibly well written manual, covering all of the issues associated with PDD-NOS. She first outlines the medical facts about the disorder, including a brief but very effective explanation of neurology, and moves on to getting a diagnosis.

Physiology of Behavior. Neil R. Carlson, 1998, Allyn and Bacon, MA (ISBN 0-205273-40-8)

The revision of this classic book for professionals incorporates the latest discoveries in the rapidly changing fields of neuroscience and physiological psychology. Comprehensive research is combined with a coherent and reader-friendly writing style. Topics covered include research, vision, body senses, chemical senses, movement, anxiety, autism, and more. Two new chapters on psychopharmacology and reinforcement and addiction have been added.

Pragmatic Language Intervention: Interactive Activities. Lynn S. Bliss, PhD, Thinking Publications (ISBN 0-930-59985-3)

This book covers specific communication skills as well as when each is to be used. The model dialogs will be very helpful for speech and language pathologists as well as teachers. As each communication skill is learned, it is then reinforced in everyday contexts. One of the most attractive features of this book is the numerous interactive activities and illustrations.

Pretending to be Normal. Liane Holliday Willey, 1999, Jessica Kingsley Publishers, London. (ISBN 1-85302-749-9)

This is an autobiographical account by an adult with Asperger Syndrome. The author holds a doctorate degree in education, is a writer and researcher specializing in the fields of psycholinguistics and learning style differences, wife, and mother of three daughters, one who also has AS. Although written about AS, in many situations you will find the similarity to NLD remarkable. A beautifully written and poignant book that parents and family members will enjoy.

Raising A Thinking Child. Myrna B. Shure, PhD with Theresa Foy DiGeronimo, MEd, 1994, Henry Holt and Company, NY. (ISBN 0-8050-2758-0)

The authors use the principles of Interpersonal Cognitive Problem Solving (ICPS) to teach appropriate skills and behavior. There are suggested dialogs, games, activities, and communication techniques that are designed for the parent to teach their child how to problem solve in a variety of situations.

Raising Careful, Confident Kids in a Crazy World. Paula Statman, 1999, Piccolo Press (ISBN 0-96400-422-4)

> For parents of the naive, trusting NLD child, this book is particularly meaningful. Important safety issues are presented, as well as sample scripts to use with the child without instilling fear. The author uses a positive, straightforward approach to topics such as how to protect a child from molestation, abduction, and other dangerous situations.

Right Hemisphere Communication Disorders: Theory and Management. Connie A. Tompkins, 1994, Singular Publishing Group, CA (ISBN 0-56593-176-9)

> Drawing on cognitive psychology, psycholinguistics, neuropsychology, and speech-language pathology, Tompkins explains the current status of knowledge about right hemisphere communication disorders and the processes presumed to underlie them. Directed to clinicians, she explains how to generate hypotheses about evaluation and management based on theory, data, logic, and patients' communicative needs.

Shadow Syndromes. John J. Ratey, MD and Catherine Johnson, PhD, 1997, Pantheon Books, NY (ISBN 0-679-43968-4)

> The authors have written a truly fascinating book about how brain chemicals and structure affect moods, personality, and other characteristics. The theme of the book is the "shadow" conditions of well-known disorders such as AD/HD and autism.

Skillstreaming in Early Childhood: Teaching Prosocial Skills to the Preschool and Kindergarten Child. Ellen McGinnis and Arnold P. Goldstein, 1990, Research Press (ISBN 0-87822-321-5)

> This book addresses the social skills deficits of youngsters, using techniques such as modeling, role-playing, and generalization of the skills. The authors have grouped the skills into six categories: Beginning Social Skills, School-related Skills, Friendship-making Skills, Dealing with Feelings, Alternatives to Aggression, and Dealing with Stress.

Skillstreaming the Adolescent: New Strategies and Perspectives for Teaching Prosocial Skills. (revised edition), Arnold P. Goldstein and Ellen McGinnis, 1997, Research Press Company (ISBN 0-87822-369-X)

> This revised edition of an excellent book in the Skillstreaming series offers terrific information for implementing adolescent social skills lessons in the following categories: Beginning Social Skills, Advanced Social Skills, Dealing with Feelings, Alternatives to Aggression, Dealing with Stress, and Planning Skills.

Skillstreaming the Elementary School Child: New Strategies and Perspectives for Teaching Prosocial Skills. Ellen McGinnis and Arnold P. Goldstein, 1997, Research Press (ISBN 0-87822-373-8)

> This selection in the Skillstreaming series focuses on teaching elementary-aged students how to deal with interpersonal conflicts and learn self-control through a curriculum of lessons in five areas: Classroom Survival Skills, Friendship-making Skills, Dealing with Feelings, Alternatives to Aggression, and Dealing with Stress.

Socially Speaking: A Pragmatic Social Skills Programme for Pupils with Mild to Moderate Learning Disabilities. Alison Schroeder, 1996, LDA, UK (ISBN 1-855-03252-X)

> The author presents a social skills program that is aimed at encouraging effective social interaction and improving self-esteem, listening skills, receptive and expressive language, and problem solving. The book includes a lesson plan for each week of the school year, each with a similar format. Assessment and evaluation procedures are included. The audience for this book is speech and language pathologists and teachers, however parents will also find the content valuable.

The Source for Nonverbal Learning Disorders. (Formerly titled, I Shouldn't Have to Tell You! A Guide to Understanding Nonverbal Learning Disorders.) Sue Thompson, MA, CET, 1997, LinguiSystems. Call 1-800-776-4332 or 1-309-755-2300.

> This is an absolute must-read book! It is a great resource for parents and teachers of NLD kids – chock full of information and strategies. The author's depth of understanding of both the disorder and appropriate interventions will have you returning to it over and over again. Every parent of an NLD child should own this book.

Star Shaped Pegs, Square Holes: Nonverbal Learning Disorders and the Growing Up Years. Kathy Allen, 1996, Unicycle Press, 1076 Lynn St., Livermore, California 94550 (or e-mail the author at Caitlin35@aol.com)

> This is a charming and warm book, written to the middle-school-aged NLD child to help them understand and cope with their disorder. There are great ideas and coping strategies throughout, written in a way that will appeal to the adolescent or young teen. The author suggests that it be read and understood with the support of a parent or professional.

Straight Talk About Psychiatric Medications for Kids. Timothy E. Wilens, MD, 1999, Guilford Press, NY (ISBN 1-57230-204-6)

> Many parents of children with NLD are faced with the issue of whether or not to use medication to deal with anxiety and/or depression. Until now, there has been precious little information available on this topic. The author does a wonderful job of explaining what parents should know about psychiatric medications for

children, along with the various classes of drugs and what they are used for. An excellent resource for parents.

Students With Learning Disabilities. Cecil D. Mercer, 1997, Prentice-Hall, Simon & Schuster/A Viacom Company, NY (ISBN 0-13-477176-1)

This textbook was written for application at university level to teach an introductory class on learning disabilities. It provides extremely comprehensive coverage of the field of learning disabilities. Parents will benefit by reading it, gaining an insight into how teachers are educated about various learning disabilities and are trained in classroom strategies.

Successful Lifetime Management: Adults with Learning Disabilities. Teresa Allissa Citro (editor), 1999, Learning Disabilities Association of Massachusetts, (Order through website, www.idam.org)

An excellent compilation of chapters by various experts in the field of learning disabilities. The book addresses areas that are, unfortunately, often overlooked when addressing the difficulties of learning disabled individuals. Topics cover items such as the impact of learning disabilities on adult social relationships, workplace issues, support services and accommodations at college and graduate school level, and communication skills of adults with learning disabilities.

Syndrome of Nonverbal Learning Disabilities: Neurodevelopmental Manifestations. Byron P. Rourke (editor), 1995, The Guilford Press, NY (ISBN 0-89862-155-0)

A collection of 18 contributions that explore the ramifications of NLD in the neuropsychology of learning disabilities and in pediatric neurological disease, disorder, and dysfunction. Among the 15 diseases and disorders covered in the book are Callosal Agenesis, Asperger Syndrome, Velocardiofacial Syndrome, Sotos Syndrome, Williams Syndrome, and traumatic brain injury.

Taming the Recess Jungle. Carol Gray, 1993, Future Horizons (ISBN 1-885-47721-X – call 800-489-0727)

The author tackles one of the major difficulties of young NLD children, the social challenges of school recess. Although the book is written for children with autism and related disorders, these children share the same social deficits as NLD youngsters. Ms. Gray identifies a variety of resources and materials that are helpful in simplifying the social demands of recess.

Teaching For The Two-Sided Mind: A Guide To Right Brain/Left Brain Education. Linda Verlee Williams, 1983, Simon & Shuster. (ISBN 0-671-62239-0)

Although written for teachers, much of what is contained within this book is interesting for a wide audience. It approaches teaching from the perspective of the left brain, right brain, and whole brain. The author presents her material in simple language, and uses excellent examples to explain what can be a difficult topic to understand.

Teaching Your Child the Language of Social Success. Marshall P. Duke, PhD, Stephen Nowicki, Jr., PhD, and Elisabeth A. Martin, MEd, 1996, Peachtree Publishers, GA (ISBN 1-56145-126-6)
> The authors, who coined the term "Dyssemia" to describe an inability to interpret and express nonverbal communications and defined it as the "body language version of dyslexia," have loaded this book with tips for improving nonverbal skills, from facial expressions, to space and touch, to gestures and postures. They also discuss how nonverbal language can be taught in a classroom setting.

Your Miracle Brain. Jean Carper, 2000, HarperCollins Publishers, NY (ISBN 0-06-018391-8)
> This book was written as an informational rather than a medical guide to explain how the brain structure and functioning of brain cells can be improved by what you eat as well as the supplements you take.

What Smart Students Know. Adam Robinson, 1993, Crown Publishers, NY (ISBN 0-517-88085-7)
> In this book, the author explains that successful students are not necessarily more intelligent than less successful students, but rather have developed an efficient approach to learning.

When You Worry About the Child You Love: Emotional and Learning Problems in Children. Edward Hallowell, 1996, Simon and Schuster, NY (ISBN 0-684-80090-X)
> There are a variety of disorders covered in this book, including specific information on NLD. This is an excellent, readable book with a host of wonderful and practical tips.

Wrightslaw: Special Education Law. Peter W. D. Wright and Pamela Darr Wright, 1999, Harbor House Law Press, VA (ISBN 1-892320-03-7) (It can be ordered through the authors' website at www.wrightslaw.com)
> This book is authored by the owners of the exceptional website for parents, attorneys, advocates, and educators known as *Wrightslaw*. This is the first in a planned series of special education law and advocacy books relating to the needs of children with disabilities.

Appendix III

Internet Resources

All Kinds of Minds

http://www.allkindsofminds.org

All Kinds of Minds is a nonprofit organization formed to further the understanding of learning differences. The institute focuses on applied research, product development, program design, and professional training to increase the understanding and appropriate support for children with differences in learning. The information at this website is based upon the work of Dr. Mel Levine and his colleagues, and is a wonderful resource.

American Hyperlexia Association (AHA)

http://www.hyperlexia.org

AHA is a nonprofit organization consisting of parents and family members of children with hyperlexia, speech and language and educational professionals, as well as other individuals interested in the mission to identify hyperlexia. This site has excellent information on hyperlexia and numerous articles on intervention.

Anxiety Disorders Association of America (ADDA)

http://www.adaa.org

ADAA was formed to promote the prevention and cure of anxiety disorders. The association includes researchers and clinicians in the field of anxiety disorders, as well as anyone interested in developing a better understanding of these disorders. They have a very comprehensive website, which includes message boards and a chat facility.

Anxiety Disorders Education Program

http://www.nimh.nih.gov/anxiety

The National Institute of Mental Health (NIMH) developed this program. The purpose is to educate public and health care professionals about anxiety – that they are real medical illnesses that can be effectively diagnosed and treated. The website has information on anxiety disorders, as well as treatment and many available resources.

Asperger Syndrome Coalition of the United States, Inc.
(ASC-U.S., Inc.)

http://www.asc-us.org

ASC-U.S. is a national nonprofit organization committed to providing the most up-to-date and comprehensive information on Asperger Syndrome and related conditions. Their website includes an NLD section.

Association of Christian Schools International

http://www.acsi.org/membership/directory/index.cfm

The Association of Christian Schools International (ACSI) has an extensive database of over 5,000 member Christian schools in the United States and Canada. There are several available search options, such as state, region, schools with special academic services, schools with homeschool services, and more.

Canadian Hyperlexia Association

http://home.ican.net/~cha/

A group consisting of concerned parents as well as professionals formed this organization. It is their mission to increase the awareness of hyperlexia and provide support for parents, children, and professionals. At their website you will find information as well as strategies for dealing with the disorder.

The Calvert School

http://home.calvertschool.org/

The Calvert School has been involved in distance schooling, or homeschooling, since 1906. They provide total curriculum packages for K-eighth grade, along with considerable support. For those wishing to pursue high school, there is a section that provides guidance on secondary education. A very reputable organization, and an excellent site for parents considering homeschooling their child.

Child Neurology Home Page

http://waisman.wisc.edu/child-neuro/index.html

This website provides information on child neurology to professionals, patients and their families. It is an excellent site for Internet resources in the field of pediatric neurology.

Children and Adults with Attention Deficit/Hyperactivity Disorder (CHADD)

http://www.chadd.org

CHADD is a national nonprofit organization that was formed in 1987 by a group of parents. They represent both children and adults who have attention-deficit/hyperactivity disorder (AD/HD). Their mission is to provide education, advocacy, and support to individuals with AD/HD, and they have a very comprehensive website.

Council of Parent Attorneys and Advocates (COPAA)

http://wwww.copaa.net

An independent, nonprofit organization of attorneys, advocates and parents established to improve the quality and quantity of legal assistance for parents of children with disabilities. At their website you will find useful legal information, as well as a directory of attorneys and advocates.

Crosswalk.com Home School

http://homeschool.crosswalk.com/learnathome/

This very comprehensive website will be a homeschool parent's favorite place. There are terrific resources, including an online newsletter, events calendar, online support group, and a great section on frequently-asked questions about homeschooling.

Developmental Delay Resources (DDR)

http://www.devdelay.org

DDR is a nonprofit organization developed to support individuals working with children who have developmental delays. Their website provides information on various disorders, and intervention options.

Dyspraxia Foundation

http://www.emmbrook.demon.co.uk/dysprax/homepage.htm

This organization was formed to support those affected by developmental dyspraxia. Developmental Dyspraxia shares many characteristics with NLD. Their website includes a description of the disorder and how it may affect the individual in school.

EDLAW, Inc.

http://www.edlaw.net

A website founded by S. James ("Jim") Rosenfield, an attorney with almost 20 years of experience in special education law. This is a website devoted to special education law where you will find briefing papers and information on federal education laws.

ERIC Clearinghouse on Adult, Career, and Vocational Education (ERIC/ACVE)

http://ericacve.org

ERIC stands for Educational Resources Information Center, and is sponsored by the U. S. Department of Education, Office of Educational Research and Improvement (OERI), and administered by the National Library of Education (NLE). ACVE stands for adult, career, vocational, and educational. ERIC/ACVE is located at the Center on Education and Training for Employment (CETE) at Ohio State University. An extensive website provides information on adult and continuing education, career education, and vocational and technical education, including employment and training.

ERIC Clearinghouse on Disabilities and Gifted Education (ERIC EC)

http://ericec.org

ERIC stands for Educational Resources Information Center, and is sponsored by the U. S. Department of Education, Office of Educational Research and Improvement (OERI), and administered by the National Library of Education (NLE). EC stands for Exceptional Children. This is one of sixteen federally funded clearinghouses. It is very large and extremely comprehensive, providing information on the education and development of individuals of all ages who have disabilities and/or who are gifted.

ERIC Clearinghouse on Elementary and Early Childhood Education (ERIC/EECE)

http://ericeece.org

ERIC stands for Educational Resources Information Center, and is sponsored by the U.S. Department of Education, Office of Educational Research and Improvement (OERI), and administered by the National Library of Education (NLE). It is a national information system designed to provide users with ready access to an extensive body of education-related literature. The EECE website is a very large, comprehensive site devoted to issues related to elementary and early childhood education.

HEATH Resource Center

http://www.health.gwu.edu

HEATH Resource Center of the American Council on Education is supported by the U.S. Department of Education, and acts as a national clearing-house providing information on post-secondary education for individuals with disabilities. Their website is an excellent resource for issues affecting this population.

Home School Legal Defense Association

http://www.hslda.org/index.asp

You'll find the section on the state laws regarding homeschooling very informative, as well as the state listings of homeschooling organizations. This site provides excellent information on the legal issues surrounding the option to homeschool.

Job Accommodation Network (JAN)

http://janweb.icdi.wvu.edu

The Job Accommodation Network is a toll-free consulting service providing information regarding job accommodations, the employment issues of people with disabilities, including information about the Americans with Disabilities Act (ADA). It is not a job placement service. Their website has many links to disability-related sites and information.

Learning Disabilities Association of America (LDA)

http://www.ldanatl.org

The LDA is a national nonprofit organization supporting individuals with learning disabilities. Their website is very comprehensive and provides information on many types of learning disabilities and education law.

LD OnLine

http://www.ldonline.org

An exceptionally comprehensive learning disabilities website servicing parents, teachers, and children. LD OnLine is a service of The Learning Project at WETA, Washington, DC, in association with The Coordinated Campaign for Learning Disabilities.

National Association of Private Schools for Exceptional Children (NAPSEC)

http://www.napsec.com

NAPSEC is a nonprofit organization made up of participating private special educational schools for children with disabilities. There is a link to all member school websites.

National Attention Deficit Disorder Association (ADDA)

http://www.add.org

The ADDA is a nonprofit organization that is staffed entirely by unpaid volunteers, and serves the needs of young adults and adults with ADD or ADHD. Their website is very comprehensive, with articles and interviews of some of the leading experts in the field.

National Center for Learning Disabilities (NCLD)

http://www.ncld.org

NCLD's mission is to promote public awareness and understanding of children and adults with learning disabilities, and to provide national leadership on their behalf, so they may achieve their potential and enjoy full participation in our society. Their website has many full text articles, and an excellent links section to additional learning disability resources.

National Information Center for Children and Youth with Disabilities (NICHCY)

http://nichcy.org

This is the national information and referral center that provides information on disabilities and disability-related issues to families, educators, and other professionals. Their special focus is children and young adults, from birth to age 22. Their website is quite large, with many articles, as well as resource sheets with state-specific information.

NLD on the Web!

http://www.nldontheweb.org

The most comprehensive NLD site on the web, and the official web presence of Byron P. Rourke, PhD, FRSC, and worldwide web headquarters of Sue Thompson, MA, CET. All of Ms. Thompson's work is on the site, as is Dr. Rourke's NLD Assessment Protocol and a "Question and Answer" section. The site is quite large, but designed so that it is easy to navigate, providing information for parents, professionals, and educators. There are numerous articles explaining NLD (grouped by reading difficulty), information on assessment, advocacy, and intervention, an extensive "library" of other suggested reading, and a comprehensive calendar of seminars, workshops, and conferences on NLD and related topics. There is also a private forum allowing for the free exchange of information, and a chat facility.

NLDLine

http://www.nldline.com

A website devoted to increasing awareness of NLD among parents and professionals. The site features articles and resource listings, personal stories, a bulletin board, and a pen-pals section for children with NLD.

OnLine Asperger Syndrome Information and Support (O.A.S.I.S.)

http://aspergersyndrome.org

This incredibly comprehensive site for Asperger Syndrome (AS) is owned and operated by the parent of a child diagnosed with AS, a disorder which has remarkable similarities to NLD. This site has become synonymous with the name Asperger Syndrome, and has become a home, or "oasis" for those interested in, or living with AS.

Petersons.com: The Private Schools Channel

http://iiswinprd01.petersons.com/pschools/

This website provides articles about private schools, and a very helpful search facility that allows you to locate private schools using various criteria, such as distance from your home, types of schools, etc.

Recording for the Blind and Dyslexic (RFB&D)

http://www.rfbd.org

A national nonprofit organization that serves people who cannot read standard print because of a visual, perceptual or other physical disability. RFB&D is recognized as the nation's leading educational lending library of academic and professional textbooks on audiotape from elementary through post-graduate and professional levels. There is a search facility at their website so that you can key in information on a particular book, and find out if it has been recorded and is available.

School Psychology Resources Online

http://www.schoolpsychology.net

An extensive listing of school psychology resources for psychologists, parents, and educators, covering such subjects as learning disabilities, ADHD, functional behavioral assessment, autism, adolescence, parenting, psychological assessment, special education, and more.

Tera's NLD Jumpstation: A Resource on Nonverbal Learning Disabilities by an NLD Person

http://www.geocities.com/HotSprings/Spa/7262

This site was created by Tera Kirk, a young woman with NLD, who is currently attending Agnes Scott College in Georgia. It provides an excellent and humorous description of NLD from the perspective of an individual with the disorder. A nice site to visit with your NLD adolescent or young teen to help them better understand their disorder.

Wrightslaw: The Special Ed Advocate

http://www.wrightslaw.com

For anyone needing accurate and up-to-date information on educational law or advocacy, this is the place. Parents, educators, experts, and attorneys visit this site for information about effective advocacy for children with disabilities. You'll find hundreds of articles, cases, newsletters, and other information about special education law and advocacy in the Wrightslaw Libraries.

Appendix IV

Organizations

Alliance for Technology Access
2175 East Francisco Boulevard, Suite L
San Rafael, CA 94901
(800) 455-7970 or (415) 455-4575
E-mail: atainfo@ataccess.org
Web: www.ataccess.org

American Council on Rural Special Education (ACRES)
Kansas State University
2323 Anderson Avenue, Suite 226
Manhattan, KS 66502
(785) 532-2737
E-mail: acres@ksu.edu
Web: www.ksu.edu/acres

American Heart Association
7272 Greenville Avenue
Dallas, TX 75231
(800) 242-8721 or (214) 373-6300
E-mail: inquire@amhrt.org
Web: www.americanheart.org

American Hyperlexia Association (aha)
195 W. Spangler, Suite B
Elmhurst, IL 60126
(630) 415-2212
E-mail: president@hyperlexia.org
Web: www.hyperlexia.org

American Occupational Therapy Association (AOTA)
4720 Montgomery Lane
P. O. Box 31220
Bethesda, MD 20824-1220
(301) 652-2682
E-mail: helpdesk@aota.org
Web: www.aota.org

American Physical Therapy Association (APTA)
1111 North Fairfax Street
Alexandria, VA 22314
(800) 999-2782 or (703) 684-2782
E-mail: practice@apta.org
Web: www.apta.org

American Speech-Language-Hearing Association (ASHA)
10801 Rockville Pike
Rockville, MD 20852
(800) 638-8255 or (301) 897-5700
E-mail: actioncenter@asha.org
Web: www.asha.org

American Therapeutic Recreation Association
P. O. Box 15215
Hattiesburg, MS 39404-5215
(800) 553-0304 or (601) 264-3413
E-mail: atta@accessnet.com
Web: www.atra-tr.org

Amicus for Children, Inc.
1023 Old Swede Rd.
Douglassville, PA 19518
(610) 689-4226
E-mail: amicusforchildren@att.net
Web: www.amicusforchildren.org

Anxiety Disorders Association of America
11900 Parklawn Drive, #100
Rockville, MD 20852-2624
(301) 231-9350
E-mail: AnxDis@aol.com
Web: www.adaa.org

Asperger Syndrome Coalition of the United States, Inc. (ASC-U.S.)
P. O. Box 49267
Jacksonville Beach, FL 32240-9267
(904) 745-6741
E-mail: info@asc-us.org
Web: www.asc-us.org

Association on Higher Education and Disability (AHEAD)
University of Massachusetts, Boston
100 Morrissey Blvd.
Boston, MA 02125
(617) 287-3880
E-mail: Carol.DeSouza@umb.edu
Web: www.ahead.org

Brain Injury Association
105 North Alfred Street
Alexandria, VA 22314
(800) 444-6443 or (703) 236-6000
E-mail: FamilyHelpline@biaus.org
Web: www.biausa.org

CdLS Foundation (de Lange Syndrome)
302 W. Main Street, Suite 100
Avon, CT 06001
(800) 753-2357 or (860) 676-8337
E-mail: info@cdlsusa.org
Web: www.cdlsoutreach.org

Children and Adults with Attention-Deficit/Hyperactivity Disorder (CHADD)
8181 Professional Place, Suite 201
Landover, MD 20785
(301) 306-7070
E-mail: national@chadd.org
Web: www.chadd.org

Council for Exceptional Children (CEC)
Division for Learning Disabilities (DLD)
1920 Association Drive
Reston, VA 20191-1589
(703) 620-3660 or (407) 367-2916 (Cynthia Wilson)
E-mail: c_wilson@acc.fau.edu
Web: www.dldcec.org

Council for Learning Disabilities
P. O. Box 40303
Overland Park, KS 66204
(913) 492-2546
E-mail: webmaster@cldinternational.org
Web: www.cldinternational.org

The Cultural Home Educators Association
2324 University Avenue, Suite 103
St. Paul, MN 55104
(651) 408-1810
E-mail: admin@happyhomeschoolers.com
Web: happyhomeschoolers.com

Easter Seals
230 West Monroe Street, Suite 1800
Chicago, IL 60606
(800) 221-6827 or (312) 726-6200
E-Mail: nessinfo@seals.com
Web: www.easter-seals.org

Epilepsy Foundation
4351 Garden City Drive, 5th Floor
Landover, MD 20785-4941
(800) 332-1000 or (301) 459-3700
E-mail: postmaster@efa.org
Web: www.efa.org

FACES: The National Craniofacial Association
P. O. Box 11082
Chattanooga, TN 37401
(800) 332-2372 or (423) 266-1632
E-mail: faces@faces-cranio.org
Web: www.faces-cranio.org

Family Resource Center on Disabilities
20 East Jackson Boulevard, Room 900
Chicago, IL 60604
(800) 952-4199 (IL only) or (312) 939-3513

Family Village, Waisman Center
University of Wisconsin-Madison
1500 Highland Avenue
Madison, WI 53705-2280
E-mail: familyvillage@waisman.wisc.edu
Web: www.familyvillage.wisc.edu/

Federation of Families for Children's Mental Health

1021 Prince Street
Alexandria, VA 22314-2971
(703) 684-7710
E-mail: ffcmh@ffcmh.com
Web: www.ffcmh.org

Home School Legal Defense Association

P.O. Box 3000
Purcellville, VA 20134-9000
(540) 338-5600
E-mail: mailroom@hslda.org
Web: www.hslda.org

Hydrocephalus Association

870 Market Street #955
San Francisco, CA 94102
(415) 732-7040
E-mail: hydroassoc@aol.com
Web: www.hydroassoc.org

Independent Living Research Utilization Project

The Institute for Rehabilitation and Research
2323 South Sheppard, Suite 1000
Houston, TX 77019
(713) 520-0232
E-mail: ilru@ilru.org
Web: www.ilru.org

International Dyslexia Association

(formerly The Orton Dyslexia Society)
Chester Building #382
8600 LaSalle Road
Baltimore, MD 21286-2044
(800) 222-3123 or (410) 296-0232
E-mail: info@interdys.org
Web: www.interdys.org

International Reading Association

800 Barksdale Road
P. O. Box 8139
Newark, DE 19714-8139
(302) 731-1600
E-mail: www.pubinfo@reading.org
Web: www.reading.org

International Rett Syndrome Association
9121 Piscataway Rd., Suite 2B
Clinton, MD 20735-2561
(800) 818-7388 or (301) 856-3334
E-mail: irsa@rettsyndrome.org
Web: www.rettsyndrome.org

Learning Disabilities Association of America (LDA)
4156 Library Road
Pittsburgh, PA 15234
(888) 300-6710 or (412) 341-1515 or (412) 341-8077
E-mail: ldanatl@usaor.net
Web: www.ldanatl.org

Leukemia Society of America
600 Third Avenue
New York, NY 10016
(800) 955-4572
E-mail: infocenter@leukemia-lymphoma.org
Web: www.leukemia.org

National Association for the Education of Young Children (NAEYC)
1509 16th Street NW
Washington, DC 20036
E-mail: naeyc@naeyc.org
Web: www.naeyc.org

National Association of Private Schools
5350 S. Western Ave., Suite 301
Oklahoma City, OK 73109
(405) 634-7778
Web: rsts.net/naps

National Association of Private Schools for Exceptional Children (NAPSEC)
1522 K Street N.W., Suite 1032
Washington, DC 20005
(202) 408-3338
E-mail: napsec@aol.com
Web: www.napsec.com

National Association of Protection and Advocacy System (NAPAS)
900 Second Street N.E., Suite 211
Washington, DC 20002
(202) 408-9514
E-mail: napas@earthlink.net
Web: www.protectionandadvocacy.com/

National Attention Deficit Disorder Association
1788 Second Street, Suite 200
Highland Park, IL 60035
Phone: (847) 432-2332
E-mail: mail@add.org
Web: www.add.org

National Center for Learning Disabilities (NCLD)
381 Park Avenue South, Suite 1401
New York, NY 10016
(888) 575-7373 or (212) 545-7510
Web: www.ncld.org

National Clearinghouse for Alcohol and Drug Information (NCADI)
P. O. Box 2345
Rockville, MD 20847-2345
(800) 729-6686 or (301) 468-2600
E-mail: info@health.org
Web: www.health.org

National Fragile X Foundation
1441 York Street, Suite 303
Denver, CO 80206
(800) 688-8765 or (303) 333-6155
E-mail: natlfx@sprintmail.com
Web: www.fragilex.org

National Information Center for Children and Youth with Disabilities (NICHCY)
P. O. Box 1492
Washington, DC 20013-1492
(800) 695-0285 or (202) 884-8200
E-mail: nichcy@aed.org
Web: nichcy.org

National Institute on Deafness and Other Communication Disorders Clearinghouse
One Communication Avenue
Bethesda, MD 20892-3456
(800) 241-1044
E-mail: nidcdinfo@nidcd.nih.gov
Web: www.nih.gov/nidcd/

National Lead Information Center and Clearinghouse
8601 Georgia Avenue, Suite 503
Silver Spring, MD 20910

(800) 424-5323
E-mail: hotline.lead@epa.gov
Web: www.epa.gov/lead

National Mental Health Association
1021 Prince Street
Alexandria, VA 22314-2971
(800) 969-6642 or (703) 684-7722
E-mail: nmhainfo@aol.com
Web: www.nmha.org

National Neurofibromatosis Foundation
95 Pine Street; 16th Floor
New York, NY 10005
(800) 323-7938 or (212) 344-6633
E-Mail: NNFF@aol.com
Web: www.nf.org

National Organization on Fetal Alcohol Syndrome (NOFAS)
418 C Street N.E.
Washington, DC 20002
(800) 666-6327 or (202) 785-4585
E-mail: nofas@erols.com
Web: www.nofas.org

National Organization for Rare Disorders (NORD)
P. O. Box 8923
New Fairfield, CT 06812-8923
(800) 999-6673 or (203) 746-6518
E-mail: orphan@rarediseases.org
Web: www.rarediseases.org

National Parent Network on Disabilities
1130 17th Street N.W., Suite 400
Washington, DC 20036
(202) 463-2299
E-Mail: npnd@cs.com
Web: www.npnd.org

National Parent to Parent Support and Information System, Inc.
P. O. Box 907
Blue Ridge, GA 30513
(800) 651-1151 or (706) 374-3822
E-mail: nppsis@ellijay.com
Web: www.nppsis.org

National Scoliosis Foundation
5 Cabot Place
Stoughton, MA 02072
(800) 673-6922 or (781) 341-6333
E-mail: NSF@scoliosis.org
Web: www.scoliosis.org

Neurofibromatosis, Inc.
8855 Annapolis Road, Suite 110
Lanham, MD 20706-2924
(800) 942-6825 or (301) 577-8984
E-mail: NFInc1@aol.com
Web: www.nfinc.org

Nonverbal Learning Disorders Association
P. O. Box 220
Canton, CT 06019-0220
(860) 693-3738
E-mail: NLDA@nlda.org
Web: www.nlda.org

O. C. Foundation, Inc.
(Obsessive Compulsive Disorder)
P. O. Box 70
Milford, CT 06460-0070
(203) 878-5669
E-mail: info@ocfoundation.org
Web: www.ocfoundation.org

Office of Special Education and Rehabilitative Services
Clearinghouse on Disability Information
Room 3132, Switzer Building
330 C Street S.W.
Washington, DC 20202-2524
(202) 205-8241
Web: www.ed.gov/offices/OSERS

President's Committee – Job Accommodation Network
West Virginia University
918 Chestnut Ridge Road, Suite 1
P. O. Box 6080
Morgantown, WV 26506-6080
(800) 526-7234 or (800) 232-9675
E-mail: bloy@wvu.edu
Web: janweb.icdi.wvu.edu

Recording for the Blind and Dyslexic (books on tape)
The Anne T. MacDonald Center
20 Roszel Road
Princeton, NJ 08540
(800) 221-4792 or (609) 452-0606
E-mail: custserv@rfbd.org
Web: www.rfbd.org

Rehabilitation Engineering and Assistive Technology Society of North America (RESNA)
1700 N. Moore Street, Suite 1540
Arlington, VA 22209-1903
(703) 524-6686
E-mail: natloffice@resna.org
Web: www.resna.org

Research and Training Center on Family Support and Children's Mental Health
Portland State University
P. O. Box 751
Portland, OR 97207-0751
(800) 628-1696 or (503) 725-4040
E-mail: caplane@rri.pdx.edu
Web: www.rtc.pdx.edu/

Research and Training Center on Independent Living
University of Kansas
4089 Dole Building
Lawrence, KS 66045-2930
(785) 864-4095
E-mail: rtcil@kuhub.cc.ukansas.edu
Web: www.lsi.ukans.edu/rtcil/catalog1.htm

Sotos Syndrome Support Association
Three Danada Square East
PMB #235
Wheaton, IL 60187
(888) 246-7772
E-mail: sssa@well.com
Web: www.well.com/user/sssa

Special Olympics International
1325 G Street N.W., Suite 500
Washington, D.C. 20005
(202) 628-3630
E-mail: specialolympics@msn.com
Web: www.specialolympics.org/

Spina Bifida Association of America

4590 MacArthur Boulevard, N.W., Suite 250
Washington, D.C. 20007-4226
(800) 621-3141 or (202) 944-3285
E-mail: sbaa@sbaa.org
Web: www.sbaa.org

Technical Assistance Alliance for Parent Centers (the Alliance) PACER Center

4826 Chicago Avenue South
Minneapolis, MN 55417-1098
(888) 248-0822 or (612) 827-2966
E-mail: alliance@taalliance.org
Web: www.taalliance.org

Tourette Syndrome Association

42-40 Bell Boulevard
Bayside, NY 11361
(800) 237-0717 or (718) 224-2999
E-mail: tourette@ix.netcom.com
Web: www.tourette-syndrome.com

The Turner's Syndrome Society of the U. S.

1313 Southeast 5th Street, Suite 327
Minneapolis, MN 55414
(800) 365-9944
E-mail: webmaster@turner-syndrome-us.org
Web: www.turner-syndrome-us.org

United Cerebral Palsy Association, Inc.

1660 L Street, N.W., Suite 700
Washington, DC 20036
(800) 872-5827 or (202) 776-0406
E-Mail: ucpnatl@ucpa.org
Web: www.ucpa.org

Williams Syndrome Association

1312 N. Campbell, Suite 34
Royal Oak, MI
(248) 541-3630
Email: TMonkaba@aol.com
Web: www.williams-syndrome.org

Bibliography

Arffa, S., Fitzhugh-Bell, K. and Black, W. (1989) 'Neuropsychological profiles of children with learning disabilities and children with documented brain damage.' *Journal of Learning Disabilities 22*, 635-640.

Asendorpf, J. B. (1993) 'Abnormal shyness in children.' *Journal of Child Psychology and Psychiatry 34*, 1069-1081.

Badian, N. (1983) 'Arithmetic and nonverbal learning.' *Progress in Learning Disabilities 5*, 235-264.

Badian, N. (1992) 'Nonverbal learning disability, school behavior, and dyslexia.' *Annals of Dyslexia 42*, 159-178.

Badian, N. and Ghublikian, M. (1982) 'The personal-social characteristics of children with poor mathematical computation skills.' *Journal of Learning Disabilities 16*, 154-157.

Baron, I. S. and Goldberger, E. (1993) 'Neuropsychological disturbances of hydrocephalic children with implications for special education and rehabilitation.' *Neuropsychological Rehabilitation, Special Issue: Issues in the neuropsychological rehabilitation of children with brain dysfunction 3, 4*, 389-410.

Batchelor, E., Grey, J. and Dean, R. S. (1990) 'Neuropsychological aspects of arithmetic performance in learning disability.' *International Journal of Clinical Neuropsychology 12*, 90-94.

Battistia, M. (1980) 'Interrelationships between problem solving ability, right hemisphere processing facility and mathematics learning.' *Focus on Learning Problems in Mathematics 2*, 53-60.

Baum, K., Schulte, C., Girke, W., Reischies, F. and Felix, R. (1996) 'Incidental white-matter foci on MRI in "healthy" subjects: Evidence of subtle cognitive dysfunction.' *Neuroradiology 38, 8*, 755-760.

Bigler, E. D. (1989) 'On the neuropsychology of suicide.' *Journal of Learning Disabilities 22, 3*, 180-185.

Brookshire, B., Butler, I., Ewing-Cobbs, L. and Fletcher, J. (1994) 'Neuropsychological characteristics of children with Tourette syndrome: evidence for a nonverbal learning disability?' *Journal of Clinical & Experimental Neuropsychology 16, 2*, 289-302.

Brumback, R. A. and Staton, R. D. (1982) 'An hypothesis regarding the commonality of right-hemisphere involvement in learning disability, attentional disorder, and childhood major depressive disorder.' *Perceptual Motor Skills 55, 3*, Pt. 2, 1091-1097.

Brumback, R. A. and Staton, R. D. (1982) 'Right hemisphere involvement in learning disability, attention deficit disorder, and childhood major depressive disorder.' *Medical Hypotheses 8, 5*, 505-514.

Brumback, R. A., Harper, C. R. and Weinberg, W. A. (1996) 'Nonverbal learning disabilities, Asperger's syndrome, pervasive developmental disorder – should we care?' *Journal of Child Neurology 11,* 6, 427-429.

Casey, J. E., Rourke, B. P. and Picard, E. (1991) 'Syndrome of nonverbal learning disabilities: Age differences in neuro-psychological, academic, and socioemotional functioning.' *Development and Psychopathology 3,* 329-345.

Chia, S. H. (1997) 'The child, his family and dyspraxia.' *Professional Care: Mother and Child 7,* 105-107.

Cohen, M. J., Branch, W. B. and Hynd, G. W. (1994) 'Receptive prosody in children with left or right hemisphere dysfunction.' *Brain and Language 47,* 2, 171-181.

Dean, R. S. (1983) 'Intelligence as a predictor of nonverbal learning with learning-disabled children.' *Journal of Clinical Psychology 39,* 3, 437-441.

Denckla, M. B. (1983) 'The neuropsychology of social-emotional learning disabilities.' *Archives of Neurology 40,* 461-462.

Denckla, M. B. (1991) 'Academic and extracurricular aspects of nonverbal learning disabilities.' *Psychiatric Annals 21,* 12, 717-724.

Deuel R. K. and Doar, B. P. (1992) 'Developmental manual dyspraxia: a lesson in mind and brain.' *Journal of Child Neurology 7,* 99-103.

Dimitrovsky, L., Spector, H., Levy-Shiff, R. and Vakil, E. (1998) 'Interpretation of facial expressions of affect in children with learning disabilities with verbal or nonverbal deficits.' *Journal of Learning Disabilities 32,* 3, 286-292.

Donders, J., Rourke, B. P. and Canady, A. I. (1991) 'Neuropsychological functioning of hydrocephalic children.' *Journal of Clinical and Experimental Neuropsychology 13,* 4, 607-613.

Ellis, H. D., Ellis, D. M., Fraser, W. and Deb, S. (1994) 'A preliminary study of right hemisphere cognitive deficits and impaired social judgments among young people with Asperger Syndrome.' *European Child and Adolescent Psychiatry 3,* 255-266.

Fisher, N. J. and DeLuca, J. W. (1997) 'Verbal learning strategies of adolescents and adults with the Syndrome of Nonverbal Learning Disabilities.' *Child Neuropsychology 3,* 3, 192-198.

Fisher, N.J., DeLuca, J.W. and Rourke, B.P. (1997) 'Wisconsin Card Sorting Test and Halstead Category Test performances of children and adolescents who exhibit the syndrome of nonverbal learning disabilities.' *Child Neuropsychology 3,* 3, 61-70.

Fletcher, J. M. (1989) 'Nonverbal learning disabilities and suicide: Classification leads to prevention.' *Journal of Learning Disabilities 22,* 3, 176/179.

Foss, J. M. (1991) 'Nonverbal learning disabilities and remedial interventions.' *Annals of Dyslexia 41,* 128-140.

Fox, A. M. and Lent, B. (1996) 'Clumsy children: Primer on developmental coordination disorder.' *Canadian Family Physician 42,* 1965-1971

Fuerst, D., Fisk, J. L. and Rourke, B. P. (1990) 'Psychosocial functioning of learning-disabled children: Relations between WISC verbal IQ – performance IQ discrepancies and personality subtypes.' *Journal of Consulting and Clinical Psychology 58,* 657-660.

Gillberg, C. (1991) 'Pediatric neuropsychiatry.' *Current Opinion in Neurology and Neurosurgery 4*, 381-390.

Glosser, G. and Koppell, S. (1987) 'Emotional-behavioral patterns in children with learning disabilities: Lateralized hemispheric differences.' *Journal of Learning Disabilities 20*, 365-368.

Goldberg, E. and Costa, L. D. (1981) 'Hemisphere differences in the acquisition and use of asymmetries in the brain.' *Brain and Language 14*, 144-173.

Goldstein, D. B. (June 18, 2000) 'Children's Nonverbal Learning Disabilities Scale.' Assessment Page: *http://www.nldontheweb.org /Goldstein_1.htm*

Gross-Tsur, V., Shalev, R. S., Manor, O. and Amir, N. (1995) 'Developmental right-hemisphere syndrome: Clinical spectrum of the nonverbal learning disability.' *Journal of Learning Disabilities 28*, 2, 80-86.

Harnadek, M. and Rourke, B. P. (1994) 'Principal identifying features of the syndrome of nonverbal learning disabilities in children.' *Journal of Learning Disabilities 27*, 144-154.

Heller, W. (June 18, 2000) 'Understanding Nonverbal Learning Disability (NVLD).' About NLD Page <http://www.nldontheweb.org/heller.htm>

Hulme, C. and Lord, R. (1986) 'Clumsy children: A review of recent research.' Child: Care, *Health and Development 12*, 4, 257-269.

Humphries, T. (1993) 'Nonverbal Learning Disabilities: A Distinct Group Within Our Population.' *Communique*, Autumn.

Johnson, D. J. (1987) 'Nonverbal learning disabilities.' *Pediatric Annals 16*, 2, 133-141.

Keith, R.W., (1996) 'Understanding Central Auditory Processing Disorders.' *The Hearing Journal 49*, 20-28.

Klin, A., Volkmar, F. R., Sparrow, S. S., Cicchetti, D. V. and Rourke, B. P. (1995) 'Validity and neuropsychological characterization of Asperger syndrome: convergence with nonverbal learning disabilities syndrome.' *Journal of Child Psychology and Psychiatry 36*, 7, 1127-1140.

Kopp, S. and Gillberg, C. (1992) 'Girls with social deficits and learning problems: Autism, atypical Asperger Syndrome or a variant of these conditions.' *European Child and Adolescent Psychiatry 1*, 2, 89-99.

Kowalchuk, B. and King, J. D. (1989) 'Adult suicide versus coping with nonverbal learning disorder.' *Journal of Learning Disabilities 22*, 3, 177-178.

Levin, H., Scheller, J., Rickard, T., Grafman, J., Martinkowski, K., Winslow, M., and Mirvis, S. (1996) 'Dyscalculia and dyslexia after right hemisphere injury in infancy.' *Archives of Neurology 53*, 1, 88-96.

Little, L. (1998) 'Severe childhood sexual abuse and nonverbal learning disability.' *American Journal of Psychotherapy 52*, 3, 367-381.

Little, L. (1999) 'The Misunderstood Child: The Child With a Nonverbal Learning Disorder.' *Journal of the Society of Pediatric Nurses 4*, 3, 113-121.

Little, S. S. (1993) 'Nonverbal learning disabilities and socioemotional functioning: a review of recent literature.' *Journal of Learning Disabilities 26*, 10, 653-665.

Lord-Maes, J. and Janiece-Obrzut, J. E. (1996) 'Neuropsychological consequences of traumatic brain injury in children and adolescents.' *Journal of Learning Disabilities 29,* 609.

Loveland, K. A., Fletcher, J. M. and Bailey, V. (1990) 'Verbal and nonverbal communication of events in learning-disabled subgroups.' Journal of *Clinical and Experimental Neuropsychology 12,* 433-447.

Mattson, A. J., Sheer, D. E. and Fletcher, J. M. (1992) 'Electrophysiological evidence of lateralized disturbances in children with learning disabilities.' *Journal of Clinical & Experimental Neuropsychology 14,* 5, 707-716.

McKelvey, J. R., Lambert, R., Mottson, L. and Shevell, M. I. (1995) 'Right hemisphere dysfunction in Asperger's Syndrome.' *Journal of Child Neurology 10,* 310-314.

Minskoff, E. (1980) 'Teaching approach for developing nonverbal communication skills in students with social perception deficits, Part 1: The basic approach and body language cues.' *Journal of Learning Disabilities 13,* 3, 118-124.

Minskoff, E. (1980) 'Teaching approach for developing nonverbal communication skills in students with social perception deficits, Part 2: Proxemic, vocalic, and artifactual cues.' *Journal of Learning Disabilities 13,* 4, 203-208.

Miyahara, M. and Mobs, I. (1995) 'Developmental dyspraxia and developmental coordination disorder.' *Neuropsychology Review 5,* 245-268.

Musiek, F. (1986) 'Neuroanatomy, neurophysiology, and central auditory assessment: Part III: Corpus callosum and efferent pathways.' *Ear and Hearing 7,* 349-358.

Musiek, F., Golleghy, K. and Ross, M. (1985) 'Profiles of types of central auditory processing disorders in children with learning disabilities.' *Journal of Childhood Communication Disorders 9,* 43-63.

Nussbaum, N. L. and Bigler, E. D. (1986) 'Neuropsychological and behavioral profiles of empirically derived subgroups of learning-disabled children.' *International Journal of Clinical Neuropsychology 8,* 82-89.

Obrzut, J. E. and Hynd, G. W. (1987) 'Cognitive dysfunction and psychoeducational assessment in individuals with acquired brain injury.' *Journal of Learning Disabilities 20,* 596-602.

Ozols, E. J. and Rourke, B. P. (1988) 'Characteristics of young learning-disabled children classified according to patterns of academic achievement: Auditory-perceptual and visual-perceptual abilities.' *Journal of Clinical Child Psychology 17,* 44-52.

Poole, N. (1997) 'Remediation of nonverbal learning problems.' The *Educational Therapist 18,* 3.

Reeves, W. H. (1983) 'Right cerebral hemispheric function: Behavioral correlates.' *International Journal of Neuroscience 18,* 3-4, 227-230.

Reiff, H. B. and Gerber, P. J. (1990) 'Cognitive correlates of social perception in students with learning disabilities.' *Journal of Learning Disabilities 23,* 4, 260-262.

Roman, M. A. (1998) 'The Syndrome of nonverbal learning disabilities: Clinical description and applied aspects.' *Current Issues in Education 1,* 1, 1.

Rourke, B. P. (1988) 'Socio-emotional disturbances of learning-disabled children.' *Journal of Consulting and Clinical Psychology 56,* 801-810.

Rourke, B. P. (1988) 'Syndrome of nonverbal learning disabilities: Developmental manifestations in neurological disease, disorder, and dysfunction.' *The Clinical Neuropsychologist 2*, 293-330.

Rourke, B. P. (1989) 'Nonverbal learning disabilities, socioemotional disturbance, and suicide: A reply to Fletcher, Kowalchuk, King, and Bigler.' *Journal of Learning Disabilities 22*, 3, 186-187.

Rourke, B. P. (1993) 'Arithmetic disabilities, specific and otherwise: a neuropsychological perspective.' *Journal of Learning Disabilities 26*, 4, 214-226.

Rourke, B. P. (2000) 'Neuropsychological and psychosocial subtyping: A review of investigations within the University of Windsor Laboratory.' *Canadian Psychology 41*, 1, 34-50.

Rourke, B. P. (June 18, 2000) 'Syndrome of nonverbal learning disabilities: Assessment Protocols.' Byron Rourke: *http://www.nldontheweb.org/nld_assmt_protocol.htm*

Rourke, B. P. and Conway, J. A. (1997) 'Disabilities of arithmetic and mathematical reasoning: Perspectives from neurology and neuropsychology.' *Journal of Learning Disabilities 30*, 1, 34-46.

Rourke, B. P. and Finlaysen, M. A. J. (1978) 'Neuropsychological significance of variations in patterns of academic performance: Verbal and visual-spatial abilities.' *Journal of Abnormal Child Psychology 6*, 121-133.

Rourke, B. P. and Fisk, J. L. (1981) 'Socio-emotional disturbances of learning disabled children: The role of central processing deficits.' *Bulletin of the Orton Society 31*, 77-88.

Rourke, B. P. and Fuerst, D. (1996) 'Psychosocial dimensions of learning disability subtypes.' *Assessment 3*, 3, 277-290.

Rourke, B. P. and Strang, J. D. (1978) 'Neuropsychological significance of variations in patterns of academic performance: Motor, psychomotor, and tactile-perceptual abilities.' *Journal of Pediatric Psychology 2*, 62-66.

Rourke, B. P. and Tsatsanis, K. D. (1996) 'Syndrome of nonverbal learning disabilities: Psycholinguistic assets and deficits.' *Topics in Language Disorders 16*, 2, 30-44.

Rourke, B. P., Dietrich, D. M. and Young, G. C. (1973) 'Significance of WISC verbal-performance discrepancies for younger children with learning disabilities.' *Perceptual and Motor Skills 36*, 275-282.

Rourke, B. P., Young, G. C. and Flewelling, R. W. (1971) 'The relationships between WISC verbal-performance discrepancies and selected verbal, auditory-perceptual, visual-perceptual, and problem-solving abilities in children with learning disabilities.' *Journal of Clinical Psychology 27*, 475-479.

Rourke, B. P., Young, G. C. and Leenaars, A. A. (1989) 'A childhood learning disability that predisposes those afflicted to adolescent and adult depression and suicide risk.' *Journal of Learning Disabilities 22*, 3, 169-175.

Schatz, J., Craft, S., Koby, M. and Park, T. S. (1997) 'Associative learning in children with perinatal brain injury.' *Journal of the International Neuropsychological Society 3*, 6, 521-527.

Semrud-Clikeman, M. and Hynd, G. W. (1990) 'Right hemispheric dysfunction in nonverbal learning disabilities: Social, academic, and adaptive functioning in adults and children.' *Psychological Bulletin 107,* 196-209.

Shields, J. (1991) 'Semantic-pragmatic disorder: A right hemisphere syndrome?' *British Journal of Disorders of Communication 26,* 383-392.

Sisterhen, D. H. and Gerber, P. J. (1989) 'Auditory, visual, and multisensory nonverbal social perception in adolescents with and without learning disabilities.' *Journal of Learning Disabilities 22,* 4, 245-249.

Spreen, O. (1989) 'The relationship between learning disabilities, emotional disorders, and neuropsychology: Some results and observations.' *Journal of Clinical and Experimental Neuropsychology 11,* 117-140.

Stellern, J., Marlowe, M., Jacobs, J. and Cosairt, A. (1985) 'Neuropsychological significance of right hemisphere cognitive mode in behavior disorders.' *Behavioral Disorders 2,* 113-124.

Stone, W. L. and LaGreca, A. N. (1984) 'Comprehension of nonverbal communication: A re-examination of the social competencies of learning-disabled children.' *Journal of Abnormal Child Psychology 12,* 505-518.

Strang, J. D. and Rourke, B. P. (1983) 'Concept-formation/nonverbal reasoning abilities of children who exhibit specific academic problems with arithmetic.' *Journal of Clinical Child Psychology 12,* 33-39.

Suzuki, L. A. and Leton, D. A. (1989) 'Spontaneous talkers among students with learning disabilities: Implications of right cerebral dysfunction.' *Journal of Learning Disabilities 22,* 6, 397-399.

Thompson, N. M., Francis, J. D., Steubing, K. K. and Fletcher, J. M. (1994) 'Motor, visual spatial, and somatosensory skills after closed head injury in children and adolescents: A study of change.' *Neuropsychology 8,* 333-342.

Thompson, S. (1996) 'Nonverbal learning disorders.' *The Gram,* Fall, a publication of the East Bay learning Disabilities Association.

Thompson, S. (1997) 'Nonverbal learning disorders.' *The Gram,* Winter, a publication of the East Bay learning Disabilities Association.

Thompson, S. (1998) 'Stress, anxiety, panic, and phobias: Secondary to NLD.' *The Gram,* Spring, a publication of the East Bay learning Disabilities Association.

Tranel, D., Hall, L. E., Olson, S. and Tranel, N. N. (1987) 'Evidence for a right- hemisphere developmental learning disability.' *Developmental Neuropsychology 3,* 113-127.

Tsatsanis, K. D., Fuerst, D. R. and Rourke, B. P. (1997) 'Psychosocial dimensions of learning disabilities: External validation and relationship with age and academic functioning.' *Journal of Learning Disabilities 30,* 490-502.

Voeller, K. K. (1986) 'Right hemisphere deficit syndrome in children.' *American Journal of Psychiatry 143,* 1004-1009.

Voeller, K. K., Hanson, J. A. and Wendt, R. N. (1988) 'Facial affect recognition in children: A comparison of the performance of children with right and left hemisphere lesions.' *Neurology 38,* 11, 1744-1748.

Weintraub, S. and Mesulam, M. M. (1983) 'Developmental learning disabilities of the right hemisphere: Emotional, interpersonal, and cognitive components.' *Archives of Neurology 40,* 463-468.

Wiig, E. H. and Harris, S. P. (1974) 'Perception and interpretation of nonverbally expressed emotions by adolescents with learning disabilities.' *Perceptual and Motor Skills 38,* 239-245.

Williams, D. L. Gridley, B. E. and Fitzhugh-Bell, K. (1992) 'Cluster analysis of children and adolescents with brain damage and learning disabilities using neuropsychological, psychoeducational, and sociobehavioral variables.' *Journal of Learning Disabilities 25,* 5, 290-299.

Willoughby, C. and Polatajko, H. J. (1995) 'Motor problems in children with developmental coordination disorder: review of the literature.' *American Journal of Occupational Therapists 49,* 787-794.

Wills, K. E. (1993) 'Neuropsychological functioning in children with spina bifida and/or hydrocephalus.' Journal of Clinical Child Psychology, Special Issue: *The neuropsychological basis of disorders affecting children and adolescents 22,* 2, 247-265.

Worling, D. E., Humphries, T. and Tannock, R. (1999) 'Spatial and emotional aspects of language inferencing in nonverbal learning disabilities.' *Brain and Language 70,* 2, 220-39.

Index